Social

Social Problems

AND

Criminal Justice

Emilio C. Viano

The American University, Washington, D.C.

Alvin W. Cohn

Administration of Justice Services, Inc., Rockville, Md.

 Nelson-Hall Law Enforcement Series

George W. O'Connor, *Consulting Editor*
Superintendent of Public Safety, Troy, New York

Nelson-Hall / *Chicago*

Library of Congress Cataloging in Publication Data

Viano, Emilio C.

  Social problems and criminal justice.

  (The Nelson-Hall law enforcement series)
  Includes bibliographical references.
  1. United States—Social conditions—1960-
2. Social problems. 3. Crime and criminals—United
States. I. Cohn, Alvin W., joint author. II. Title.
HN59.V5   364'.973   74-11500
ISBN 0-88229-115-7

For
Sherry Lee and Sara
and in memory of
Maria Luisa Rondini and Berta Mann

Contents

Part IV: Social Control

Preface

The kinds of social problems that will confront society in the final decades of the twentieth century appear almost insurmountable and more than perplexing. The alleged breakdown of the family, drug abuse, poverty, alienation of youth, juvenile delinquency, adult crime, political interference in company with graft and corruption, racism, and sexual promiscuity are among popular subjects for discussion in homes, schools, and churches and on television.

Citizens, social workers, psychiatrists, politicians, and judges face daily the consequences of social problems and their effects on the maintenance of social order. They must confront the problems, attempt to deal with them, and find ways of reducing their harmful or negative impacts on society. Michael Harrington (1969) observed: "The sixties posed problems, but the solutions to them were left up in the air. The seventies will deal with them, or else" (p. 47).

The policeman, as much or more than others, plays a frontline role in dealing with social problems on a daily basis. Further, because he is close to the real problems and the real people associated with the problems—delinquents, unemployed, poor, criminals, the mentally ill, militants—he also is frequently associated with the causes of the problems. Much has been written on law enforcement and on social problems, but little, if anything, has been written on both from a unified point of view. Therefore this book will explore some social problems in society now, particularly those that we believe influence daily policing.

In effect, although all the problems that afflict society are related to the delivery of social services, they interface at the same time with the criminal justice system. This interrelationship is a reality not yet, we believe, fully recognized through systemic management. However, the National Advisory Commission on Criminal Justice Standards and Goals (1973 *c*), in its summary report, *A National Strategy to Reduce Crime*, concentrated on improvement in the delivery of social services as one of four basic priorities in combating crime. It also emphasized ". . . the need for all elements of the criminal justice system to plan and work together with the social service delivery system" (p. 3).

In the Introduction we present a general orientation to the study of social problems. Our objectives also are discussed. Part I considers sociocultural problems—that is, problems that derive from the rapid changes in values and perspectives today. Issues related to racial relations (chap. 1), to the commitment of members of society to contribute to the society (chap. 2), and to one of the basic institutions of society, the family (chap. 3), are examined. Part II is concerned, instead, with problems that are economic in origin—poverty and unemployment (chap. 4), white-collar crime (chap. 5), and environmental issues (chap. 6).

Deviance and personality problems are discussed in Part III. For example, in chapter 7 violence is examined as an integral part of the American experience; crime and its consequences are carefully detailed in chapter 8; and juvenile delinquency and youth crime, problems related to mental health and the so-called victimless crimes, and issues that involve the victims of criminal situations are laid out in chapters 9, 10, 11, and 12, respectively. Finally, in Part IV the administration of criminal justice is discussed as a system in need of major changes. In particular, chapter 13 contains a valuable historical overview of the development of mechanisms of social control and important theoretical insights into current practices.

The conclusion focuses on the universal responsibility for working toward the understanding, relief, and control of social problems. We do not offer any panaceas or ready-made solutions but attempt, rather, to outline, both for the layman and for persons in criminal justice administration, steps everyone in society ought to take to help alleviate the conditions we call social problems.

Acknowledgments

We wish to thank several persons for their assistance in completing this work. We owe a special debt of thanks to Mrs. Lou Wissler for her invaluable editorial assistance. She was willing to devote many hours to the task of editing the manuscript, contributing her professional skills with enthusiasm and keen interest. Mrs. Artie B. Parlor and Miss Dorothy O'Callaghan have our warmest appreciation for their help in preparing the manuscript. Finally, we are grateful for the assistance provided by the Center for the Administration of Justice at The American University, and in particular by Mrs. Jenny McGough, when the manuscript was being typed.

Introduction: Orientation to the Study of Social Problems

Perspectives in the Study of Society

Wilbert Moore (in Rose 1970) has written:

> Many of the significant components of man's social existence are persistent even if examined over considerable periods of time. The daily, weekly, and annual schedule of man's activities shows a remarkable consistency, as do the forms and patterns that deal with life's major events, such as birth, marriage, and death. The persistence of patterns gives order and constancy to recurrent events. [P. 832]

Strong evidence suggests that without some coherent patterning, social life would be utterly chaotic and intolerable. Yet although persisting patterns do provide stability, no society is absolutely static. Population shifts, internal tensions, clamor against inequities, competition for power, and other dynamic factors always threaten to subvert or to redefine established ways.

xv

For certain elements any change deemed threatening to the status quo may generate a reactionary movement to maintain or to reestablish the old order. For others, even the remote possibility of another way of life may provoke revolutionary fervor and attempts to remake society. The goals of certain social and political movements, for example, are to change the norms of society in order to provide greater opportunity to those barred from full participation, as in the struggle for women's rights during the nineteenth and twentieth centuries. Sometimes basic values are questioned, and attempts are made to overturn existing regimes or at least to alter their social structure and reorient their political course. Recently we have witnessed dramatic expressions of these processes not only in underdeveloped countries—the third world—but in the United States as well. The image of a secure and tranquil democracy shatters as those who are dissatisfied with, and perhaps alienated from, the American Way of Life angrily face those who claim they "never had it so good" and want to preserve the social world as it is.

While this raucous dialogue rages on, basic ideas and tenets about society, culture, human institutions, and centuries-old solutions are questioned and challenged. Thus a society may be studied either as it is, through its dominant institutions, its ideological systems, its expressions through art and literature, its technological advances, and its most prominent personalities, or from the point of view formed by some major social problems. A close, even predictable relationship exists between a culture's recurrent social problems and its characteristic values and institutions.

In this book, then, we intend to study American society from the perspective of social problems. More particularly we will explore the significance of these problems for contemporary law enforcement practice and will deal with numerous problems that we think accurately reflect the current American scene: race relations; alienation and deviance; family disorganization; poverty and unemployment; white-collar and organized crime; vested interests, pressure groups, and Big Business; violence and crime; juvenile delinquency, mental health, and suicide; crimes without victims; and the victims of crime. We also will discuss problems related to the administration of justice and to the environment.

A Problem Is in the Eye of the Beholder

Is each problem mentioned important? Are all recognized as significant social problems? These are difficult questions to answer, for they imply value judgments. For example, many may agree that unemployment, poverty, and housing are major social problems in today's society; yet a few people would disagree. Spokesmen for real estate interests insist that no real housing shortage exists. Some claim, often on the basis of religious beliefs, that poverty is spiritually beneficial; some rich people often have stated that poverty is good for (other) people. Government officials, certain economists, and a few employers remark from time to time that a certain amount of unemployment is good in that it creates competition and a general situation favorable to management, or that without Big Business, we could not enjoy our present prosperity.

Even though most people agree that certain issues constitute major social problems, agreement on their solutions does not necessarily follow. For example, many people think that racism is a social problem, but to some the solution lies in complete black emancipation, while to others the solution is in keeping or putting blacks back "in their places." Because sickle cell anemia is a serious public health problem, particularly among blacks, several programs have been developed to combat the disease, but the results are generating anxiety, confusion, and hostility. People who have tested positive in community screening programs often panic, not realizing they may have only the trait and not the disease. Those who have the trait and many who have the disease can work; yet misinformed employers deny them jobs, and insurance companies will not insure them. In 1974 sickle cell screening became mandatory for children entering the District of Columbia and Virginia public schools, even though most medical experts and community spokesmen are opposed to the new laws. Thus strong disagreement is growing over the proposed solutions to a situation recognized as a problem.

Also, agreement on the probability that a condition constitutes a social problem does not necessarily mean agreement on how much of that condition represents a problem. For example, a general acceptance of the population explosion as a problem carries with it widespread disagreement on what the optimum growth rate should be. Some advocate zero population growth; others advocate different rates. In the same way, unemployment experts are at odds in deciding what rate of unemployment should be considered unhealthy for the economy. Thus opinions differ not only on what the social problems are but also on the point at which they become problems. The determination depends in part on various frames of reference. That is, a government economist may place unemployment within normal limits; a person who must feed a hungry family but cannot find a job may view the problem in considerably more negative terms.

Similarly, in discussing drugs or alcohol, people may agree that drug abuse or excessive consumption of alcoholic beverages is a problem, but they may strongly disagree on the use of drugs and alcohol—that is, where the boundary between use and abuse lies. Some would ban both altogether. The social drinker hardly sees this problem, but the policeman who investigates an accident that resulted from "driving while under the influence" may view it from a far different perspective.

Thus it appears that disagreements occur because in most cases society accepts as unobjectionable, and sometimes even good, the crucial aspects of social problems. That alcohol is a problem in American culture is inseparable from alcohol's performance of a social function in scores of contexts, ranging from cocktails before dinner to wedding receptions to formal diplomatic gatherings. Similarly, a clear relationship exists between certain problems and life in the city or population growth. For centuries fertility was both necessary and functional for the preservation of society, but advances in medical knowledge, better nutrition and hygiene, and better predictability of economic cycles have transformed the population increase into one of society's most serious challenges.

Hence, conflicts arise among different groups in terms of defining the social problem and in planning strategies of control, but when law enforcement is involved, as in alcohol and drug abuse, delinquency, and civil disobedience, the conflicts may become even more complex and difficult to resolve. People want no interference in their own lives; they demand it only for the other guy. Racial desegregation is an example. Twenty years ago several people saw southern de jure segregation as a problem. Their concern initiated the civil rights movement, which gained momentum in the 1960s. To correct the situation, legislation was passed and efforts were made to implement it. This action, in turn, created new social problems as citizens disagreed on the substance of the matter or on the methods of implementation. Thus, the attempt to solve one problem begot another problem.

Such controversies are particularly strong when they involve issues of morality and religious values—abortion, premarital sex, or legalized gambling. How do we know, then, that the topics we discuss here are recognized as social problems? We know because the general consensus among social scientists, civil leaders, and government officials and in several public opinion polls indicates that our topics represent areas of concern that can be made less acute if dealt with in a timely fashion; they represent issues that confront the modern-day policeman.

We do not suggest that these are the only significant problems in present-day America or even that all are among the most vital. However, they undoubtedly constitute some of the most compelling issues that people now encounter in their daily lives and that demand serious consideration.

Social Problems Defined

Social problems are viewed here as those significant interruptions in the socially or morally desired scheme of things that involved persons believe should be alleviated through appropriate social action (Nisbet 1966; McDonagh & Simpson 1969). Thus social problems pertain to human relationships, and anywhere the prevailing relationships among members of society frustrate the important personal goals of a large number of people, a social problem exists. And who, more than a policeman, must deal on a daily basis with persons who feel the impact of these significant social problems? Further, social problems represent areas that appear to seriously threaten the structure of society because of society's inability to regulate relationships among people. In other words, a social problem is a problem in human relationships that threatens society itself or frustrates the important aspirations of many people (Raab & Selznick 1964).

Three Great Revolutions in American Society

What causes a given social problem? In a society as complex and differentiated as ours, no simple or single answer is possible. All that we, as social scientists, can do in an introductory statement is to identify, hopefully, some of the more general processes that have occurred in American society and that can be pointed out as possible forces in the generation of social problems.

American society has experienced three great revolutions: the political revolution in the eighteenth century; the industrial revolution of the nineteenth century; and the urban-suburban revolution in the mid-twentieth century. Thus during the eighteenth century some of the country's most serious concerns were political tyranny (as well as political unity), persecution because of religious differences, and the struggle to find a national identity. During the nineteenth century working conditions, economic exploitation, slavery, the unpredictability of economic cycles, and the assimilation and acculturation of immigrants became serious problems in the United States. Today, though some of the concerns of the two previous centuries are still sensed, numerous new problems are immediate and real: poverty, minority status, violence and urban disorders, family instability, drug abuse, the status of women, population control and distribution, and involvement in major world affairs. Most of these problems are distinctly urban in origin. The twentieth century has witnessed a massive internal migration from country to city, from city to suburbs, and from southern to northern and western regions of the country.

Social and Public Health Problems

Some people seem to equate social problems with public health problems and to see social problems as the embodiment of patently evil elements that are easily identifiable and subject to disposal. Unfortunately, this view is rather simplistic.

First, even public health problems that appear to be relatively simple have numerous causes that require years of painstaking research to identify. For example, malaria, once a serious public health problem, has many causes: the bite of a malaria-carrying mosquito, the number of open-water breeding places in the area, nonscreened houses, ignorance and lack of concern, poverty that permits such conditions and ignorance to exist, the failure of governmental agencies to tackle the problems effectively, and finally, the germ itself. Although the germ is the immediate and specific cause of malaria, it could have no effect unless the other proximate conditions existed.

Second, a social problem differs from a physical disease in that no single factor in the genesis and development of a social problem can be isolated. The causes of social problems appear to be many and diverse, and the relationship between them unclear and difficult to predict. Therefore, in order to study and understand social problems we must investigate the total situation that breeds a particular problem instead of looking at a single, specific cause.

Thus, the image that many people have of society and its problems—a healthy organism invaded by a single alien substance—is not correct, and consequently, the solutions they propose often are equally incorrect. Many persons, for example, see the legislator or policeman as a kind of a physician who can remove the spreading cancer quickly and effectively, destroy the infection-carrying germs, and leave untouched the overall condition of the organism itself. Using this simplistic approach, people expect the school and the church, say, to deliver immunization shots and the prisons to exercise surveillance over or to isolate those affected by the disease. In reality, the major conditions in which social problems originate are identified as industrialization, urbanization, geographic mobility, class and occupational mobility, the consequent population changes (birthrate, death rate, age patterns, variety of the population), the impact of technology and science, and the consequent breakdown of tradition. Obviously, the "St. George and the Dragon" approach to the study and solution of social problems does not stand up in the face of such complex social realities.

Social Disorganization

The impact of such conditions has made it very difficult for society to order relationships among people in a constant and timely fashion. A society is not just an aggregate or mass of individuals; it presupposes the forming of individuals into some kind of order. As a form of organization, society demands interaction among its members and a certain degree of interdependence among them, and it exists as long as these ties of association and interdependence are maintained. This societal form of organization has been devised so that the chances of surviving and multiplying are increased (Lenski 1970). Its success depends much more on its members' common acceptance than on forced compliance or police power.

In a rapid and constantly shifting way, the changing social conditions already noted have undermined the prevailing rules of relationship in American society. These changes have occurred, according to some, mainly because traditional social groups, such as the family, have broken down, and a conflict has developed between rules and aspirations as well as between goals and means. Thus social disorganization has occurred as society has become increasingly unable to efficiently reconstruct the web of social relationships, and social problems, such as delinquency and crime, are a natural consequence.

Psychological Factors

As historians emphasize the massive social changes that are still occurring in American society, and as sociologists are concerned with the social disorganization that accompanies such changes, psychologists direct their attention to another component—the personality factors in social problems. They have a major interest in studying and understanding why the process of socialization fails for certain persons as it succeeds for others who may belong to the same family.

Every member of society develops within a general give-and-take process between the individual and society. This process—or compromise, if you please—is important because it serves the need for social control. In fact, it is through such a process that humans learn how to conduct themselves in socially acceptable ways. As sociologists have noted, if individuals do not assume responsibility for policing their own conduct, no society can operate effectively and attain its goals. It would be unrealistic, though, to assume that this process can take place without struggle and resistance; hence every society has devised a system of rewards and punishments to motivate individuals to act in socially approved ways and has designated certain people—policemen—to enforce the rules and norms. But the potential for some members to effectively resist in various ways is ever present and becomes real in different forms of crime and delinquency.

Distribution of Social Problems

Although the causes of social problems cannot be compared to those of public health problems, it is important to understand how those factors described above affect the community life so as to produce social problems. Therefore, the study of social problems must involve an epidemiological component; that is, we need to know the possible impact of situation and environment on the development of social problems. For example, values, aspirations, and behavior are learned, the personality is developed, and the influence of society at large is transmitted and filtered in such places as schools, churches, neighborhoods, and executive offices of Big Business as well as in families and peer groups. Their study contributes to an understanding of where, when, and how social problems are generated (epidemiology) and what remedial measures (social action) can be taken.

Approaches to the Study of Social Problems

We mentioned the four main analytical approaches to the study of social problems in discussing the study of causation. We will once again briefly emphasize them here.

First, the concept of *social change* arises when the relationships among persons or groups are modified. Social change, often identified with innovation, is particularly useful in studying problems related to urbanization and the impact of technology.

Second, the theories of *social disorganization* are especially useful in understanding the problems that stem from the breakdown of conventional expectations and norms, such as in families.

Third, the study of *deviant behavior* has stimulated research in the individual manifestations of social problems. For example, why is it that some people are homosexuals or are poor or become involved with drugs?

Finally, the *epidemiological approach* to social problems involves a study of relative risks. The epidemiologist estimates the risk of a condition's appearance in one population group and compares it with the risk of its appearance in another group. Although social problems are not viewed as epidemics, they nonetheless resemble epidemics in that they may be distributed unevenly throughout the population, and it is important to know how and why. For instance, epidemiological methods are well adapted to the study of juvenile delinquency, which is not an epidemic as is cholera but resembles one since it is unevenly distributed throughout the population. Certain groups of people seem to have a high risk of delinquency, in much the same way that certain people once had a high risk of contracting cholera, but the causes of delinquency are more complex. The causes of delinquency, unemployment, poverty, crime, or illegitimacy rates cannot be traced to any germ.

These four approaches are not mutually exclusive but are, on the contrary, complementary in that they aid in supplying parts to the causation jigsaw puzzle.

Objectives

In this book we will attempt to look at social problems as they interface with the administration of justice in the United States, particularly problems that are directly relevant to contemporary law enforcement practice. We will ignore or only touch on problems that are peripheral to the field of law enforcement.

The role of the criminal justice agent vis-à-vis the major social problems is extremely important because the law enforcement officer day after day is forced to confront the issues, to uphold the law, and to deal with the people affected. At the same time he has his own personal belief system, the result of his own socialization into society, which has significant influence on task performance and job satisfaction. A better understanding of social problems will prove an invaluable asset for the police officer who strives for professional performance and wants to be a part of the process of shaping a better society now and for the future. An understanding of social problems can be equally useful to other workers in the administration of justice.

This is not a how-to-do-it book, though. Since the causes of social problems are complex and varied, it is quite difficult, if not impossible, to offer prescriptions that are realistic and effective in varying places and situations. Rather, we provide a descriptive survey of selected social problems and attempt to illustrate their importance for law enforcement and other criminal justice administration practices.

We aim particularly at making police officers aware of the main social problems and at providing a good store of factual knowledge about social problems in order to facilitate a general understanding of them. We also show, where appropriate, the relationship between theory and practice. On the one hand, every practical policy is derived from the real world; on the other, every theory has implications for control, treatment, and practical intervention. To attempt to separate them in the name of being practical simply reveals a lack of awareness of the theories and assumptions that underlie decisions and actions. To overlook experience as a source of information and to deny the necessity of action-oriented recommendations are equally foolish.

Another objective of this book is to provide a sense of perspective. The study of social problems upsets some people. A few interpret such discussion as an attack on their country, and they react by vigorously denying that any problems exist or that there is a relationship between the problems and society's existing institutions and values. For such people social problems are the sole fault of those whom they affect. That is, people make their own problems; society does not cause them. Other persons become ardent crusaders for social reform. We attempt to place each problem in a reasonable perspective in order to help the reader avoid both kinds of extremes and develop, instead, a realistic attitude conducive to effective action.

Hopefully this book will give readers some appreciation for the role of the expert. Although most people defer to expert opinions in such matters as health or taxes, some people think knowledge of social problems, their causes, and strategies for effective control is intuitive. Unfortunately, what applies to any other field of knowledge and inquiry applies also to social problems; that is, the layman's and the expert's opinions and explanations are not the same. To disregard or to distrust the expert may be wrong as well as unwise. Folklore and guesswork may be effective in certain situations, but in reality they are without any solid scientific foundation. At the same time, disregard for the layman's concerns or beliefs may be equally wrong and certainly unwise.

Finally, we hope this book will guide its readers to become agents of constructive change. People who study social problems often experience a feeling of futility and helplessness. If the origins of social problems are so complex, what can one individual do? Certainly one person cannot do much alone, but changes in social policy stem from attitude changes among large numbers of people. Fosdick (1947) said: "Are we part of the problem or part of the answer?" In other words, are we among those whose indifference, prejudice, ignorance, and selfishness are the real roadblocks in the path of a just social policy? Or are we among those whose interest, knowledge, open-mindedness, and receptivity make it possible to promote a just social policy?

Part I

Socio-Cultural
Problems

CHAPTER 1

The Struggle for Equality

Racism Illustrated

In 1954 the United States Supreme Court issued its historic *Brown* v. *Board of Education* decision, thereby outlawing racial segregation in the public schools. The decision, aimed at de jure segregation, stated that it was unconstitutional to separate students according to race—in effect, simply, that the age-old separate-but-equal doctrine could no longer be used in this country. Although the decision was concerned with statutes that attempted to legally separate the races, its impact was, and still is, felt where de facto segregation also existed—segregation based not in law but in actual practice.

In 1973, almost two decades after the *Brown* decision, the state of Virginia (Virginia Education 1973) admitted that the failure rate among its black students was exceptionally higher than that among whites because special education classes were used as a "dumping ground and a segregation weapon in the state's school system and that some school systems used the classes to set blacks apart" (p. 1).

These results came to light after the state completed a racial-ethnic survey, which also indicated that although blacks accounted for 24 percent of the school population, ". . . 47 percent attend special education classes in grades three, six, nine, and twelve, . . . [and that] 42 percent of all failures are black" (p. 1). The same report revealed that:

> Some teachers and educational officials contend that the rate is high because most blacks come from a poor economic-social life or that they feel their chances are limited in a majority-white America. Black students say white teachers are intolerant of their cultural differences and too quick to fail them for that reason. [P. 3]

In a border state until a few years ago, all delinquents that juvenile courts committed to training schools were sent to segregated facilities. Examination of the number of commitments revealed that before desegregation of the facilities judges were committing almost equal numbers of whites and nonwhites, but after desegregation the number of committed nonwhites almost doubled, while the number of whites almost halved. Although nonwhites, predominantly black, earlier were being committed in numbers disproportionate to their actual ratio within the population, the disproportion increased significantly after desegregation, leading some observers to conclude that though judges still attempted to meet their responsibilities they nonetheless acted in racially biased ways. The judges could be considered as intentional or unintentional racists.

A black veteran rejected on his first attempt to register to vote checked and rechecked but was unable to locate the error the white registrar had found in his application. When he got up to leave he inquired,

> "Ma-am, would you do one thing for me?"
> "What is that?"
> "Will you tell me the mistake I made?"

"Oh, sure. You underlined Mr. when you should have circled it."
[U. S. Civil Rights Commission 964]

This sort of testimony helped to pass the civil rights law in February 1964. The historic legislation contained eleven major provisions intended to:

> ... assure all citizens, regardless of race, color, religion or national origin, their equal rights: in voting; in access to hotels, restaurants, theaters and other places of public accommodation and to such other places as libraries and parks; in education; in Federally-assisted programs; and in employment. To accomplish this the bill ... [gave] the Justice Department additional powers, ... [established] two new agencies—an Equal Employment Opportunity Commission and a six-man Community Relations Service—and ... [extended] the life of the United States Civil Rights Commission. ... [U. S. Civil Rights Commission 1964, p. 1]

The civil rights law, passed primarily to redress wrongs against blacks, also served to remedy the wrongs against all other minority groups. President Johnson (1963) stated: "We have talked long enough in this country about equal rights. We have talked for one hundred years or more. It is time *now* to write the next chapter, and to write it in the books of law."

During testimony on the civil rights bill some people attempted to sweep under the rug the amount and kinds of discrimination against blacks, alleging that northern liberals were greatly exaggerating southern discrimination. However, investigation revealed quite the contrary.

Voter Registration

The numerical difference between white and black voter registration in certain states of the deep South was so enormous that racial discrimination was the only possible explanation. A government sampling of counties in old Confederate states revealed that while some counties had more registered white voters than the actual number of white inhabitants, no blacks at all were registered (U. S. Civil Rights Commission 1964).

In a typical county the white population over the age of twenty-one totaled 2,624; yet there were 2,810 registered white voters, or 107.1 percent of the population. No one in the qualified black population of 6,085 was registered. In another county that contained 1,900 white persons over twenty-one, 2,250, or 118.4 percent, were registered voters. None of the 5,122 blacks of voting age was registered. In a third county with a white voting population of 4,116, registered white voters numbered 6,130, or 148.9 percent. Here only fifty-six, 6.1 percent of the 909 blacks of voting age, were registered voters (U. S. Civil Rights Commission 1964). Although such registration patterns existed in northern states, they were generally not so extreme.

The drive to obtain voting rights for blacks and other minority groups was expensive in terms of emotion and human life. In Belzoni, Mississippi, the minister who led a black voting drive was shot down on the courthouse steps in broad daylight by men who had warned against carrying on his campaign. In Gadsden County, Florida, 300 black teachers were told they would lose their jobs if they tried to vote.

Almost a decade ago, in Selma, Alabama, hundreds of blacks ran a gauntlet of armed state troopers and stood in line eight hours without food or water in an attempt to register. In Fayette County, Tennessee, blacks who registered suffered serious economic retaliation and lost their jobs, according to the 1961 Civil Rights Commission report (1964):

A list of the "culprits" was circulated. White merchants quit trading with them. Pressure was brought to prevent suppliers in Memphis from selling to them. Their credit was stopped; their loans called; their mortgages foreclosed. They could not buy the necessities of life. One white banker was quoted as saying, "My secretary's got the names of the 325 who registered. I tell them, anybody on that list, no need coming into this bank. He'll get no crop loans here. Every store has got that list." [P. 2]

On July 1, 1963, Attorney General Robert Kennedy testified before the Senate Commerce Committee:

White people of whatever kind—prostitutes, narcotics pushers, Communists, or bank robbers—are welcome at establishments which will not admit certain of our Federal judges, ambassadors, and countless members of our Armed Forces.

Outlawing Discrimination

Kennedy was testifying in order to have written into the civil rights bill a prohibition against discrimination in most public facilities, such as hotels, motels, restaurants, theaters, sports arenas, barber shops, and gas stations. He and other proponents argued that no other form of discrimination touches people so directly in every aspect of daily life, and none is more violative of the human dignity perceived to be every American's birthright. Testimony also pointed out that although blacks suffer most from discriminatory practices, the same kinds of blatant discrimination are directed against almost all religious, racial, and minority groups that are not white Anglo-Saxon protestants (WASPS).

Additional provisions of the bill outlawed discrimination in such areas as education and federally assisted programs and provided for equal employment opportunities. President Eisenhower (1953) once remarked:

I will say this—I repeat it, I have said it again and again: wherever Federal funds are expended for anything, I do not see how any American can justify—legally, or logically, or morally—a discrimination in the expenditure of those funds as among our citizens. All are taxed to provide those funds. If there is any benefit to be derived from them, I think they must all share, regardless of such inconsequential factors as race and religion.

In a message to Congress ten years later, President Kennedy (1963) declared:

I ask you to look into your hearts—not in search of charity, for the Negro neither wants nor needs condescensions, but for the one plain, proud, and priceless quality that unites us all as Americans: a sense of justice. In this year of the Emancipation Centennial, justice requires us to insure the blessings of liberty for all Americans and their posterity—not merely for reasons of economic efficiency, world diplomacy, and domestic tranquility—but above all, because it is right.

Ten years after the historic march on Washington, D.C., in August 1963, when Martin Luther King delivered his "I Have A Dream" speech, several commentators indicated that the problem of racism had not been abolished. Roger Wilkins (1973) noted:

> It has been a long decade since that August of 1963 and neither white nor black Americans possess this summer the freedom from guilt, anger, and future pain that a sustained national purpose of eliminating racism would have given us. The grievances were too deep, the imbalances too great and racism too normal and American for love and legislation to plant the nation firmly on the road to absolution and racial decency in one short decade.... The race problem— though some wish it were gone—is still with us and the consequences of ignoring it multiply against future tranquillity. In a lot of barren and forsaken places in this country the grim clocks still tick. A third of black Americans are still poor and more than 40 percent of black children live in poverty.

Poverty and Racism

Racism in the United States touches people in many ways, including economics, criminal justice services, employment, and social relationships. Blacks and other minorities tend to be the poorest persons, but even these who are most deprived still look for better ways of life and greater opportunities for their children, at the very least.

The *Task Force Report: Juvenile Delinquency* (President's Commission on Law Enforcement and the Administration of Justice (1967*c*) observes the following:

> Living as he does in a neighborhood likely to be among the city's highest in rates of crime, ... [the slum dweller] worries about and wants police protection even more than people living in the same city's safer regions. He may not have much formal education ... and he may hesitate to visit teachers or attend school functions, but studies show that he too, like his college-graduate counterpart, is vitally interested in his children's education [see, e.g., Coleman et al. 1966; Cloward & Jones 1963]. And, while some inner-city residents, like some people everywhere, may not be eager to change their unemployed status, it is also true that many more of them toil day after day at the dullest and most backbreaking of society's tasks ... without hope of advancement. Very likely by his parents ... left

home ... looking for a better life, only to be absorbed into the yet more binding dependency and isolation of the inner city. [P. 42]

And a noted black author (Brown 1965) has commented:

The children of these disillusioned colored pioneers inherited the total lot of their parents, the disappointments, the anger. To add to their misery, they had little hope of deliverance. For where does one run to when he's already in the promised land? [P. 8]

That comment is concerned primarily with the plight of poor blacks but holds true for other minorities, such as Chicanos, Puerto Ricans, and American Indians. In fact, the American Indian is the most impoverished of *all* citizens. A comprehensive 1970 United States Census Bureau survey (1973) shows that Indian family income falls below that of other minority groups and far below that of the nation as a whole. The report also states that the Indian lags behind other Americans in almost every social and economic measurement except education. In terms of income, the report adds, the median for American Indian families in 1969 was $5,832. By contrast, the median income of persons of Latin-American origin was $7,534, and for blacks it was $6,308, in all considerably less than the national median of $9,590. The 1970 U.S. census survey (1973) also discovered that 40 percent of Indian families live on incomes below the poverty level; 32 percent of all black families are below it; but only 14 percent of all American families are below the poverty level.

Racism and Criminal Justice Administration

As indicated earlier, racism is not always a malicious or organized effort at discrimination, particularly in the criminal justice system. Studies have shown that the police, courts, and correctional agencies often treat minority group members less favorably than their white counterparts. For example, in the San Francisco Project (1965), which looked at sentencing practices in a northern California federal district in the mid-1960s, it was discovered that nonwhites and the poor received less probation and longer prison sentences than did white offenders.

Others have studied police reaction to offenders in regard to race and have reported that the black suspect is much more likely to be arrested and dealt with formally than is the white, especially if youthful (see, e.g., Piliavin & Briar 1964; Goldman 1963). In a review of *Delinquency in a Birth Cohort,* the reviewer (Lubeck 1973) states the following:

> Throughout the study, race emerged as the factor most highly related to delinquency.... The authors found that race was related to a nexus of factors indicative of disadvantaged social position. Nonwhite delinquents were most likely to have come from a low socioeconomic category, to have a greater history of residential and school mobility, to drop out of school, and to exhibit the lowest IQ's and school achievement levels.... Police decision-making appeared to be strongly influenced by racial considerations. Nonwhites were much more likely than whites to receive severe dispositions regardless of ... offense type or offense seriousness. While these results suggested that differential disposition was a function of racial prejudice, the authors lacked sufficient data to make definite conclusions in this area. [Pp. 78–79]

The black policeman himself sometimes feels the racial prejudice of his white colleagues. In a study of black policemen, Nicholas Alex (1969) reported:

> [Some] of the men interviewed felt that white policemen responded to them (as black policemen) simply in terms of racial categories and attributed to the Negro policeman all the stigmas implied by racial prejudice. In this situation, the white policeman completely accepts the stereotyped response to Negroes, and the uniform of the Negro policeman does not in any way change these feelings.... By ignoring the Negro as much as possible the white policeman removes himself from contact with him, and this lack of interaction relieves the white police officer from expressing hostility against the Negro policeman. However, this does not work, for situations do occur which require interaction. Consequently, the white police officer must fall back on other social devices to isolate himself from his own hostility. [Pp. 92–93]

Historical Developments

In *Strangers in the Land,* John Higham (1967) traces the historical development of racism in the United States and relates it to patterns of nativism:

Absent from the strictures of the eighteenth century nationalist, notions of racial superiority and exclusiveness appeared in the mid-nineteenth, but they were to undergo a long process of revision and expansion before emerging in the early twentieth century as the most important nativist ideology. [P. 131]

He notes that racial nativism forms only a segment of the larger evolution of the race consciousness that has occurred in recent times, and that what has come to be called race prejudice came about as a result of

... the extension to European nationalities of that sense of absolute difference which already divided white Americans from people of other colors. When sentiments analogous to those already discharged against Negroes, Indians, and Orientals spilled over into anti-European channels, a force of tremendous intensity entered the stream of American nativism. [P. 132]

The entire story of modern racial unrest, nativist and otherwise, has two basic levels—one emotional, the other intellectual. Most of the emotions flow from a reservoir of continuing suspicion and distrust accumulated over the span of American history toward human groups stamped by obvious differences of color. The ideas, however, depend on speculations on the nature of races.

Higham believes that the distinction between the two may be partly artificial. "[T]he spirit of white supremacy, or what may be labeled race-feeling, has interlocked with race-thinking at many points. Indeed, their convergence has given the problem of race its modern significance" (p. 132). The issue also becomes confused at times over the distinction between *ideas* and *practices*, for such a distinction determines the difference between prejudice and discrimination. Prejudice connotes an attitude or an opinion; discrimination implies an act or practice.

A once-common view, one still not completely abandoned, interpreted discrimination primarily as a consequence of a person's prejudices toward various other groups (Glenn 1963). But according to others (Freeman & Jones 1970), "We now know from a large set of studies in various fields that there is only limited correspondence between prejudice and discrimination. Attitudes and behavior, thoughts and actions are not the same thing" (p. 151).

Traditional religious beliefs, hardly spelled out or articulated, nonetheless served the practical purposes of the early American colonists who enslaved blacks and who "scourged Indians as Satanic agents" (Freeman & Jones 1970, p. 151). However, the evolution of white supremacy into a comprehensive philosophy of life required a great deal of work from philosophers and intellectuals concerned with race. Since such prejudice was not innate, race thinkers had to convince others to be hostile toward people who were different by reason of skin color or national origin.

Concepts of Race

Writers on race fell into two basic groups—those who believed that the races differed physiologically and those who believed the problem was cultural. Stimulated by scientific discoveries, men in the seventeenth and eighteenth centuries began to study human types systematically in order to catalog and explain them. They used physiological characteristics such as skin color, stature, and head shape to distinguish one type from another. Higham (1967) remarks, "Quite commonly [they] ... associated physical with cultural differences and displayed, in doing so, a feeling of white superiority over the colored races" (p. 134).

At the end of the nineteenth century significant waves of immigrants from European countries flowed toward American shores. While immigration to the Promised Land had always existed, the amount rarely had much impact on economics. In fact, the immigrant's inexpensive labor and commitment to learning American ways proved a boon to wealthy American nativists in positions of authority. But among the new immigrants were many who held views contrary to those of long-established citizens; in fact, many were anarchists, some were communists, and others simply by their presence threatened the status quo.

Consequently many writers began to suggest that these European "races" were of lower quality than Americans, and these ideas gained wide acceptance. According to Higham, several prominent writers began campaigns of foreign and racial agitation in order to convince the public that immigrants were severely threatening the American way of life. Hence racism and nativism became interchangeable, and discrimination against anyone who was different or who appeared to be different became commonplace. Further, considerable violence was associated with these beliefs (see chap. 7).

Scientific inquiries and studies led several persons to assert the notion of racial superiority, particularly the superiority of the white race over all others. In fact, in the early 1900s, Madison Grant, an intellectual who took pride in his ancestry, wrote *The Passing of the Great Race*, in which he stated flatly that different races cannot blend, and that any attempt at such assimilation would only lead to deterioration of the white race. Higham says, "Grant, relying on what he thought was scientific truth, made race the supreme value and repudiated all others inconsistent with it. This, at last, was racism" (pp. 156–57). Grant and others then helped to spur vicious attacks on Orientals (the "Yellow Peril"), blacks, and any other persons not of "pure blood," as in the "Nordic type."

Definitions

Webster's New World Dictionary (1970) defines race as "any of the different varieties of mankind, distinguished by form of hair, color of skin and eyes, stature, bodily proportions, etc. . . . The term has acquired so many unscientific connotations that in this sense it is often replaced in scientific usage by *ethnic stock* or *group.*" Dentler (1967) provides this explanation:

Ethnicity refers to a social characteristic of a population. Its root, *ethnikos*, means nation, and writers originally employed the term to describe behavior and attitudes associated with country of origin. Today, however, an ethnic group includes persons who, by virtue of commonly perceived physical and cultural traits, are self-conscious of special group membership and subject to differential treatment by persons outside the group.

The term "ethnicity" is akin to, yet broader, intellectually more accurate, and politically more responsible than the idea of race. Race is fundamentally a biological concept. It grew out of the untested assumption that the human species consists of branches which are

biologically distinct from each other. The shortcomings of the concept of race are so great that most social scientists prefer to work with
other more exact conceptions of group characteristics which are
essentially social and cultural. [P. 163]

Biological principles for defining and identifying races vary
and cannot be applied scientifically or consistently. Realistically,
people classify others through location, language, style of life,
and other criteria that generally have no relationship with biolo-
gy or physiology but are often thought of as racial. Dentler
(1967), then, states that the idea of race in terms of *science*
should be eliminated because the biological delineation is poor
and does not correspond with common social usage, even where
it may have relevance.

This position seems especially applicable in interpreting social
conflict. Ethnicity, not race, arises out of contact between historically separate human groups, and physical differences initially
are probably of little consequence. Dentler adds:

Skin color, stature, body type or hair texture, among other features,
may be singled out in the course of contact between groups and used
to make distinctions. But physical appearances by themselves seldom
if ever lead to the establishment of group differences. Proof of this
comes directly to mind: within many socially homogeneous populations there are substantial differences in physical appearance that do
not lead to cleavage or differential treatment. [P. 164]

Most social scientists today believe that in terms of biological
inheritance all races are alike in everything that really counts.
They recognize differences in skin color, facial features, and
bodily proportion, "but according to all evidence available, these
have no effect upon learning or behavior. With the exception of
several very small, isolated, inbred primitive tribes, all racial
groups seem to show the same distribution of every kind of
ability" (Horton & Leslie 1970, p. 352).

Thus the evidence seems to indicate that from a biological
point of view all races or ethnic groups have the same learning
abilities, but the apparent differences in personality, behavior,
and actual achievement are purely the result of social, cultural,
or environmental factors. "Such differences (for example, igno-

rance and shiftlessness among Negroes) are cited by the majority group to justify its discrimination which, in turn, perpetuates those very differences. Thus a vicious cycle is completed, and an illusion of innate race differences is preserved" (Dentler 1967, p. 352).

Attacking Stereotypes

Notwithstanding overwhelming evidence to the contrary, several respected scholars and intellectuals claim that inherent ability differences between the races indeed exist (see, e.g., Shuey 1958; van den Haag 1964; Jensen 1969). For the most part, however, other reputable scholars researching the field continue to attack their conclusions. In spite of the evidence, though, many people cling to their stereotyped thinking about others who appear to be different, and others act out their prejudices in discriminatory ways. Members of ethnic groups even today are discriminated against in housing, employment, education, and social relationships. Although equal opportunity is proposed as the hallmark of the democratic tradition, study after study reveals that more often than not the opposite is true. Legislation and social pressures have softened discrimination in the United States, but prejudicial action still exists, not only in isolated sections of the country but also in urban and metropolitan areas.

In order to counteract discrimination, various groups over the years have been involved in lawsuits, protest demonstrations, and ghetto riots, and have urged public hearings for legislative purposes. Considerable violence in recent years has involved radical whites and blacks, Black Panther incidents, charges of police brutality, and assassinations of prominent black and white leaders. These events illustrate the depth of feeling associated with the process of racial change in the United States. They also expose the bitter resistance to change that some white Americans show as well as some black Americans' desperate insistence on change. While the white-black incidents appear most dramatic, serious discriminatory problems exist for other ethnic groups as well—Chicanos, Indians, Orientals, and persons of certain national origins and religious persuasions.

Prejudice

In a historic work, *The Nature of Prejudice,* Gordon W. Allport (1954) analyzes relationships between groups and suggests that they are conditioned by six basic and interconnected factors. According to him, each forms a different but necessary approach to the understanding of prejudice. These factors are: *historical, socio-cultural, situational, personality, phenomenological,* and *stimulus-object.* Allport states, "There is no master key. Rather, what we have at our disposal is a ring of keys, each of which opens one gate of understanding" (p. 208).

Thomas F. Pettigrew (1971) has adapted Allport's work into the schema shown in Figure 1.1. Pettigrew notes that "the six approaches form a lens model that focuses down from the broadest approach, the historical, to the main stimulus-object of the process" (p. 408).

FIGURE 1.1

	six approaches to the study of race relations
	historical
social factors	sociocultural
	situational
	personality
individual factors	phenomenological
	stimulus-object

SOURCE: Thomas F. Pettigrew, "Race Relations," in *Contemporary Social Problems*, 3d ed., ed. Merton and Nisbet (New York: Harcourt Brace Jovanovich, 1971), p. 409. Adapted from Gordon W. Allport, *The Nature of Prejudice* (Cambridge, Mass.: Addison-Wesley, 1954), p. 207 (Figure 11).

The Six Approaches to Understanding Prejudice

The Historical Approach. The broadest approach examines historical factors and incidents, such as slavery, segregation legislation, and socioeconomic forces that may be linked to the development of prejudice.

The Socio-cultural Approach. The cultural and institutional factors that produce the context in which race relations take place are examined here. General questions raised include the numbers and types of ethnic groups, how well they do economically, the kinds of occupations open to them, and such sociological considerations as housing and educational patterns.

The Situational Approach.   In this set of factors the analysis becomes narrower and more specific in considering certain ways in which groups encounter one another. Here the historical and socio-cultural factors, on the one hand, and the individual factors, on the other, come together and "conditioned by particular circumstances, produce 'race relations' as such" (Pettigrew 1971, p. 409).

The Personality Approach.   Attention here begins to center on the psychology of the individual. Questions are raised about the need for scapegoating (common in the United States), why people have closed minds, and what are the psychological processes of attitude development.

The Phenomenological Approach.   Now the analysis becomes even more specific as explorations and analyses are made about individual experiences, contacts, and occurring phenomena. Racial stereotypes, perceptions, and belief systems are studied.

The Stimulus-Object Approach.   The most specific approach examines the focus of the issue—the person against whom the prejudice is directed—not just as the victim of prejudice and discrimination but also as a reactor to such oppression. Explorations include studies of the object's behavior as a possible cause of prejudice and discrimination and of others' reactions to that behavior.

Other Approaches to the Problem

Aaron Antonovsky (1964) suggests that too much emphasis has been placed on psychological explanations of discrimination. He argues for a more sociological approach and adds:

> The failure to perceive that discrimination is a system of social relations underlies the overemphasis of research on the psychological factor of prejudice. Whatever its psychological origins, discrimination takes place largely outside the realm of the conscious decisions and the freedom of choice of individual persons. It is more than the sum of the individuals who discriminate; it is an institution with a life of its own. [Pp. 410–11]

Antonovsky defines discrimination as:

> ... the effective injurious treatment of persons on grounds rationally irrelevant to the situation. Individuals are denied *desired* and *expected* rewards or opportunities for reasons that have no relation to their capacities, merits, or behavior, but solely because of membership in an identifiable group. [P. 409]

He says that even though we do not have enough evidence to fully understand the social arrangements that create and continue discrimination, at least six *theoretical* notions can help us to understand the search.

First, the *weight of the past* describes traditional patterns that seem to serve some function and so are not easily changed. Sale of a house to a black family in an all-white neighborhood is an example.

Second, social behavior appears to be predominantly *role-playing*. Thus a person acts in expected ways appropriate to a position occupied, regardless of personal beliefs and values. A real estate broker probably will not show a black family a house for sale in a white neighborhood if the community does not expect such action, regardless of the broker's own beliefs.

Third, according to Antonovsky, *isolating mechanisms* operate to prevent the victims of discrimination from obtaining relief or access to the necessary tools to break down the barriers. Not being shown houses for sale, voting restrictions, and inadequate educational and recreational facilities are examples.

Fourth, law and other *social sanctions* often abet discrimination, which reflects the climate of opinion and the dominant values of the community. Vested interest group pressures, restrictive covenants, and voluntary business association practices illustrate the point.

Institutionalized evasion of antidiscriminatory policies is often ignored in studies of race relations. Intentional evasion of school desegregation mandates, apathetic law enforcement, and ineffective communications between government agencies are prime examples.

Finally, *anticipatory fears*, held by neighbors, colleagues, work groups, and the public in general, often operate to prevent changes in discriminatory practices. Fears about the possible breakdown in community values because of school bussing or about possible devaluation of property as a consequence of sales to nonwhites—whether real or rationalizations—are included.

Effects of Discrimination

Although Antonovsky argues for a sociological perspective he takes, in reality, a social-psychological approach to the problem of discrimination. Nonetheless, he believes that one of the worst aspects of discrimination as an institution is its "feedback character" or what others have called the "self-fulfilling prophecy" and the "principle of cumulation" (Myrdal 1944; Merton, 1951). Antonovsky (1964) writes:

> Discrimination vitiates the power and knowledge of its victims, so that they may often be unable to take advantage of the facilities and opportunities which do exist to combat it. It may lower their levels of aspiration, and it produces a degree of objective support for the original rationalizations. It would be an oversimplification to assume that this vicious circle encompasses all factors; for then, we would expect discrimination to spread and harden into a caste system. Other factors modify these tendencies, but they negate neither the significance of the feedback nor its consequences. [P. 412]

Despite all efforts to understand discrimination and major attempts to end it, it continues to exist. Theoretically, discrimination might be eliminated if the victimized minority groups would relinquish their claims and aspirations to equal opportunities in the struggle for life chances. That is, if they would accommodate to a caste status, and, according to Antonovsky (1964), that is exactly what happened in the North and in the South at the end of the nineteenth century.

A second alternative, one that has been widely received and practiced in the last decade, is the establishment of quota systems through which specific percentages of minority groups are admitted to universities, hired or promoted, or moved into neighborhoods where they were previously unwelcome. Since this procedure has not been fully tested it has raised considerable concern and anxiety; yet it continues to be applied on both formal and informal bases.

A third alternative seems to have been most prominent in the 1960s but is less used today—violent confrontation. This method was advocated by many white and nonwhite militants who believed that the only way to end discrimination was to violently oppose persons and agencies that seemed to discriminate the most. Reasoning people, thought the militants, would realize the evils and wrongs inherent in discrimination and thus would become an effective force in bringing about responsible change. What many of these people failed to realize, or accept, was that a significant backlash could ruin their hopes. Indeed, in many instances the results of some elections along with the failure of some proposed bills to pass through some legislatures proved that such a white backlash did, in fact, occur.

Working for Change

Today experiments, programs, proposals, and courses of action suggest that peaceful working relationships, education, and positive experiences of various groups working together on specific issues and causes all bear on the lessening of discrimination and bigotry. Shouts of "police brutality" are significantly fewer, even though many people still consider verbal abuse of ethnic minorities almost as offensive as physical abuse. Racism in schools and employment, in housing and recreational facilities, and in all other areas of life still exists. Laws have essentially eradicated de jure segregation, but de facto segregation still exists because many Americans are not yet ready to change lifelong beliefs and practices.

Some social analysts have argued that as a significant black middle class emerges discrimination against blacks will become a thing of the past and that other minority groups also will be less discriminated against. Unfortunately, the evidence for such a position, according to Freeman and Jones (1970), ". . . is not entirely convincing and the argument is, at present anyhow, untenable" (p. 156). They argue, along with others, that it is really not the lower class blacks and other nonwhites who have the worst economic problems; rather, it is the middle class nonwhites, who have considerable education but cannot buy the house they want or live in the neighborhood they choose.

After several violent summers and the passage of considerable civil rights legislation it appeared that America was well on the way to ending discrimination against ethnic minorities and was moving toward an integrated society. Today, the trends are contradictory. Certainly nonwhites are making headway in obtaining jobs, education, housing, and political influence, but also society appears to be more separated. Horton and Leslie (1970) point out: "Polarization of viewpoint, alienation of the races from each other, and mutual hostility and distrust are growing" (p. 405).

The National Advisory Commission on Civil Disorders (1968) announced as its basic conclusion that "Our nation is moving toward two societies, one black, one white—separate and unequal" (p. 1). In 1969 two highly respected organizations, Urban America, Inc., and the Urban Coalition, published a new study, *One Year After*, in which they concluded that "we are a year closer to being two societies, black and white, increasingly separate and unequal." Although a few of the many recommendations of the National Advisory Commission have been followed, for the most part no massive revision of our national priorities has occurred. In fact, some would argue for regression.

It is probably safe to predict that halfway and halfhearted measures will not work. Token integration, grudging concessions, and a dribble of expenditures will not bring racial peace; in fact, such actions may bring about further polarization as ethnic minorities realize more and more the gap between what they are entitled to have and what they are actually receiving. But to do nothing is to encourage even greater polarization and the drift toward two societies.

Clearly massive integration in housing or the elimination of de facto school segregation cannot possibly be accomplished in the near future. It is equally foolish to assume that the mere opening of employment opportunities is going to have a dramatic impact on the problems of discrimination. The remedy requires more than a simple increase in the number of Equal Opportunity Employers or union acceptance of nonwhite members.

Freeman and Jones summarize the current American atmosphere:

Given the climate of the white community today, it is doubtful that their values will change to the extent required to promote integration and freedom of choice in education, housing, and social relations, federal laws and programs notwithstanding. While gains undoubtedly will be made, they will remain small and sporadic with the continuing risks of violence and the proliferation of radical movements. Perhaps the application of rational Black Power will trigger the solution, but one cannot be completely optimistic about the chances for ending discrimination in the contemporary American community. [P. 173]

CHAPTER 2

Alienation and Anomie

The Dropout Society

Throughout recorded history individual members of every civilized society have vocally opposed their governments and rulers. Sometimes operating alone, sometimes in groups, these people have expressed disagreement, conflict, and outrage over practices, issues, policies, and political developments. In a sense, then, individuals and oppressed groups have been alienated from the societies in which they have lived.

Shortly after World War II, and particularly after the Korean conflict in the early 1950s, greater attention and concern seemed to center on those who were dropping out. Beatniks, hippies, teenieboppers, heads—all, no matter what the name, who had become estranged from society—became targets of ridicule and social action programs. As society grew more technocratic, more bureaucratic, and more materialistic, the dropout rate appeared to rise. The exact amount of spread in such alienation is impossible to determine simply because few persons were that concerned about the isolated individual. It was not until dropout groups became activists that others began to take notice.

Additionally, the alienated had always been viewed as persons from the lower class "who just didn't have it." However, the 1960s, and especially the heights of the Vietnam conflict, clearly revealed that alienation was affecting not just lower socioeconomic groups but middle and upper classes as well. Thus when middle-aged, comfortable people, children of the wealthy, and others thought to have made it in society began to join blacks, Chicanos, and other oppressed groups, society began to express concern about alienation.

Definitions

Alienation is a difficult term. However, social and behavioral scientists, who use the word most frequently, have defined alienation as either a psychological or social estrangement or separation between a part or the whole of the personality and significant aspects of the world of experience (Gould & Kolb 1964).

Although numerous philosophers have discussed alienation as a form of deviance, social scientists have looked to Marx (1959) and Merton (1957) and behavioral scientists have looked to Freud (1953) for inspiration and explanation of the concept.

According to Marx, economic production and the system of class domination alienates humans from the mainstream of life. He believed that every human has a right to share in profits derived from labor, but the disproportionate sharing that results from the class system alienates man from his work, nature, and himself.

Merton, whose thinking derives from Durkheim's earlier work (1952), uses the term *anomie* in treating estrangement or alienation as a consequence of instability, demoralization, and deinstitutionalization. In discussing American society Merton attempts to account for the different rates of deviance in various locations in American society in terms of the kinds of opportunities for achievement of goals or success. He suggests that the lower social strata and certain racial and ethnic subgroups represent the disadvantaged social locations in American society that are not able to achieve socially desirable goals through legitimate means. Stress and strain in the pursuit of normal goals force persons who represent these groups to engage frequently in illegitimate behavior in order to achieve success or cope with failure.

Freud, although concerned with social values and norms, nonetheless placed greatest emphasis on the individual and his ability to cope with stresses and strains of daily living. Freud suggested that alienation occurs when the individual is unable to reconcile societal demands with personal needs and desires. When the inability to reconcile such differences becomes stressful, the individual becomes neurotic (acts out unconscious desires) and may become psychotic (withdraws from society itself). However, Marcuse, a Marxist philosopher, finds in Freud the suggestion that where class domination is prevalent, the individual's pathological behavior worsens (Marcuse 1955).

Depending on the writer's values, literature suggests that alienation is a phenomenon concerned with man's estrangement from the society he lives in or his estrangement from himself. In other words, alienation is either a social condition or a psychological state of affairs for the individual. In either instance, one who is, or appears to be, alienated is one who is deviant.

Alienation and Deviance

The person who is unable to achieve a relatively stable existence in society and for some reason appears to deviate in thought or behavior is viewed as a social outcast. In its mildest form such deviance is viewed as eccentricity; in its most severe form it is labeled as crime or delinquency. The mild form alarms few people, for the eccentric is viewed as someone merely different or weird. An eccentric may be a hermit, a recluse, or any harmless person who does things differently.

The severe form alarms society because sometimes the deviancy is actually harmful to other persons. Crime and delinquency frequently result in physical harm, and no one (except a masochist) enjoys being hurt. Therefore, although deviance can take various forms, societal reaction determines the deviant's fate. The eccentric is generally left alone to be dealt with only by family members. However, for crime and delinquency society has developed systems of social control.

People are concerned with control and lessening of harmful deviance, whatever its causes. Throughout history society has attempted to deal with different forms of deviance and alienation; today, a general systems approach is popular. In *Cure for Chaos*, Simon Ramo (1969) summarizes the approach:

> In the systems approach, the concentration is on the analysis and design of the whole, as distinct from analysis and design of the components or the parts. It is an approach that insists upon looking at a problem in its entirety, taking into account all the facets, all the intertwined parameters. It is a process for understanding how they interact with one another and how these factors can be brought into proper relationship for the optimum solution of the problem. The systems approach relates the technology to the need, the social to the technological aspects; indeed, it starts by insisting on a clear understanding of exactly what the problem is and of the goals that should dominate the solution and lead to the criteria for evaluating alternative avenues. As the end result, the approach seeks to work out a detailed description of a specified combination of men and machines —with such concomitant assignment of function, designated use of material, and pattern of information flow that the whole system represents a compatible, optimum, interconnected ensemble for achieving the end desired. (P. 107)

Ramo suggests that alienation and deviance should not be viewed as either social or psychological ills affecting society or the individual; instead, they should be viewed in their totality. Their causes and their cures should be viewed systematically, or our inability to understand or "cure" them will remain. Ramo continues:

> Typical problems we now face are growing in complexity at an increasing rate. In many important facets of our society our choice now is clear: either we take the systems approach route and perform well, or we accept absolute and utter confusion and chaos. In some instances it simply will not do at all to let the problem build up, to let the operation grow as a group of uncoordinated elements, safe in the

feeling that all penalty we incur is a small deviation from optimum. In some situations you cannot have a less-than-good system. For certain classes of problems, if you take away the compatibility, the harmony of the ensemble, if you fail to insure the appropriate kind of interactions—in short, if you don't work the problem as the systems problem that it really is—then you will have an absolute failure, not merely an inefficient compromise. [P. 122]

In *The Politics of Therapy*, forensic psychiatrist Seymour Halleck (1971) suggests that one reason for our failure to control crime and delinquency is our overemphasis on the causes of deviancy within the individual and lack of emphasis on the interaction of society and individual. In discussing juvenile justice, for example, he says:

If reforming a small injustice in the juvenile court system does not help society much, the planner will have to direct his attention to our total system of justice and eventually to the relationship of the judicial system to the rest of society. (Pp. 184–85)

Positive Values

Up to this point we have suggested that alienation and/or deviancy, in the form of individual eccentricity or criminal behavior, is a negative phenomenon and one that sometimes elicits from society harsh and punitive reactions. But not all deviance should be so viewed, including crime and delinquency, which are at times even healthy for society. Are we condoning crime and delinquency—even urging their increase? Certainly not. We are suggesting, though, that some deviance, even crime, is absolutely functional and important in a changing, prospering society. Durkheim (1950) suggested the same notion many years ago when he said that crime is normal, "for a society exempt from it is utterly impossible." He explains:

Crime is ... necessary; it is bound up with the fundamental conditions of all social life, and by that very fact it is useful, because these conditions of which it is a part are themselves indispensable to the normal evolution of morality and law.

Durkheim is not really accepting crime but, rather, suggesting that a crime-free society could be repressive—that is, one in which individuals could not voice complaints and grievances. Crime, he adds, is merely a label; as community standards and sentiments shift, someone or some act always will be viewed as deviant or considered criminal. Murder, rape, and burglary are not popular forms of deviancy, but Durkheim believes that when they occur, they nonetheless indicate a healthy society; individuals are not so suppressed as to be not "free" to behave in ways that meet their own needs.

If the notion that murder and rape suggest a healthy society is difficult to accept, we need only think of the importance to a society of persons who are willing to break the law in order to bring attention to its possible injustices. For example, Martin Luther King, Jr., and his followers, who were willing to violate the law, commit criminal acts, probably hastened by years the correction of the injustices in de jure discrimination. Durkheim suggests that collective sentiments change only when someone brings attention to them; laws change when community morality changes. Unfortunately, these changes do not always come by peaceful means.

Deviancy in the forms of crime and delinquency is often perceived with alarm but tolerated at times either because it is "a way of life" or because "it really doesn't hurt anyone." Thus Daniel Bell (1953) noted: "While Americans made gambling illegal, they did not in their hearts think of it as wicked—even the churches benefited from the bingo and lottery crazes. So they gambled—and gamblers flourished" (p. 217).

Laws and Politics

Laws change simply because legislators and courts change them. They are changed, Durkheim would argue, because a society is composed of individuals free to behave often in criminal ways in order to bring attention to the need for change. Thus collective sentiments and moral judgments change over time. Acts previously not criminal become criminal; acts previously criminal may become noncriminal. At one time in some areas of the United States the law forbade the seating of whites and blacks at the same lunch counter; today the law forbids restaurants to discriminate because of race. At one time those who insisted on racial mixing at lunch counters were deviant; today those who refuse service because of race are the criminals.

The labeling of an act as deviant is seen as a political act, but so is the labeling of the person who commits a deviant act political in nature. In *Radical Non-Intervention: Rethinking the Delinquency Problem*, Edwin Schur (1973) says:

> Crime and delinquency are inherently political phenomena. This is so for at least two reasons: because public policy decisions of various sorts shape the social structures and value systems within which such behavior occurs; and because ultimately the substance of crime and delinquency laws is . . . a matter for political decision. [P. 139]

Two others suggest that public policies and laws are formulated by those who hold power (Quinney 1970 b) and that ". . . deviance is the name of the conflict game in which individuals or loosely organized small groups with little power are strongly feared by a well-organized, stable minority or majority who have a large amount of power" (Lofland 1966, p. 14).

Schur argues that because of the significant changes that have occurred recently in American society and because of rapid social change it is not always possible to draw a simple line between individual deviance and social or political conflict. For political and social reasons, groups have violated laws to further their own goals, while "persons we earlier would have labeled individual deviants (drug addicts, homosexuals, ex-prisoners) are organizing and engaging in political action in support of their collective interests" (p. 140).

This heightened concern for one's individual and collective rights, regardless of labels others may apply, has initiated an era in which some persons and groups are questioning the social significance of some forms of deviance (e.g., drug consumption, gambling, adult homosexuality, abortion). Others—namely, those who hold power—merely want to consider deviance as an individual matter that needs and ought to be controlled. Groups of youths who are antiestablishment seek significant changes in the social structure of society; persons who hold power look for ways to control alienated youths who are merely "acting out adolescent rebellion."

Youth Culture

The so-called youth or teen-age culture and the ways various segments of society, including the youth themselves, view the contemporary situation may illustrate the conflict between socially significant and individual deviance.

Growing up has always been difficult, but by and large the process has been an individual experience to be endured alone. Certainly, an adolescent shares his experiences with others, frequently behaves as a part of a small group or a cohort, often commits delinquent acts with peers, but generally such growing up has been viewed as something one must do and eventually will accomplish more or less successfully.

However, not until the end of World War II and later in the fifties were adolescents recognized as a distinct subcultural group. Youth collectives, such as gangs, clubs, and organizations, had always existed, but they had never been seen as an all-encompassing group. Of course, heightened materialism, technocracy, and other developments in society enhanced the subculture, for merchants became quite willing to recognize an increasingly affluent group that could purchase their products and become legitimate consumers. An analysis of record and clothing industry sales techniques shows that even though adolescents still cannot be said to have single purposes and goals, merchants have treated them that way and have contributed largely to the so-called youth culture of today.

As society broke out of the silent fifties into the active sixties, adolescents moved from a culture to a counterculture. Roszak (1969) suggests that this youthful counterculture results from a pervasive alienation from and questioning of the technocracy, bureaucracy, and materialism of the adult society.

The Task Force Report *Juvenile Delinquency and Youth Crime,* prepared for the President's Commission on Law Enforcement and the Administration of Justice (1967 c), asserts that adolescents today live in a distinct society of their own. This society, however, is not easy

> . . . to understand, to describe, or, for that matter, to live in. In some ways it is an intensely materialistic society [and] . . . it is an intensely sensual society; its members are preoccupied with the sensations

they can obtain from surfing or drag racing or music or drugs. In some ways it is an intensely moralistic society; its members are preoccupied with independence and honesty and equality and courage. On the whole it is a rebellious, oppositional society, dedicated to the proposition that the grownup world is a sham. At the same time it is a conforming society; being inexperienced, unsure of themselves, and, in fact, relatively powerless as individuals, adolescents to a far greater extent than their elders conform to common standards of dress and hair style and speech, and act jointly, in groups—or gangs. [P. 41]

Youthful rebellion has always been viewed as a part of growing up and generally has been accepted by the older generation. It is something that every parent has himself experienced and, in turn, expects of his offspring. Such rebellion has been explained in psychological terms, and efforts to understand and control it tended to be a private family matter. Of course, schools, church groups, and law enforcement agencies, among others, have always been concerned with adolescent rebellion, for not uncommonly this kind of acting out takes the form of delinquency. Thus adolescent turmoil caused concern, but it was never viewed as a cultural activity that took on a political tone.

Adolescent Rebellion

During the sixties, adolescent rebellion took on new forms as youths throughout the country began to voice most actively their disenchantment with the society inherited from their parents. Perhaps beginning with the free-speech movement in Berkeley, youths engaged in oppositional and revolutionary activities. No longer were they just trying to grow up; they were trying to change the society they lived in. The Vietnam issue became pervasive as youths collected their resources and became a strong and viable force for change. They began to reject anything and everything associated with the status quo, especially the existing power structure or the establishment.

According to Flacks (1971), in the behavior of youth today we are witnessing ". . . a subculture . . . that looked at first like a deviant group but turned out to be a vanguard" (p. 51). Flacks further suggests that the youth culture today remains as rebellious as that of yesterday but now is a collective force dedicated to societal change. No doubt youthful attacks against the material and moral decay of our society have had significant impact on our political system. The bitter and frequently well-organized antipathy toward the war in Vietnam is perhaps the most dramatic example of all.

Separation of the youthful rebellion associated with growing up from the organized rebellion associated with youth groups and organizations is not always possible. Some people, for example, have wondered at youths who jump on so many reform bandwagons that they cannot possibly believe in all the issues with equal strength. Adults, who frequently pick one or two issues to fight, are unable to understand the nondiscriminating youths who march and picket and demonstrate for every issue that comes along. Thus it has been argued that some youths rebel for the sake of rebelling and not because they are truly committed to the actual issue.

Deviance and Innovation

We have said that certain kinds of deviancy—often associated with those who seem to be the most alienated or most deviant—are healthy for society, especially as they bring about needed changes in laws, attitudes, and values. From a sociological perspective, we can say that some deviance is "functional" for society, especially since it brings about creative and innovative change. Some deviance may form the basis for new institutions that are better equipped to function than are older ones. Without protest and organized concern among consumers, for example, corporations would continue to ignore consumer desires. Automobile manufacturers today appear to be more responsible in the areas of safety and pollution reduction, perhaps in large measure because of protest.

Thus protest apparently deviant in nature in relation to cultural norms frequently is innovative and likely to be dynamic. But Gross (1959) asserts, "Social dysfunction is not a latter-day terminological substitute for 'immorality' or 'unethical practice' " (p. 182).

Sometimes, according to Coser (1962), the norms of the group actually may be at fault and not the innovator who rejects them. To an unknown extent, some deviation from current norms probably is functional for the basic goals of the group.

Regarding society's views on those who are most alienated and turn their alienation into protest and change, Merton (1966) wrote:

> In the history of every society, one supposes, some of its culture heroes eventually come to be regarded as heroic in part because they are held to have had the courage and the vision to challenge the beliefs and routines of their society. The rebel, revolutionary, non-conformist, heretic, or renegade of an earlier day is often the culture hero of today. Moreover, the accumulation of dysfunctions in a social system is often the prelude to concerted social change that may bring the system closer to the values that enjoy the respect of members of the society. [Pp. 822–23]

Moral Entrepreneurs

Sociologist Howard Becker (1963) coined the term "moral entrepreneur" to describe "outsiders" to the mainstream of society who promote in the society the idea that something is deviant and needs to be changed. In seeking change, particularly in law, such people try to convince others that their ideas about the change and how people should approach it are correct. Moral entrepreneurs sometimes create a movement, which can take the form of an organization, and work actively in its cause. Most of their entrepreneurial behavior is directed at those in power, particularly the state, as they attempt to write into criminal law the range of deviance for which the courts may impose sanctions and penalties. Historical examples include consumer laws, drug abuse laws, and the Prohibition Amendment.

In *Social Deviance,* Daniel Glaser (1971) comments on the moral entrepreneur, drawing a distinction between deviants who prey on victims and deviant acts that may be said to be victimless in nature:

> One important observation that should be made on moral entrepreneurship, however, is that the laws against predation (preying on innocent victims) have a history quite different from that of the laws against deviant consumption, selling, performance, belief, or status.

The definition of predation as deviant has been crescive (increasing), while the definition of other acts and statuses as deviance has been episodic. Because in-group predations create clear-cut victims and threaten the security of person or property, popular sympathies aroused by them vary more in intensity than in direction. Rarely if ever do people try to repeal a law against predation; they only try to alter the penalties or the definitions. Insurance companies and others with special interests, rather than the types of persons or movements usually regarded as moral entrepreneurs, have been the main promoters of new definitions or sanctions for predation, particularly on property offenses. [Pp. 93–94]

In the last few years some reverse moral entrepreneurship has been practiced as groups have attempted to change criminal laws in terms eliminating some laws, reducing penalties, and/or promoting court decisions that have the effect of changing existing practices and procedures. An excellent example is the work being done to repeal or otherwise reduce criminal penalties for drug abuse, especially possession and use of marijuana. Again, the American Friends Service Committee (1971) seeks to decriminalize and otherwise overhaul the American criminal justice system, particularly corrections.

The moral entrepreneur generally must persuade others to define as criminal those acts first perceived only as atypical, especially deviant acts other than predation, since such acts do not particularly threaten anyone in terms of harm to body or property. In order to bring about change and interest in the issue, however, the moral entrepreneur must convince others that the act or status is indeed threatening.

For successful persuasion, according to Glaser (1971), the moral entrepreneur must promote three crucial contentions:

... (1) the deviant injures himself, either in this world or in an afterlife; (2) the deviance is contagious (if not eliminated it will spread to our children or even to us); (3) the deviance, though not predatory in itself, is conducive to predation, and is thereby threatening. [P. 94]

The arguments for change become exaggerated as the moral entrepreneur attempts to seduce citizens into support of his belief systems. Thus he seeks to convince others that without additional penalties for marijuana use, for example, users will become more depraved and will "eventually rape our children." Further, drinking will lead to molestation of women and children; prostitution and homosexual behavior are not only immoral but also will lead to more depravity, sin, and eternal damnation. It is interesting to note how often those who demand more statutes and penalties for acts associate the deviant act with sexual promiscuity, diminution of morality, and a general decline in society.

Changing Society

If a society, then, is free and nonrepressive it allows dissent and experiences deviance to the right and the left of the political spectrum. That is, the society is always in the middle of extremist points of view. Some forces seek to repeal all drug laws, say, by invoking the belief that what one does to one's own body is that individual's concern and not society's. At the very least, some would argue, addiction should not be dealt with on a criminal law basis but, rather, handled as a medical problem. Others would argue, conversely, that the only way to reduce immoral behavior is to define it as a crime and provide the strongest possible penalties for violation. These forces would reject the notion that addiction should be dealt with medically, although some would accept such treatment if all addicts were locked up until "cured."

In a free society, then, not only are conflicting values and beliefs expressed but adherents also try to persuade bystanders that one particular view is more just and appropriate than another. Vested interests make a dynamic society; when they clash they frequently produce change. Society is almost never stagnant: it changes as one group manifests greater power over another group; it changes as it shifts its values and beliefs.

Change, however, poses a special dilemma for many segments of society. The youth, for example, are never sure which values their elders most treasure and are thus most likely to enforce. Police may feel the same dilemma, for they are the official representatives of society and must enforce the laws of the community. Obviously it is not possible or practical to enforce all laws with equal vigor at all times. Thus law enforcement is necessarily selective—selective primarily as a response to the enforcer's perception of which values society holds most dear.

Police become both the agents and the victims of social control. Whether or not to arrest prostitutes, adult homosexuals, or draft-card burners is not always a simple decision, especially since various vested interest groups influence many police department policies. Control of mass demonstrations poses another dilemma, in terms not just of "good" policing but also of the general community's tolerance of various kinds of disturbances and deviance. Curfew laws frequently are not enforced. Late-night gatherings of youth may not arouse the community at a particular drive-in restaurant, but if such loitering upsets local businessmen or if delinquent behavior ensues, curfew laws are more likely to be enforced. Somewhere along the line the police are called to make value judgments that in large measure reflect moral judgments—what is best for you, and what is best for society, notwithstanding what the laws do or do not say.

Law and Morality

Arguments about morality and criminal law are especially acute; consequently, an active debate is being carried on now. The issue began to receive considerable attention in 1957 when the so-called Wolfenden Report (Committee on Homosexual Offenses and Prostitution 1957) was issued. A British governmental committee to examine the laws on prostitution and homosexual behavior prepared the report, which included a recommendation that penalties for private homosexual activity between consenting adults be removed. Support for the recommendation lay in the belief that criminal law should not be used to enforce moral standards or as a mechanism for social control, especially in matters related to citizens' private lives. The report, however, made an exception: the law may rightfully intrude where necessary to preserve public order and decency, to protect individuals from offensive and injurious behavior, and to guard against exploitation and corruption, particularly of those who might be most vulnerable. The report stated:

Unless a deliberate attempt is to be made by society, acting through the agency of the law, to equate the sphere of crime with that of sin, there must remain a realm of private morality which is, in brief and crude terms, not the law's business. To say this is not to condone or encourage private immorality. [P. 24]

This laissez-faire policy for citizen behavior has stirred up considerable debate in both Britain and the United States. Lord Patrick Devlin (1965) argued that "the criminal law as we know it is based upon moral principle. In a number of crimes its function is simply to enforce a moral principle and nothing else" (p. 7). Conversely, legal philosopher H. L. A. Hart (1963) argues that when individual liberty is considered, the law should be very carefully limited. Hart further contends that any justification for imposing criminal penalties to regulate what can be considered moral behavior must be compelling. Devlin, however, counters that the status quo—that is, the continuing right of the state to impose moral values on citizens—justifies not changing the law. Further, he argues that the responsibility for providing justification for a change must rest with those who seek such change.

Contemporarily, Schur (1973) claims that the Hart and the Wolfenden Report positions appear to be winning the argument:

This is so not simply because of its possible philosophic merits, but also because of a great deal of evidence showing the ineffectiveness (and actual harmfulness) of overextending the criminal law. . . . Such evidence is especially plentiful in crimes without victims. [P. 144]

Schur says that the effects of using morality as a base for criminal law produce a number of difficulties both for society and for law enforcement agencies. He suggests that in victimless crimes (e.g., homosexual behavior, drug use, and gambling) only consensual transactions are involved, for a participant probably would not complain to law enforcement authorities. "The absence of a complaining victim and the consequent difficulty in obtaining evidence hampers enforcement activity tremendously and forces police to rely on highly questionable techniques such as the use of informers, decoys, and electronic surveillance" (p. 144).

About society, Schur says:

. . . given the consensual and usually private nature of the transactions, and the supply-demand factor that frequently raises the economic incentive for illicit 'suppliers' (i.e., drug importers and distributors, illegal abortionists), there is virtually no possibility of effective enforcement. And not only are these laws blatantly unworkable, but they set the stage for much secondary crime (theft by addicts to support their habits) and drive many potentially law-abiding citizens into criminal roles and increasingly antisocial outlooks. [Pp. 144–45]

(For more discussion on the concept of victimless crimes, see chap. 11.)

Law Enforcement and Future Prospects

Alienation, or deviance, whether in the form of individual beliefs and behavior or collective or group action, may not be more pervasive in our society today than in the past, but more persons have become increasingly concerned with its causes and effects. Certainly, law enforcement officials, who are legally authorized to enforce the laws of the state, are caught in the middle, for they are the ones who deal most frequently with certain categories of the alienated or deviants. The law enforcement agency is more concerned with enforcement than is any other facet of the criminal justice field. Since enforcement is a frontline action of the agency it may possibly become an important medium for evaluating and analyzing contemporary values and beliefs.

Whether or not a police agency should attempt to influence laws, regulations, and beliefs is hotly debated. That the police do indeed influence community belief systems goes without saying, for internal policies determine which laws will or will not be stringently enforced. Police departments, of course, do not have complete autonomy in such matters. However, in the absence of direction from the courts, legislative bodies, and elected officials, police departments are, in effect, often forced to decide which moral issues take precedence.

The debate over the right of the police to make such decisions will continue for a long time. Responses of individual officers and departments in this controversy, of course, will make an impact on social standards and community values. The labeling of the alienated—the deviant—and the way in which social control agencies respond to them will most likely change in the future. The specificity and extent of these future changes simply cannot be predicted.

CHAPTER 3

The Outlook for
the American Family

Defining the Family

In *A Dictionary of the Social Sciences* (Gould & Kolb 1964), the human family is defined as "an institutionalized bio-social group made up of adults (at least two of which, unrelated by blood and of the opposite sex, are married), and children, the offspring of the maritally related adults..." (p. 257). However, according to R. D. Laing (1971), the human family cannot be satisfactorily defined:

> We identify, as families, networks of people who live together over periods of time, who have ties of marriage and kinship to one another. The more one studies family dynamics, the more unclear one becomes as to the ways *family* dynamics compare and contrast with the dynamics of other groups not called families, let alone the way

families themselves differ. As with dynamics, so with structure (patterns, more stable and enduring than others): again, comparisons and generalizations must be very tentative. [P. 7]

In recent years the literature on the concept, definition, purpose, and function of the so-called nuclear family has increased. Although the literature explores contemporary values, beliefs, and mores in the role of the family, no conclusions can be reached, nor, especially, does any evidence suggest that the family is a dying institution, as some claim. If anything, the family in one form or another is as viable and dynamic as it ever has been, even though it may now be viewed in a perspective slightly different from the historic and traditional Judeo-Christian concept.

Today, broadly speaking, homosexual unions (some even by marriage) and the adoption of children by single adults and purposefully childless couples are included in the concept of family in American society. Social and behavioral scientists, therefore, have considerable difficulty in dealing with the concept, especially since any analysis must include situational, biological, and cultural factors. Consequently, any attempt to define family disorganization must include the problem of family definition and all the ramifications of such a definition.

R. M. MacIver (1937) wrote, "A family is a group defined by a sex relationship sufficiently precise and enduring to provide for the procreation and upbringing of children" (p. 196). MacIver's definition tends to stress the biological component, but it also hints at certain cultural factors, especially the institutionalization of the family in societal functions. However, his definition ignores the many personal functions of the family, especially the ways parents teach their children, how various members relate to one another, and how they help one another. Burgess and Locke (1953) attempt to cover MacIver's omissions when they speak of the family in transition from "institution to companionship" and definable as a "unity of interacting persons."

Cavan (1953) skirts the issue of definition but indicates that the American family has two important aspects: "as a social institution charged with important functions related to the public welfare; and as a mode of personal living for husband, wife, and children" (p. 3). She says that in terms of public welfare the family is called on to support fundamental and traditional values of society, such as legitimacy in birth, regulated sexual activities, the training and education of children, and enforcement of laws and moral codes.

In personal living Cavan recognizes family responsibility for providing for the personal needs of its members, including love, protection, assistance, and the provision of utilitarian necessities. She adds, "The institutional and personal aspects of marriage and family life are interrelated" (pp. 4–5), but that over the course of time and in different places emphasis varies on which aspect of family life is more important.

Although a precise definition of the family in America today is difficult, several variables seem to affect all definitions. Always included are some kinds of biological as well as social components, in which the traditional family is viewed as having bond and purpose. The relationships of family members usually are spelled out by law and are affected by cultural or societal values—law and values themselves frequently interrelated. Finally, a definition should recognize that meaning, belief, and tradition associated with the family change over periods of time.

Thus the so-called nuclear family of the past—husband, wife, and children—still remains basic, but other kinds of unions, families, and social arrangements today also are called families and recognized as such, sometimes by mere acceptance, sometimes in law. A union of homosexuals and their adoption of children is possible now; a few years ago it would have been unthinkable. An unmarried woman who has an illegitimate child now is more likely than ever before to rear her child in her own home because the stigma attached to such a birth is no longer so repugnant to the community as it once was. Adoption agencies are increasingly considering single-parent adoptions that previously were against the law.

Societal Values

Western society's values and traditional beliefs obviously are in a state of transition. The modern family unquestionably feels the impact of such change, for it may be in a state of flux as great as that of any other Western institution. But the extent to which the family has changed and is changing is open to speculation. Max Lerner (1957) points out:

> The American family has been caricatured by both American and foreign observers, and in one sense it is a caricature of itself, since it always seems to be parading its excesses.... With all its weaknesses and excesses the American family is a going concern reflecting less the disintegration of the culture than its mobility and genius for innovation.... If the American family is sick, then the class system must also be sick, and the whole economy, the democratic idea, the passion for equality, the striving for happiness, and the belief that there can be free choice and a future of hope. For it is on these that the American family is founded ... the point [being] ... that the American family is part of the totality and reflects its virtues as well as weaknesses. [Pp. 550–51]

Lerner then traces the historical development of the traditional family in America, commenting that the usual elements have been largely stripped of their functions. The American family is primarily based on European tradition, in which the father was the unquestioned head of the family; he was the ruler of his farm or had a clear status in his society. In America, however, the father now does not hold such absolute power nor is he able to control his offspring as did his forebears.

Children leave home to advance their educations or to begin their own families. Fathers till the soil less and increasingly choose, instead, to live in the city.

> Thus the traditional family—large, three-generation, patriarchal, attached to the land, closely integrated in performing the collective economic functions of farm homestead or small shop or small business—has almost gone out of the picture. It is more likely to be small, two generation, mobile, whole-family-centered, equalitarian. The family no longer performs to the same degree the old functions of economic production, religious cohesion, kinship continuity, educational and cultural transmission. [Lerner 1957, p. 551]

Lerner does not seem to imply that the American family has found nothing to replace what it has given up of these functions. No longer a production unit, however, the contemporary but traditional family has become a more demanding consumption unit based on the earning power of both husband and wife and the spending power and tastes of all family members, especially the children. The family is still a basic residence unit, even though every year it becomes more mobile, and even though older children sometimes move out to live in their own dwellings. The family probably has become more a cultural entity and less an educational and religious unit, and has permitted, perhaps abdicated in favor of, outside institutions assuming these functions.

The family today probably is a group of individuals with more personal freedom than was possible in the old traditional family —individuals striving more for companionship than for unchangeable roles. Lerner suggests, although as an overgeneralization, that the family "is cemented, if at all, by the pursuit of happiness rather than the exercise of authority" (p. 532). But he explains:

> I have no alack and alas for this. The oldest function of any family, that of producing and caring for children, it still performs. The relationship between husband and wife, between parents and children, between brothers and sisters, is less traditionally regulated than it once was. But who will say that bonds of kinship maintained in a spirit of free commitment, with a continuous inquiry about their meaning, are any less strong for that fact? Given the necessary elements of obligation and tradition, the American has fashioned anew the features of his family institutions, as he does everything else about him—his clothes, income, technology, production, government, class system, laws, occupations, ideas, and opinions. The result may seem chaotic, but only because it is revolutionary. [P. 552]

Types of Families

Notwithstanding our problems of definition, the American culture probably contains at least six distinct family types, four of which are still largely traditional.

First, the rural family exists primarily in the Midwest and New England. The rural family tends to be large, and the children, who do field and household chores, do not leave the basic family residence until they come of age, graduate to higher education, or marry.

Second, the old-family unit is common especially among elites who have accumulated wealth over a long period of time and have considerable status in the community but little geographical mobility.

Third, the family that consists of second- and third-generation immigrants, especially from central and eastern Europe, has residual traditional elements of the old culture or the historic ways of doing things. This type of family has had a great deal of cohesion, but recent signs indicate a breakup as the youngest members become more assimilated into the general American culture.

Fourth, the lower class, poor, black family has been shaped by the plantation-heritage caste conditions of the South. In recent years this once rural family type has experienced tremendous geographical and social mobility in the North. It has been described as essentially matriarchal and large, and has its own distinct set of cultural values (United States Department of Labor 1965).

Fifth, the lower class, poor, white family is essentially rural in character but, like the southern black family, has moved to the North in search of greater opportunity. The family tends to be large and patriarchal, with mostly mobile, undereducated, and laboring or semiskilled fathers.

Sixth, the middle class, big city, small town, or suburban family is dominant now in the United States. The father may be a transient figure because of his white-collar job; the mother is the stabilizing influence. Both parents tend to be reasonably well educated, willing to move in order to better their position in life, committed to higher education for their children (to continue the family's upward mobility), and frequently active in community affairs. This kind of family has increased in numbers and community influence, as the technological revolution has turned America from a farming, largely rural society into an urban and suburban one. Technology has freed the female from continuous chores and household duties, and has permitted her to obtain education and employment in offices, businesses, factories, and government agencies. The family also received impetus as the social and sexual revolutions gained support and made wives and mothers more equally important in terms not only of family responsibilities but also of achieving family goals of happiness, material goods, and wealth (Lerner 1957).

Social and Sexual Revolutions

The social and sexual revolutions within the American family probably made their greatest gains during and immediately after World War II. More women than ever before continued their educations, and young people remained dependent on parents longer as they gained more knowledge and delayed marriage until later years. Today female emancipation is becoming widespread as many join the women's liberation movement.

Thus as the family moved from farm to city and as the father found employment in offices or factories, the family became middle class oriented. The American father began to lose his authority and was unable to exercise the continuous direction required in the old patriarchal family. Although theoretically his authority is still recognized, as family members gain more equality the father becomes generally no more than a court of last resort on questions of discipline. Further, because of changes in religious values he is no longer backed up by the paramount authority of religious sanction. In all probability the father of the middle class family no longer has the will to assert such authority. Lerner summarizes:

On daily matters his wife is his deputy, and under the absentee sovereignty of the husband the deputy becomes king—only to give up her authority on weekends to the husband or at times to the children themselves. Thus the libertarian tradition is reinforced by the changes in the inner authority structure of the family. The children think in terms of claims and rights, more than of duties and obedience. Their world is not that of deference to authority but of "talking back" to parents and bargaining to exact a set of rewards for their surrender to family rules on food habits, manners, and behavior. [P. 354]

As a consequence of all these social, sexual, technological, and cultural changes, the American family is still altering, and many kinds and variations are developing, some in reaction against changes, some in order to remain contemporary. The family now is quite vulnerable; its heavy burden is to make society function and to help the democratic way of life to survive. The burden is placed on all families, small or large, broken and disorganized, inner-city or suburban.

Types of Family Disorganization

Although the family in some form has endured as an institution in almost all societies, and especially in Western society, breakup and disorganization have increased. The American divorce rate, for example, has been steadily increasing in recent years. According to the Department of Health, Education and Welfare, the divorce rate in 1968 was 2.9 per 1,000 total population. In 1969, the rate rose to 3.2 and then to 3.5 in 1970. In 1971 the rate was 3.7; in 1972, the latest year for which data are available, the rate was 4.2, an almost 44 percent increase over a four-year period (National Center for Health Statistics, 1973*a*).

The marriage rate, though, has been quite stable over almost the same period of time. The rate was 10.6 (per 1,000 population) in 1969 and 10.9 in 1972 (National Center for Health Statistics 1973*a*). Thus while people are marrying in the same proportion, they are divorcing at a significantly higher rate.

Clinard (1971) defines a state of disorganization as "one in which there is a 'breakdown of social controls over the behavior of the individual' and a decline in the unity of the group because former patterns of behavior and social control are no longer effective" (p. 77). Goode (1971), although not contradicting Clinard, emphasizes member roles rather than social control breakdown: "[F]amily disorganization may be defined as the breakup of a family unit [or] the dissolution or fracture of a structure of social roles when one or more members fail to perform adequately their role obligations . . ." (p. 468).

Goode classifies six major forms of family disorganization:

1. The uncompleted family unit: *illegitimacy.* Although the family unit may not be said to "dissolve" if it never existed, illegitimacy may nevertheless be viewed as one form of family disorganization for two reasons: (1) the potential "father-husband" conspicuously fails in his role obligations as these are defined by the society, mother, and child; and (2) the role failure of members of the families of both mother and

father, especially with regard to social control as a major, but indirect, cause of illegitimacy.

2. Family dissolution by virtue of the voluntary departure of one
spouse: *annulment, separation, divorce, desertion. Job desertion* may
also be included here when the individual uses the excuse of a job to
stay away from home for a long period.

3. Alterations in role-definition resulting from differential impact
of cultural changes. These may affect relations between husband and
wife, but the major result is a *parent-youth conflict.*

4. The *empty shell* family, in which individuals live together, but
have minimal communication and contact with one another, failing
especially in the obligation to give emotional support to one another.

5. The family crisis caused by *external events,* such as the temporary or permanent involuntary absence of one of the spouses because
of death or incarceration in jail or prison, extended medical or mental
hospitalization, or because of such impersonal catastrophes as flood,
war, and depression.

6. *Internal catastrophes* that cause involuntary major role failures
through mental, emotional, or physical pathologies, including, for
example, severe mental retardation of a child, psychosis of the child
or spouse, or chronic and incurable physical conditions. [P. 469]

This rough classification emphasizes that the family is basically
an organization of roles and that a consistent pattern of role
performance is necessary for the family's continued existence, at
least in the traditional and conventional mode. The classification
does not hold in some instances if the original role pattern is
unconventional or different, as in homosexual and single-parent
adoption families. Once the basic family is defined, however, any
changes in basic role patterns or performances will lead to dissolution and/or disorganization. The classification, although not
specific, nonetheless demonstrates that the larger society in
which the family exists expresses more concern about certain
kinds of family dissolution than about others. For example:

... (the family of the deserter ... receives more sympathy than that
of the prisoner); ... the society furnishes social patterns for certain
participants, but not others, to follow (death, although more tragic
than divorce, is more acceptable in some circles); ... it avoids any
inquiry into some forms which may nevertheless be emotionally
important to the participants (the "empty shell" family, or the family
adjusting to the strain of the severe pathology of one of its members);

and . . . even when the society does concern itself with the problem, it may focus on only one of the participants (the deserter or the illegitimate father), not on the entire family. [Goode 1971, pp. 469–70]

The various forms of family disorganization are found in all societies, but the rates of family dissolution vary among societies. The rates, of course, vary over time as a result of societal influences; thus during periods of war and depression, and according to changes in values and mores, rates may change. Additionally, the ways in which individuals adjust to these forms and values also vary.

Causes of Family Disorganization

No doubt, families individually and collectively react emotionally to issues and problems; therefore, individual family member reactions to disorganization experiences are highly specialized. A child feels the death of his own mother or father in a way far different from the death of some other child's mother or father. A spouse recently divorced looks back on a series of conflicts in ways different from those of other divorced spouses. Each family member, too, sees a catastrophic illness in a different way, reacting emotionally according to personal psychological makeup. Each event is, of course, unique, especially if viewed in all its particularity and detail.

However, when social scientists research large numbers of similar cases, common patterns emerge to help others explain and understand their significance. Armed with such information counselors, social workers, physicians, and others are able to help people adjust to their disorganizing experiences. Professional and self-help groups deal with special kinds of problems, such as those associated with divorce, serious medical and mental pathologies, and problem-type children. These groups operate on the premise that many problem situations, although unique to each family unit, have been experienced in other families; thus the troubled family can be helped because the helpers have had experience in dealing with others who have had similar problems.

Goode (1971) maintains that in research into family disorganization and provision of help for troubled families a distinction must be made between the disorganization of a family *unit* and that of the family *system* in a particular society. Further, both of these forms must be distinguished from *change* in a family system:

> All enduring marriages inevitably end with death of one or both spouses, but the family *system* which is common throughout that society is not thereby affected. The family customs of the society may continue without change, and indeed they contain provisions for the contingency of death. A society may also have a high divorce rate, but the family *system* may remain unchanged.... Wherever the world's population is experiencing industrialization, family systems are also undergoing some changes, though not all these are being recorded. This means that at least some of the elements of the old family patterns, such as arranged marriages in China, are dissolving. Of course, if a family *system* is undergoing change, the rates of occurrence of certain forms of disorganization, such as divorce, separation, illegitimacy, or desertion, may change. [Pp. 470–71]

Generally, families are autonomous in being able to do as they please and in relating to people outside the family only as they choose. No one outside the family has rights in the family's deliberations and decisions. Relatives involved in any family situation vary from one family system to another, but in general the state may interfere only when: (1) family members themselves initiate state action (as in an application for welfare or social services or commitment to a mental hospital); (2) someone in the family is officially reported to be receiving inadequate care (such as involvement of a juvenile court in matters of neglect or dependency); or (3) the state intervenes as a result of law violation or a suspected public health problem brought to the state's attention by someone outside the basic family unit, such as the police, a neighbor, or a public health nurse.

Increasing industrialization is breaking down the extended family (several generations living together), and often other responsible relatives no longer express so much concern as they once did for complete welfare of their family members. Hence the breakup of a family unit, regardless of cause, is more likely to deprive one or more of its members of anyone who feels any responsibility for even their physical care. Consequently the state intervenes more, and such intervention is more often welcomed. Because of their basic philosophy of *parens patriae*, juvenile courts have expressed increasing initiative in looking after the welfare of dependent, neglected, and delinquent children.

Societal Influences

Another factor in family disorganization should be mentioned now. Many families break up as a result of personal factors and reactions to specific situations—alcoholic spouses, nonsupporting spouses, desertion. But families also dissolve because the values, pressures, and structure of society itself sometimes help to create the problems that family units, or at times some social agency, must solve—illegitimacy, incarceration, war, divorce.

An outstanding example of how society, or one of its agencies, can create problems for a family unit is the no longer existing policy of welfare departments to deny assistance under the category of Aid to Dependent Children if the father of the family resided in the home. The law basically provided assistance only to children whose fathers were absent from the home, regardless of the reason for that absence; hence fathers who were in the home but unable to provide for the children frequently deserted to gain the needed care. Welfare departments even organized secret midnight raids on suspected violators, thereby ultimately ensuring desertion. Recent policy changes, however, allow fathers to remain in families that receive funds.

Divorce

As Americans have increasingly tolerated sexual promiscuity and illegitimacy, they also have begun to accept divorce. The increasing rate of divorce, according to Brinton (1959), reflects in part the inevitable disappointments of a sexual relation exalted into something which cannot possibly be achieved:

> [I]n itself our high divorce rate is not a sign of sexual looseness or promiscuity; indeed, as continental Europeans accustomed to such age-old institutions as the mistress like to point out, our American addiction to divorce is in itself a tribute to our high standards for

marriage. The really grave aspect of the whole American sex problem is not so much one of sex morality in its narrow sense, but of its part in the larger context of our discontents and fears. . . . [P. 386]

Divorce grows out of dissension and creates additional conflict on both sides of the family line. Marriage agreements are broken, and harmonious relationships among in-laws are disrupted. Frequent problems involve custody of minor children, child support, and remarriage. The mechanisms for avoiding or reducing marital conflict, though, cannot in any society enable every couple to tolerate marriage. Divorce, then, is one of the safety valves for the inevitable tensions of married life. Goode (1971) maintains:

> At present we cannot say why a particular society adopts the pattern of divorce rather than that of separation, or of living together but enlarging the household to take in additional wives, but divorce is clearly a widespread solution for the problems of marital living. Moreover, the alternative solutions that various societies offer are only a variation on the pattern of divorce. [P. 481]

Of course, the women's liberation movement might take Goode to task for even suggesting that only the male in the household should be able to take on additional mates, but Goode might maintain the attitude that that would be only a variation on the pattern.

More divorces are granted during the second or third years of marriage than at any other time, and half of all divorces occur within the first six years of marriage (Glick 1957). Apparently, major adjustments must be made early in marriage when couples are learning to live together harmoniously, and many couples simply are unable to make such adjustments. Similarly, satisfactory early adjustments seem to increase the likelihood that adjustments made in later years will be successful, or at least that if divorce does not occur in the early years of marriage it is less likely to happen later on, no matter what other adjustments might be required (Horton & Leslie 1970).

Divorce has long been considered much more probable in childless marriages than in child-producing marriages, because unhappy marriages are less likely to produce children anyway, and once born, children tend to deter divorce. Research, however, calls these generalizations into question, for a recent study reveals that nearly 60 percent of all divorces involve minor children present in the home (U.S. Department of Health, Education and Welfare 1964).

Effects of Divorce

The assumption until recently has been that divorce is apt to produce severe emotional trauma in children, and ample impressionistic evidence indicates that both parents and children sometimes react to divorce with other obvious symptoms of maladjustment (Waller 1967). However, in a study of divorce in metropolitan Detroit most of the 425 mothers divorced for periods ranging from two to twenty-six months believed both themselves and their children to be better off than before the divorce (Goode 1956). These data may indicate that as divorce becomes more common and less stigma is attached to it, the more serious emotional reactions to divorce will become less common.

The risk of divorce appears greater in low income than in higher income families. This finding came as rather a surprise to social scientists, who had long assumed that lower class families lacked the know-how and financial resources to make divorce common. The Detroit study, however, showed that divorce rates were higher among the lowest ranked occupational groups and lower among highest ranks (Goode 1956). A second study that used occupation as the criterion also indicated that the highest divorce rates are associated with lower status occupations (Kephart 1955).

These findings have at least two plausible explanations. First, insufficient income and the lesser status rewards of lower ranked jobs are themselves serious problems that tend to be reflected in people's inability to separate their marital adjustments from financial and status adjustments. Second, divorce reflects a general disregard for the importance of marriage among lower class groups. According to the Moynihan Report (U.S. Department of Labor 1965) this observation tends to hold, for the highest divorce rate over all ethnic minorities occurs among blacks, whose divorce rate (in urban areas only) approximates 5.6 percent. For urban whites the percentage is 4.0.

The common belief that lower class persons enter and leave nonlegally sanctioned "marital" relationships at will extends to a belief that they tend also to break legally sanctioned relationships that prove more troublesome than rewarding. Although this conception contains some elements of stereotyping, it seems more likely that divorce is not considered so serious a step at lower income levels as it is among the middle classes (Horton & Leslie 1970).

It is also important to note that changing values related to sex and morality have significantly affected the concept and practice of marriage and divorce in modern times. More frequently than ever before, not just lower class persons but those in the middle classes as well view divorce with less seriousness. Additionally, more young persons than ever before on all income levels are living together without benefit of marriage and with considerably less stigma than was attached just a decade ago. According to the National Center for Health Statistics (1973*b*), the number and rate of divorces granted in the United States in 1972 increased for the tenth consecutive year—an 82 percent increase over the decade. We cannot know, however, whether the annual number of divorces would increase significantly over the approximately 839,000 granted in 1972 if persons living together without legal sanction chose to marry.

Illegitimacy

Changing values in sex and morality and the ways couples choose to relate to each other, frequently without a marriage bond, may have some impact on the illegitimacy rate, but no accurate determination can be made. We do know, however, that the illegitimacy rate from 1965 through 1968 (the last year for which national data are available) has remained relatively stable (U.S. Public Health Service 1968).

Many years ago anthropologist Bronislaw Malinowski formulated his rule of legitimacy: every society has a rule that each child should have a legitimate father to act as its protector, guardian, and representative in the society. (See, e.g., Calverton & Schmalhausen 1930). This rule, like all other rules, is violated, with apparently increasing frequency even though the rate may be relatively stable. In legalistic, moralistic, and repressive societies, where the rule is strongly enforced, the illegitimacy rate has tended to be low. In such instances, nonconforming individuals and their illegitimate children tend to suffer serious sanctions.

The regulations that form and sustain the family system motivate men and women to marry and to place the child in a definite position in a unit within the kinship and social structure. Another regulation requires the specific family unit to be responsible for the child's maintenance and socialization. These regulations tend to define legitimacy and thereby illegitimacy (Goode 1971). Crane Brinton (1936) has condensed the close relation between legitimacy and illegitimacy:

> Bastardy and marriage in this world are quite supplementary—you cannot have one without the other. In another world, you may indeed separate the two institutions and eliminate one of them, either by having marriage so perfect—in various senses—that no one will ever commit fornication or adultery, or by having fornication so perfect that no one will ever commit marriage. [Pp. 82–83]

In the United States and in Western society generally, illegitimacy is condemned partly because it is obvious evidence of sexual intercourse outside marriage. The relationship is not unusual, however, for in about 70 percent of known societies (Murdock 1949) some degree of premarital sexual license is found, but childbirth outside marriage is not approved. Hence most societies probably are more concerned with illegitimacy than with sexual intercourse outside marriage. Public opinion places stronger condemnation on illegitimacy than on a simple violation of the norms of sexual conduct. In fact, disapproval of sex relations outside marriage is weaker when a marriage between the couple is imminent than when a union is unlikely or even impossible. Further evidence to support this conclusion is found in the relatively low rates of adult arrests on charges of fornication and adultery. Although youths are more condemned than adults for premarital sexual activity, even here, in today's society, it is assumed to be occurring with greater frequency, and with more publicity, than ever before.

Marriage and Sexuality

The question Kingsley Davis (1939) posed becomes pertinent: Why does society not "solve" the problem by requiring the use of contraceptive methods and, when these fail, abortion? His answer, although perhaps outdated, is that to break the normal relationship between sexuality and the family, so that adults would as a matter of course decide rationally whether they would enjoy sex within or outside the family, would also lessen the motivation to marry and found a family. He concludes that the radical changes necessary to almost completely eliminate illegitimacy probably would come close to eliminating the family system, too.

However, evidence in support or rejection of Davis's hypothesis is uncertain. We know that more people are living together and engaging in premarital sexual intercourse, but the marriage rate has remained fairly stable. In other words, the United States population has been increasing, but the marriage *rate* has remained the same, which may, in effect, even suggest that proportionately *fewer* people are marrying. Whether or not this theory supports or contradicts Davis cannot be determined at this point, especially since we do not know whether current sexual behavior is a passing fad or is reflective of a new morality that will endure.

Notwithstanding these changing social values, numerous persons and groups continue to speak against illegitimacy and abortion; indeed, public outcry has been far more strident than the facts suggest. The striking change in the United States over the past generation is that illegitimacy is no longer a personal or family problem but a *social* problem, especially as state and private agencies have become far more concerned with the fate of the illegitimate child and mother, providing them with help, counseling, and even support. In fact, the recent passage of laws that make abortion easier to obtain is, in part, a reflection of society's changing values and willingness to provide help where such help is indicated and personally desired.

Even though society now is willing to help mother and illegitimate child, many persons in society are unwilling to help the woman who *continues* to have illegitimate children. The "black woman on welfare," assumed to be most promiscuous of all

American women, is most frequently cast in this image. In fact, though, while the rate of illegitimacy among nonwhite women is significantly higher than the rate for white women, the nonwhite rate has been steadily decreasing as the white rate has been increasing. Another common belief that younger women have more illegitimate births than do older women has been disproved by data that indicate women over twenty-five have significantly more such births than do those younger (U.S. Public Health Service 1968).

Changes in Codes of Conduct

The changing social, moral, and sexual climate together with the various liberation movements have complemented one another and perhaps have permitted a relaxation in former strict codes of conduct. As more Americans strive for middle class status and as more people "do their own thing," nonstandard behavior previously viewed as seriously deviant and immoral is better tolerated among whites and nonwhites, old and young. Divorce, homosexuality, abortion, adultery, premarital sexual intercourse, and illegitimacy are no longer so condemned as they once were. Churches and others who monitor moral behavior express alarm, but greater tolerance apparently has not diminished the family and the so-called moral fiber of the country.

If anything, the notion of the family has changed, but historians at a future date must judge whether the change is good or bad since lack of evidence makes such a judgment impossible at this time. Schur (1964) says, "The social scientist cannot 'prove' values—he simply cannot demonstrate scientifically what is right and what is wrong. He can hopefully . . . provide us with as broad an understanding as possible from which to make whatever determinations face us" (p. 14). Thus Horton and Leslie (1970) conclude:

> Current family problems must be seen in the context of transition from a large, stable family system oriented toward agriculture to a small, individualistically oriented family, functioning in an urban setting. The transition has disrupted traditional ways of adjusting and has produced value conflicts. Conflict focuses on individualistic versus familistic goals and on relationships between the generations. [P. 223]

Part II

Economic Problems

CHAPTER 4

Poverty and Unemployment

Poverty as a Social Problem

Poverty has always been considered an economic problem. However, depending on time, place, and society, it also has been viewed in terms of morality, religious belief, and human philosophy about caring for the "less fortunate." Unlike other societies, Americans have not accepted poverty as inevitable but have in fact tended to regard it as an abnormal condition.

Because we tend to have a hopeful view of human nature, we believe that want is unnatural and unnecessary. Our faith in our society's unlimited resources and our pride in the productive achievements of the American economic system have strengthened this view.

An optimistic outlook has not always served us well in dealing with the misery that has existed despite all our resources. Sometimes we seem to have expected distress to cure itself, or have assumed that spiritual discipline could treat economic ills. Confidence in the eradicability of poverty has nevertheless been a dynamic force for reform in the United States. In fact, Bremner (1956) points out:

> Because of our assumption that want is man-made, not God-made, we have never lacked earnest critics to call us to account for both our individual and our social failings. In every generation they have reminded us that poverty is shameful, not only to those who suffer from it, but also to the society that allows it to exist. [P. xi]

Social workers, church officials, economists, and government authorities have from various points of view expressed concern about the nature, causes, and possible solutions of poverty in the United States. During the 1930s when the Great Depression affected innumerable people, significant attention was paid to the hungry and the poor. Aside from that period, the contemporary significance of poverty went unnoticed until Michael Harrington (1962) wrote *The Other America.*

> In a nation with a technology that could provide every citizen with a decent life, it is an outrage and a scandal that there should be such social misery. Only if one begins with this assumption is it possible to pierce through the invisibility of 40,000,000 to 50,000,000 human beings and to see the other America. We must perceive passionately, if this blindness is to be lifted from us. A fact can be rationalized and explained away; an indignity cannot. [P. 25]

War on Poverty

Two years after publication of *The Other America*, in his State of the Union message, President Johnson declared a war on poverty. He said that the per capita income of some 35 million Americans in 1962 had been only $590, compared to a national average of $1,900. By 1968, according to the Census Bureau, the number of people classified as poor had dropped to 25.4 million —13 percent of the population, down from 22 percent in 1961 (Feagin 1972, p. 101).

The idea of waging a war on poverty is not new. The sentiments expressed in the 1964 Economic Opportunity Act echoed those that David Lloyd George expressed in his budget message to the Parliament of Britain in 1909:

> This is a war budget for raising money to wage implacable warfare against poverty and squalidness. I cannot help believing that before this generation has passed away, we shall have advanced a great step towards that good time when poverty and the degradation which always follows in its camp, will be as remote to the people of this country as the wolves which once infested its forests. [In Waxman 1968, p. xi]

In 1966 Sargent Shriver, then director of the Office of Economic Opportunity, stated that poverty could be eliminated in the United States by 1976. Two weeks later he qualified his statement by saying that poverty could be eliminated, but "it might run somewhere around $3 billion or $4 billion [a year], maybe a little more" (in Waxman 1968, p. xi). OEO, now being dismantled as revenue sharing and other forms of federal aid go directly to local jurisdictions, subsequently issued a statement that eradicating poverty would be a Herculean task and comparable to hunting an elephant with a peashooter.

Historical Developments

Our history of dealing with the poor is long and varied and, like so many other facets of our culture, much in the British tradition. In the Middle Ages, during the reigns of Edward III and Richard II, concern for the poor was expressed almost entirely in terms of discouragement, or at least regulation, of begging, and in the control of the laboring class. De Schweinitz (1943) points out, "The king and his lords saw begging, movement, and vagrancy, and the labor shortage as essentially the same problem to be dealt with in one law" (p. 6).

Subsequent to the passage of that law in 1349, the Poor Law, which had its beginnings in the reign of Henry VIII, established a pattern for dealing with the poor that has survived to this day. The Poor Relief Act of 1601, the so-called Elizabethan Poor Law, was a recodification of earlier legislation and included provisions that influenced the administration of relief to the poor for the next 350 years, not only in England but in the United States as well (Leyendecker 1955, p. 22).

The Elizabethan Poor Law expressed for the first time the concepts that: government was responsible for care of the poor; public tax money would be used to help the poor; an administrative agency would be established to administer poor relief; and distinctions would be made between the able-bodied and the impotent poor. The law recognized that not all able-bodied could find work, and a "means test" was developed to determine who was eligible to receive aid (Leyendecker 1955, pp. 22–23).

It was apparent that government could not assist everyone who needed help. Consequently, during the medieval period an extensive, though unintegrated, program of charities filled the gap. Most notable among private agencies was the church, which even now provides some support and assistance for the poor.

The strong emphasis on charity, particularly as a responsibility of the churchgoer, led to the founding of many institutions specifically for care of the sick and the poor. Churches, religious orders, and lay brotherhoods frequently administered hospitals and almshouses established through charitable bequests. Guilds, formed to protect members, often set aside funds for care of the poor. Additionally, individuals gave and made charitable donations to specific families and persons known to be in need.

In America, the English colonists naturally used the Elizabethan Poor Law as the model for care of the poor. As early as 1692, Plymouth Colony passed a law mandating the government to assume such responsibility. However, the situation in America differed in many respects from that in England. In America work was available to all who had physical stamina, but many were unable to meet the rigors of colonial life and some needed considerable time to find homes and provisions.

Consequently, Leyendecker (1955) notes:

> The necessity of coming to terms with these problems [about the poor] led in short order to that almost inextricable intermingling of poor relief with enforcement of public order and morality, and with the promulgation of rules regarding the conditions under which persons could enter, move about in, or become established members of the community. [P. 31]

These attitudes toward the poor, their regulation, and the marriage of assistance with morality are today's legacies: we still believe that the poor can and should care for themselves, and, according to the Horatio Alger legend, each person should be able to find success in the Promised Land.

Colonial Traditions

During and for years after colonial days the poor rarely received aid at home but were, instead, usually farmed out or apprenticed, especially dependent children. Boston erected its first almshouse in 1660, but it was not until 1734 that New York established an institution with the all-embracing title House of Correction, Workhouse, and Poorhouse. In 1727, Connecticut opened a "colony workhouse," primarily for "vagabonds, idle persons, and beggars" (Capen 1905, p. 61).

Because poverty usually was assumed to result from one's personal shortcomings, little effort was made to understand its causes or the need for variation in its treatment. Kelso (1922) says: "Poverty was not differentiated from chronic pauperism, and pauperism was akin to crime. The sturdy beggar, the idiot, the drunkard and the widow who was only poor were herded together under the same roof, the chief source of anxiety being the net cost of the establishment" (p. 101).

Reform Movement

By and large most people in this country were and perhaps remain indifferent to the plight of the poor. But as industrialism and large urban centers grew in the nineteenth century, some reformers and altruists began to express public dissatisfaction with the ways the poor laws were administered and particularly with the inadequate care such laws and programs provided for certain helpless and dependent groups: children; the deaf, dumb, and blind; the feebleminded and insane.

This dissatisfaction was expressed first through the establishment of private institutional facilities for children—the so-called "orphan asylums," and, later, in the second and third quarters of the nineteenth century, by institutions for other groups mentioned. Although the child-caring institutions were largely private, other institutions were usually operated under public auspices—generally by the state. *Thus the first challenge to the poor law resulted not in efforts to reform or replace it but rather in removing certain groups from its jurisdiction* [emphasis added]. [Leyendecker 1955, p. 40]

As institutional programs grew and flourished throughout the United States, governments became entangled in organizations for their administration. Generally, special boards of managers were created to administer specific institutions and were answerable to governors and legislatures. As services became more complex, the need for some integration of services and programs became apparent. Massachusetts in 1863 was first, with its State Board of Charities; in 1867, New York established the Board of State Commissioners of Public Charities. Unlike the Massachusetts board, which had governing powers, the New York board was advisory and inspectional only. By 1873, ten states had established state boards of charity, and by 1931 only five states were without some central state agency concerned with matters of social welfare. Today every state has an administrative agency responsible for the administration and regulation of charitable and welfare programs, but they vary widely in function, structure, and legal bases of operations.

New private welfare agencies usually were designed to assist certain segments of the population rather than to provide welfare for all classes. Special interest groups were begun for children, the aged, persons with particular ethnic or religious backgrounds, or according to occupational categories. Many of these groups and organizations united to establish the National Conference on Charities and Corrections, which considered national issues and problems. They also sought reform:

The system [of relief] tends to excite hostility to the state itself. First, relief educates a large class to look to government for help; and when this is received the feeling of dependence increases.... As the State excites hope which it cannot fulfill, a time comes when the pauper is a public enemy.... As the State cannot distribute its funds fairly, discontent is aroused in the neighborhood where aid is given.... Having been educated by the State to be a beggar, he turns upon the State because it does not recognize his demand for support to be based on "natural rights." None of these considerations weighs against personal and voluntary charity, which is a favor and not a legal obligation, and which may be suspended when the demand is made in the name of right. [Brown 1940, p. 43]

Organized Private Charity

Organized private charity came into being for two basic reasons: to supplement government efforts during depression periods and to ease the consciences of charitable people who were distressed about the mistreatment of so many "worthy" poor. Many private agencies, however, were just as vulnerable as the public programs to bureaucratic difficulties and indiscriminate giving. They often did not adequately assess need, and professional beggars learned how to get the money, leaving the legitimately poor without assistance. The Charity Organization Society (COS) movement, born late in the nineteenth century, was designed to improve the administration of private welfare activities through research and information sharing related to proper ways of determining need and assisting persons truly in need. Thus the COS movement "gave impetus, and a sense of purpose and direction, to private charitable agencies. They saw the philosophy and method being evolved by the movement as the answer to the vexing problem of . . . relief" (Leyendecker 1955, p. 49).

Not long after the private agencies had begun to campaign to eliminate the inadequacies of relief programs, certain categories of needy persons, including the blind, aged, and widows with dependent children, began to receive a new form of aid—pensions. European developments in social insurance and pension programs probably inspired this new method of assistance. Special interest groups advocated pension programs, but many within the organized welfare systems, including social workers, opposed them. Those who were against the new programs claimed that they would be nothing more than liberalized forms of relief and that no matter what safeguards were instituted, "the programs would be affected by the same abuses as those that had discredited outdoor (noninstitutionalized) relief under the poor law (Leyendecker 1955, p. 53).

Although objections to the programs were raised, urbanization, unionism, and industrialization contributed to a growing demand for pensions. In 1903, Illinois enacted the first program of financial aid to the needy blind; in 1911, Missouri passed the first mothers' aid legislation; and in 1923, Montana's old-age assistance law became the first to survive the challenge of constitutionality.

> Social workers soon recognized their mistake in opposing this movement. While still adhering to their conviction about the undesirability of public outdoor relief for the great mass of the needy, they saw that the blind, the aged, and widowed mothers were clearly not in the labor market and, therefore, were not likely to be pauperized or made "work shy" by this form of public aid. In spite of the fact that some of the earlier programs were poorly conceived, the spirit in which most of them were administered did much to allay their fears of corruption and inefficiency. They even began to advocate more liberal measures and to take part in administering the programs. [Leyendecker 1955, p. 54]

Government Action

Progress in pension assistance was quite slow. Until passage of the Social Security Act in 1934, only twenty-four states had programs of aid to the blind, twenty-eight had old-age assistance, and forty-two states had some form of mothers' aid. None of the state programs, according to Leyendecker, covered residents in all counties, the programs were frequently quite restrictive, and the grant size usually was small.

The concept of these specialized programs, called categorical assistance, is now well established in this country. Although such assistance strongly resembles the Poor Law, especially in determining need and government responsibility for care of the poor, it is basically seen as a radical departure from traditional relief methods.

> With respect to philosophy, structure, standards, and finance it operated within an entirely new frame of reference and required a fundamental revision in established habits of thought regarding public responsibility for the care of the needy. The translation of these proposals into effective legislation also involved important constitu-

tional issues so that it is not surprising that progress was slow, and that the resulting legislation was based on many compromises. [Leyendecker 1955, p. 54]

Immediately after World War I, America entered a period of great industrial expansion accompanied in many areas by social reform that affected the workingman. The need for reform appeared to be over; prosperity seemed available to everyone, especially those who were willing to work. The eclipse of reform in the 1920s did not signify a weakening of the national faith in the possibility of overcoming poverty but, in fact, reflected the widespread assumption that poverty in the midst of plenty had been almost eliminated. Because poverty seemed to be a thing of the past, many said no additional reform was needed. Government and private agencies, sometimes working collaboratively, had been doing "a good job," so it was thought.

Political conservatives boasted that because of amiable relations between Big Business and government in the Harding and Coolidge administrations, the American dream of material abundance was fast becoming reality (Bremner 1956, p. 260). During the 1928 campaign, Herbert Hoover referred to the automatic solution of social problems by means of business processes as "our American experiment in human welfare." He cited the progress made in the preceding seven years as proof that this experiment had brought the United States "nearer to the abolition of poverty, to the abolition of the fear of want, than humanity has ever reached before" (Bremner 1956, p. 269).

Those who did not agree with Hoover's assessment of the end of poverty and want indicated, well before the 1929 stock market crash, that his view was based on an improper reading of the evidence (see, e.g., Worcester 1929, pp. 337–53). But not until many months after the crash did either Hoover or the nation as a whole acknowledge the full extent and seriousness of the country's economic situation.

By that time "the abolition of poverty, the abolition of the fear or want" had become in a very real sense the major concern of the American people. The Hoover administration then undertook such measures to promote recovery as were consistent with the President's philosophy of government. Even so, the Administration retained the outlook of the 1920's and, as Franklin D. Roosevelt observed, the program it adopted to meet the emergency delayed relief and neglected reform. . . . Before the decade was over the voters had repeatedly expressed their confidence in a new administration, which was as firmly committed to reform as to recovery, and which recognized . . . that the basic faults in the economy were insecurity, insufficient income, and low standards of living. [Bremner 1956, p. 261]

Public Welfare

In the aftermath of the Depression, the Roosevelt administration spearheaded passage of numerous public welfare acts designed to end poverty and assist Americans in their quest for a decent standard of living. The Social Security Act was one of the most prominent pieces of legislation passed during the New Deal period. The various bills proposed were as much concerned with economic reform as with humanitarian objectives because they were aimed at increasing workers' buying power by raising their incomes.

In retrospect, the New Deal program apparently was not carefully planned but, rather, characterized by experimentation, compromise, and frequent policy shifts, which is understandable in view of the enormity of the problem. According to Brown (1940):

> In May, 1933, when the Federal Emergency Relief Act was passed, some eighteen million persons (four million families) were receiving emergency aid of one kind or another. In some states 40 percent of the population was on relief; in some counties the rate was as high as 90 percent. The low standard of assistance resulting from inadequate funds, moreover, denied assistance to many people whose need was acute. [P. 145]

Although the entire nation was acutely conscious of economic problems and poverty during the 1930s, very little attention seems to have been devoted to such issues from 1940 to 1960. Like the 1920s, these were decades of unparalleled prosperity. The middle class came into its own, especially as a result of business successes during and immediately after World War II. At the same time the poor became more isolated from the mainstream of American life. According to Galbraith in his book *The Affluent Society* (1958), public preoccupation with the increasing affluence of the middle class both obscured poverty and outmoded the definitions applied to it decades before.

Measuring Contemporary Poverty

The federal government in the last decade has paid a great deal of attention to the problem of measuring poverty, but experts cannot provide a commonly agreed on standard. In the depression years before World War II, the Bureau of Labor Statistics of the Department of Labor produced minimum subsistence budgets. Several years ago it again determined estimates of income levels, before taxes, needed to maintain a "modest but adequate" standard of living for families of four in twenty key cities in the United States.

At 1964 price and income levels, the Bureau's budgets ranged from $5,000 to $6,000 per year, depending on location. According to an August 1973 Bureau of Labor Statistics (1973a) report, a lower class family of four needed approximately $7,500 and a middle class family $11,500 for minimum subsistence.

Few people would argue that four-person families with incomes below $7,000 are poor, and the Bureau of Labor Statistics indicates that its figures represent cutoff points for deprivation, which is generally considered to be one stage above poverty (Faltermayer 1964, p. 119). But income alone does not provide a completely satisfactory definition of poverty. Great deprivation can exist even with moderate money income. According to one study, in Harlan County, Kentucky, 59 percent of the families had automobiles (hardly seen as luxuries in the 1970s), while half of the houses lacked inside toilets, and children as well as adults suffered from malnutrition (Horton & Leslie 1970, p. 323).

The issue obviously becomes complex and confused, depending on the source of the basic data as well as the family's location. It is more expensive to live in New York City than in Little Rock, Arkansas. Food may be cheaper where it is produced; however, clothing and household supplies as well as equipment may be more expensive.

Although the Bureau of Labor Statistics indicates that an average low income family of four needs approximately $7,500 per year for subsistence, a June 1973 Bureau of the Census report indicates that the average family of four in 1972 needed $4,275 to survive adequately. This report also states that the poverty rate cutoff line was up from $4,137 in 1971, and that, according to its classification, 24.5 million Americans can be ranked among the poverty-stricken. These figures, incidentally, are based on data collected under intergovernmental auspices and on a formula devised in the 1960s in relation to the Consumer Price Index.

In years past, the poor comprised, for the most part, the aged and infirm and immigrants who expected to work as unskilled or semiskilled laborers in an expanding economy. But according to Harrington (1962), today's poor are eternal aliens in the affluent country of their birth:

> They are the rejects of their past. They are the people who have been driven off farmlands, workers displaced by technological advancement, old folks who face poverty in their declining years, women left alone to raise their children, unemployed teenagers and youths who have dropped out of school but cannot find jobs. This is a new kind of poverty in a new kind of society. This is the first poverty of automation, the first poverty of the minority poor, and a poverty that under present conditions could become hereditary, transmitted from generation to generation unless the typical cycles of poverty are broken. [P. vii]

Thus the poor are not only the unemployables but also those who want to and do work but are unable to earn enough to provide a reasonable standard of living for themselves and their families. It is not possible to measure poverty only in terms of amount of income necessary for survival. Relative inequities and double standards also have their effects. Orshansky (1965) points out:

> ... there cannot be one standard universally accepted and uniformly applicable by which it can be decided who is poor. Also inevitably a single criterion applied across the board must either leave out of account some who should be there or include some who, all things considered, ought not to be classified as indigent. [P. 3]

Inequities and Discrimination

It is well known that as family income increases, expenditures for basic essentials, such as food and housing, decrease proportionate to total expenditures. Therefore, a larger proportion of total gross income of high earners can be used for other items, such as television sets, vacations, and expensive clothing. Too, the more affluent have greater resources for high quality medical and dental care, better schools, and more advanced education for their children.

The poor, in contrast, must use proportionately more of their gross incomes for taxes as well as goods and services. In a recent study, Caplovitz (1963) notes that people with small incomes lack not only ready cash for discount purchases of major durables, but also substantial credit opportunities. Because many of these families have highly mobile residence patterns and poor work histories, they do not meet the good credit rating requirements—that is, a stable job, home ownership, and friends who can vouch for them. Hence they are forced to pay high markups on low quality goods, the major device merchants use to protect themselves against the risks of doing business with low income customers.

Freeman and Jones (1970, p. 85) point out that such discrimination is only the beginning. In addition to being exploited or, at the very least, subjected to unusual inequitable business practices, the poor frequently are at the mercy of door-to-door salesmen who abound in low income areas. In fact, even the local outlets of chain store supermarkets and department stores either charge higher prices or sell inferior quality merchandise at advertised prices.

Because the poor have few financial resources and little power to redress wrongs, the system not only forces them to live literally on the brink of starvation but also imposes conditions that increasingly exclude those with marginal and minimal incomes from the consumer opportunities the rest of the population normally enjoy.

A disproportionate number of poor in the United States are nonwhite; thus the social planners must consider, in addition to the poverty problems, the interplay between discrimination and poverty. The combination of social problems represents a threat to the lives and property of all community members, as riots and civil disorders lead to vandalism, destruction, and looting.

Freeman and Jones (1970, pp. 85–86) indicate that these conditions of economic unrest and violence have further hastened the departure of middle income families from the centers of major cities. Inner-city problems then are compounded by the association, if not actual causal link, of poverty and lower socio-economic status with many forms of individual deviant behavior, including crime, delinquency, and mental illness.

Employment and Unemployment

Virtually every institution of social welfare and control encounters difficulties and deficiencies that have immediate bearing on the poverty problem. While the nation suffers from tremendous manpower shortages, especially in technology and the professions, the poor suffer from incredibly high rates of unemployment and underemployment.

According to the Bureau of Labor Statistics (BLS) (1973b) in June 1973 out of a total labor force (persons over age sixteen and not institutionalized) of 148 million, over 91 million were employed. These figures reflect civilian as well as military employed. BLS data for July 1973 also reveal an unemployment rate of 4.7 percent, or a total of 4,196,000 persons. Adult men (over age twenty) are unemployed at the rate of 3.0 percent; adult women are unemployed at a 4.9 percent rate.

As indicated earlier, professionally and technologically trained and educated persons have the highest rate of employment and also earn the highest salaries. This fact is complicated in part by the unemployment rate of 2.9 percent for white-collar workers compared with 5.3 percent for blue-collar workers.

Although the overall unemployment rate is 4.7 percent, teen-agers (between the ages of sixteen and nineteen) constitute the largest group of unemployed—14.4 percent. This group includes persons who have dropped out of school, have not joined the military, and are probably among the least educated and least skilled vocationally. It also includes those who, caught in a vicious cycle, are poor, undereducated, and without substantial marketable skills.

The relationship between poverty and discrimination also enters an examination of the differences in unemployment between whites and blacks and other nonwhites. The jobless rate for whites is 4.1 percent; the rate for nonwhites is a high 9.3 percent.

In commenting on the relationship of race to poverty, Freeman and Jones (1970) state:

> This massive number of people, including high concentrations of blacks and other minority groups, represents large segments of the population who do not participate in the social or the political life of the country, who are not related to the upward mobility pattern common in society, who are unusually susceptible to the unscrupulous influences of some charismatic leaders, and who constitute among their number a potentially destructive group in the community. It is clear to most social planners . . . that unless the community mobilizes efforts to break the cycle of poverty, the risks are great that the poor may indeed be organized in ways that result in chaos and massive destruction and disorganization within the community. Witness the riots of the past several Summers. [Pp. 86–87]

Federal Assistance

Associated with poverty and unemployment are the public welfare programs administered by the federal and state governments. The number of persons on public welfare is difficult to determine. If reporting systems were accurate and reliable it might be possible to determine the exact numbers of persons who receive different kinds and types of grants from public funds. The complicating factors, though, are that many people receive different kinds of services and, contrary to popular notions, many families require public assistance only sporadically (Harris 1973).

Some families are only partially supported, since someone in the household is gainfully employed, even though the income may be insufficient to meet basic needs. Those who receive the greatest amounts of assistance are the aged and one-parent households with one or more children (Orshansky, 1965, p. 14).

A series of social welfare studies prepared for the congressional Subcommittee on Fiscal Policy of the Joint Economic Committee contained an analysis (Storey 1972) of the numbers of persons who received benefits from various public income transfer (public assistance) programs, including aid to families with dependent children, aid to the blind, aid to the permanently and totally disabled, and old-age assistance. The report indicates that many persons receive benefits from more than one such program, in the form of cash, medical care, subsidized housing, and free or reduced-price food. In fact, the report estimates that twenty-six of the largest federally funded income transfer programs and the major nonfederal programs

> ... which are expected to have a gross total of 119 million beneficiaries in fiscal year 1972, will actually be aiding no more than 60 million different individuals. The gross number of 64 million recipients in the 10 Federal programs and the non-Federal programs basing assistance on need criteria is probably about 25 to 30 million different individuals. This figure reflects the true size of the "welfare rolls" today. [Storey 1972, p. 1]

The report maintains that although many assistance programs are available with benefits that reach large numbers of people, many recipients are living in poverty conditions. Still other low income people receive no assistance at all. "When cash incomes were last measured by the Bureau of Census, it was found that 25.5 million Americans, 13 percent of the population, had incomes below the poverty threshold" (Storey 1972, p. 1).

The report also states that the generally inadequate benefits under the basic cash assistance programs for the poor have led to more programs aimed at improving the lot of the poor. Often the politics of welfare legislation dictate that supplementary aid be provided in a form other than cash and to specific sectors of the low income population.

> Unfortunately, the ways in which each new modification of the welfare system would later interact with existing programs were not always well understood, resulting in what must seem to the average taxpayer to be random effects in terms of income adequacy and equity among different groups of people. [Storey 1972, p. 1]

People receive benefits under several programs generally because they avail themselves of benefits to which they are entitled and for which they make legal application; multiple benefits do not imply wrongdoing or illegal behavior. But total expenditures for fiscal 1972 for the twenty-six major federally funded income transfer plans and the nonfederal programs, including public assistance, social insurance, and veterans' cash benefit programs, and the major programs that offer assistance in kind were estimated to cost $100 billion. This staggering sum might lead one to ask why such enormous expenditures do not eliminate poverty. However, the twenty-five to thirty million Americans who are described as in need received only $24 billion (Storey 1972). The actual breakdowns among the various categories of program expenditures are shown in Table 4.1.

Poverty and Stereotypes

Although the aged and chronically ill receive a considerable percentage of available public money, families with dependent children comprise another significant group. Theoretically, the family program is designed to be *habilitative*—that is, designed to change dependency into productivity. The concept suggests that with adequate numbers of social workers, occupational and social training programs, counseling services, and the like, the poor can be changed into productive citizens, able to care for themselves and their families. The concept further suggests that the need for assistance should be only temporary.

Such aims have not been realized, however, and both defenders and critics of the program are quick to offer explanations for its failure. Some critics maintain that the welfare recipient is a shiftless, lazy, ne'er-do-well who lives off the fat of the land at the expense of the middle income taxpayer. The welfare recipient is seen as one who could work if he would look for a job, but he does not simply because welfare "pays for everything, so why should he work."

The facts, however, prove otherwise, for it is possible to only barely survive under the terms of most public assistance grants, "and the evidence suggests that a large proportion of welfare clients want desperately to escape from their current way of life"

TABLE 4.1

Benefit Outlays under Public Income Transfer Programs,
Fiscal Year 1972

(in billions)

| | Benefit Outlays, Fiscal Year 1972 | | |
| | | | State and |
Program	Total	Federal	Local
Income-tested programs:[1]			
Aid to families with dependent children	$ 6.7	$ 3.7	$ 3.0
Old-age assistance	2.5	1.7	.8
Aid to the blind	.1	.06	.04
Aid to the permanently and totally disabled	1.5	.8	.7
General assistance[2]	.7		.7
Veterans' pensions	2.5	2.5	—
National school lunch program (free or reduced-price lunches)	.5	.5	—
Food stamps	2.0	2.0	—
Food distribution (to individuals and families)	.3	.3	—
Public housing	.8	.8	—
Medicaid	7.0	3.9	3.1
Total, income-tested programs	$24.6	$16.3	$ 8.3
Other income transfer programs:			
Old-age and survivors' insurance	$34.5	$34.5	—
Disability insurance	4.0	4.0	—
Railroad retirement	2.1	2.1	—
Civil service retirement	3.4	3.4	—
Other federal employee retirement[3]	4.0	4.0	—
State and local retirement[4]	3.3	—	$ 3.3
Unemployment insurance	6.4	6.4	—
Workmen's compensation[5]	3.0	.2	2.8
Veterans' medical care[6]	2.2	2.2	—
Veterans' compensation[7]	3.6	3.6	—
Medicare	8.5	8.5	—
Total, other programs	$75.0	$68.9	$ 6.1
Total, all programs	$99.6	$85.2	$14.4

[1]These programs base benefits on the current needs of recipients.

[2]Data on general assistance payments are for calendar year 1970.

[3]Military retirement and six other retirement programs.

[4]Data on benefits paid by state and local retirement systems are for calendar year 1970.

[5]Data on workmen's compensation benefits under state programs are for calendar year 1970 and include both cash benefits and reimbursements for medical expenses.

[6]The Veterans Administration's medical care program is in part an income-tested program, since any veteran who signs a "pauper's oath" can get free care in VA hospitals. However, many VA patients are entitled to treatment for reasons related to military service and receive care without regard to their financial resources.

[7]Benefits are income tested for a small number of parents who are survivors of deceased veterans.

SOURCE: *Budget of the United States Government, 1973*, "Special Analysis L: Federal Income Security Programs."

(Freeman & Jones 1970, p. 110)—even in New York City, which provides the highest amounts of welfare assistance. Investigations have shown that the number of welfare chiselers is exceedingly small, for most welfare recipients are truly in need, and most able-bodied men who can find work support their families and resort to welfare assistance in only the most rare instances (Matza 1966).

Even with facts to disprove it, the notion that most if not all persons on the public dole are cheats, chiselers, and not actually in need dies hard. Indeed, the Department of Health, Education, and Welfare (HEW), which has primary responsibility for administering federal welfare programs, recently issued new rules that again permit secret state investigations of welfare applicants and recipients, a practice abolished in the 1960s. The sweeping changes and assumptions on which the reinstituted policy is based, according to the Department of Health, Education, and Welfare, were made to upgrade procedures for determining relief eligibility, fair hearings, and recovery of overpayments. The new rules, it is assumed, will save the taxpayers hundreds of millions of dollars annually.

> The purpose of these regulations is to make sure welfare funds get to those in need, and to help restore the public's faith in our welfare system. The longer large overpayments and payments to ineligible recipients continue, the more people in real need are deprived of funds intended for them. [DHEW 1973]

Welfare rights groups, recipients, and legal aid groups argued that a return to secret probes might lead to harassment and invasion of privacy. A spokesman for HEW responded: "[C]onstitutional rights are to be observed and protected ... I have an awful lot of confidence that states and counties are going to do right by their poor" (DHEW 1973).

Gordon (1973) summarizes in part the reissued policy, which reflects the capitalistic and Protestant Ethic philosophy that one must earn what he obtains and that he must obtain it legally: "[A]lthough rights of property are protected, capitalist societies do not guarantee economic security to most of their individual members. Individuals must fend for themselves, finding the best available opportunities to provide for themselves and their families" (pp. 174–75).

Certainly some people are chiselers. Gordon (1973) indicates that "driven by the fear of economic insecurity and by a competitive desire to gain some of the goods unequally distributed throughout the society, individuals may eventually become 'criminals' " (p. 174). Almost every study on the subject contains enough evidence to indicate that the numbers of persons who cheat or chisel in order to obtain public assistance are very small, while the numbers of persons on welfare who seek employment and want to get off the rolls are substantial. The studies show that most people who are receiving some kind of welfare are indeed needy and deserving, and public funds are their only resource for survival. The funds they receive generally are meager and insufficient; that is, survival may be guaranteed, but becoming wealthy remains no more than a dream.

Economic Reform

According to Feagin (1972), a survey published in 1972 reveals that Americans are dragging their feet on the road toward welfare-statism "and that their reluctance is closely related to strong beliefs about the meaning of economic failure. Persons who hold a man responsible for his own poverty, giving little credence to social or economic factors, also tend to have negative attitudes toward existing welfare programs and to oppose new anti-poverty proposals" (p. 129).

Feagin adds that as long as large numbers of Americans attribute social problems, including poverty, to the character defects of individuals rather than to social defects as well, "massive economic reform will be extraordinarily difficult ... [for] major improvements in the American economic structure (such as redistribution of income) may require—among other things—a major shift in American attitudes and values" (p. 129).

In *Challenge to Affluence*, Gunnar Myrdal (1963) summarizes the current American situation:

> The fact is, of course, that there is a very large volume of crying elementary needs in America which, if they were translated into effective demands, could sustain rapid economic growth of production for a long time to come. They could do this even without the efforts of the advertising industry to induce the really affluent Ameri-

cans to ever more fancy consumption patterns which stand in such blunt contradiction to the nation's inherited Puritan ideals. [P. 58]

Myrdal discusses the need for reform in the United States in order to help the needy and deserving poor; he believes that with such reforms economic progress can expand in a rapid and steady course. "Never in the history of America has there been a greater and more complete identity between the ideals of social justice and the requirements of economic progress. The latter goal is not attainable if large-scale policy measures are not inaugurated to reach the former goal" (pp. 64–65).

CHAPTER 5

Public Enemy Number One: White-Collar Crime

A Definition

Crime in the streets gets the headlines, but funds lost in white-collar crime, such as fraud, embezzlement, tax evasion, and bribery, amount to much more than all the loot taken in robberies, burglaries, and muggings. Experts warn that illegal business activity is growing rapidly; thus concern among government officials, businessmen, and consumers is mounting. Law enforcement agencies are being asked to step up efforts to catch white-collar crooks and to increase the severity of the penalties. Senator Alan Bible, chairman of the Senate Select Committee on Small Business, has stated:

> White-collar crime is the type of crime that can have a serious influence on the social fabric of the nation and is costing the American

consumer millions of dollars in higher prices and lost tax revenues. ... We have heard it said that a little man can steal a bottle of milk from a doorstep, and he goes to jail in a hurry. But a business tycoon can steal thousands of dollars and probably won't ever see the inside of a prison. [In *U.S. News and World Report,* March 12, 1973, p. 53]

White-collar crime existed for a long time outside the sphere of popular attention to crime and unnoticed in scientific investigations of crime and criminality. Edwin H. Sutherland (1940, 1949) was among the first social scientists to ask that white-collar offenses be included in the data that criminologists analyze. He defined white-collar crime as "a crime committed by a person of respectability and high social status in the course of his occupation" (pp. 1–12; 9).

Sutherland's definition was valuable in pointing out the double standard that still exists in the criminal justice system—that is, the mild treatment a respectable, well-to-do offender receives versus the harsh treatment often meted out to a poor, disadvantaged one. However, in emphasizing the violator rather than the violation, Sutherland failed to account in his definition for crimes committed outside an occupation, such as personal income tax evasion or credit buying without intention to pay, or crimes that persons of lower socioeconomic status commit in the course of their occupational roles, such as repairmen who intentionally overcharge, embezzlement, or employee fraud. Thus violations of financial trust, such as embezzlement, and offenses that violate the well-being of the national economy, such as black market operations, were included in the definition of white-collar crime (Cressey 1950; Clinard 1952).

Edwin Schur (1969) characterizes white-collar crime as nonprofessional fraud—nonprofessional because fraud is not the violator's primary means of earning a living. Kwan, Rajeswaren, Parker, and Amir (1972) expanded the definition of white-collar crime. They held white-collar crime to be "any endeavor or practice involving the stifling of free enterprise or the promoting of unfair competition; a breach of trust against an individual or an institution; a violation of occupational conduct or the jeopardizing of consumers and/or clientele" (p. 13).

Although this reinterpretation of white-collar criminal behavior is less restrictive and emphasizes the offense rather than the offender, it is primarily business-oriented. Edelhertz's (1970) definition appears to cover all of the most important facets. He holds that white-collar crime is "an illegal act or a series of illegal acts committed by nonphysical means and by concealment or guile to obtain money or property, to avoid the payment or loss of money or property, or to obtain business or personal advantage" (p. 3).

Common Elements of White-Collar Crime

In some respects, it is easier to state what white-collar crime is not rather than what it is. The term refers to a vast array of offenses, some with physical evidence, others with little or no physical evidence.

Illegal or unethical practices discovered include an investment fund manager's placing interest-free deposits in a bank in return for loans to shaky companies in which the fund holds stock, and company officials' conspiring with accountants to falsify reports of the firm's present and potential earnings, thus raising its stock price and allowing participants to profit from sales. In another instance a mutual fund manager buys large amounts of stock through a broker, who then repays the favor by informing the manager on hot stock issues, which the manager buys for himself. Again, company executives learn of developments that will raise or lower the value of the firm's stock, and they buy or unload shares before the information becomes public.

Regardless of the disparity of the crime, offender, or victim, certain common elements apparently are basic to most or all types of white-collar crime. These elements include, for example, the intent to commit a wrongful act or to achieve a purpose inconsistent with law or public policy—not unique to the area of white-collar crime. Disguise of purpose or intent also is common but not limited to white-collar crimes. Disguise of purpose is essential to the perpetrator of white-collar crimes because it assures the carelessness and/or ignorance of the victim. Carelessness or ignorance may be entirely a calculated effect on the offender's part, as in falsification of stock reports, drug tests, or income tax returns. Advertising frauds rely on both the ignorance and cupidity of the buyer. An important corollary to the victim's ignorance and carelessness is his belief in the true nature and content of the dealings.

Acquiescence can be either affirmative or negative: mail frauds require the victim's affirmative acquiescence in placing an order; slum dwellers may negatively acquiesce to landlords' shoddy treatment because they are unaware of landlord-tenant laws.

Another common element of white-collar crime is concealment. The perpetrator may use a variety of methods to ensure that victimization is concealed as long as possible, and very often the victim never realizes that he has been taken.

The usual form of concealment is the lulling tactic, whereby the victim, through a time-consuming scheme of letters, telephone calls, and other means, is tired out and eventually gives up. Cooling the mark—that is, quieting a swindle victim who realizes what has happened—is one of the fine arts of professional hustlers. Other methods of concealment include the limitation of possible evidence and the creation of vast paper organizations to confuse victims and create legal knots for any who may seek legal recourse (Edelhertz 1970).

Categories and Interrelationships

Just as white-collar crime differs greatly from conventional, professional, or organized crime, considerable differences exist among types of white-collar criminality. The categories of white-collar crime range from those individually perpetrated occasionally to those that are the central activity of a business. Some crimes are violations of trust—bribery, computer fraud, employees' larceny—perpetrated in the course of a person's occupation; some crimes are not the central purpose of business but are "incidental to and in furtherance" of the business. Some types of white-collar crimes, such as counterfeiting, may occur in any of these categories. In addition, an interplay often exists between white-collar and conventional crimes. A thief who steals several credit cards does not use them but sells them to a fence. The fence in turn resells them, and the purchaser uses the cards to commit forgery or credit card fraud.

Financial Impact of White-Collar Crime

Because of the low visibility, high impact nature of white-collar crime, an exact amount of dollars lost is almost impossible to calculate. It is generally agreed, however, that the financial impact of white-collar crime dwarfs the combined costs of all other types of criminal behavior (Task Force Report 1967; Schur 1969; Edelhertz 1970).

Six years ago a presidential commission estimated annual losses in the United States at more than $1.3 billion from fraud and $200 million from embezzlement—approximately five times the loot from conventional robberies and burglaries. Sheer numbers of persons caught indicate that business crime is rapidly increasing. The Federal Bureau of Investigation reports that, nationwide, arrests for fraud and embezzlement increased by 86 percent between 1960 and 1971. Arrests for forgery and counterfeiting rose by 50 percent during the same time. In 1972 the U.S. Securities and Exchange Commission made 893 surprise inspections of stockbroker-dealers and found 1,030 violations.

In June 1973, at the opening of a Senate committee hearing on the traffic in stolen and counterfeit securities and their use in worldwide swindles, the total amount of stolen or unaccounted for securities was put at $50 billion. U.S. Postal Service officials report that mail fraud cases in 1972 were up 40 percent over the decade. Officials of the U.S. Department of Housing and Urban Development say that complaints about land deals increased from an average of fifty a week to three hundred weekly during the last part of 1972.

Financial costs can be divided into several more specific areas. Individual losses are the most directly felt and have perhaps the most damaging effect. The individual consumer who buys faulty or mislabeled merchandise, or is duped by false or misleading advertising, rarely has adequate recourse in recouping financial losses. The individual also bears the financial burden in security frauds, professional malpractice, and land frauds.

The financial impact of white-collar crime adversely affects business and corporate operations. Unfair labor practices, price fixing, or other devices that undermine competition and effectively weaken the free enterprise system have a detrimental effect on all business. Such practices smother competition, often force closings of smaller business operations, and increase the price the consumer pays. In fact, the consumer bears a major portion of the economic impact of white-collar crime. Everyone suffers when industry stifles research and development that would revolutionize or significantly affect an obsolete technology, commits environmental breaches to further profits, or designs obsolescence into a product. Advertising or merchandising frauds, price-fixing schemes, and industry-created shortages of goods also victimize the consumer public, particularly the poor and elderly.

Governments—local, state, and federal—also feel directly the financial costs of white-collar crime. Tax avoidance and evasion are so widespread that Schur (1969) says, "Honest payment by everybody liable to income tax would enable the government to decrease the general tax burden by 40 percent" (p. 165).

Physical Impact of White-Collar Crime

Most people believe that white-collar crime inflicts no physical harm on the victim; the criminal's actions are intended, rather, merely to gain for him a more favorable economic position (Kwan et al. 1972; Edelhertz 1970). But many types of white-collar crime do in fact present the risk of injury or death. For example, knowingly marketing tainted or adulterated foods is not an uncommon practice; or druggists may sell outdated pharmaceuticals. The thalidomide tragedy illustrates the serious consequences in a drug company's release of an inadequately researched and tested product. In Britain alone, use of the drug resulted in the births of 432 malformed and deformed babies.

Violations of fire, building, and safety codes have resulted in heavy loss of life. Shoddy construction practices have caused injury and death. In addition, disregard of pollution control regulations contributes heavily to the general deterioration of a biologically sound environment.

Social Impact of White-Collar Crime

The tremendous price that white-collar violations exact from society definitely does not allow them to be considered as morally neutral acts. Some white-collar crimes can and do maim, injure, and kill; others impose oppressive financial burdens on the victim. But the most serious damage in this type of crime is inflicted on the nation's social, economic, and political institutions (President's Commission 1967).

White-collar criminal activity is by its nature a violation of trust. Its very operation hinges on guile and concealment. When acknowledged community leaders participate in such violations of trust as business swindles, dishonest advertising, unfair pricing, and rental or construction of substandard buildings, the entire moral climate of society is adversely affected. The impression that political corruption is now a way of life in the United States is justified at times. A cartoon has indicated that the era of the New Deal and the era of the Fair Deal have given way to the era of the deal.

Criminal cases that involve city officials are under way in many cities—New York, Chicago, Miami, New Orleans—and state officials are being prosecuted. Recent convictions include: former U.S. Senator Daniel Brewster, sentenced to a prison term for taking an "illegal gratuity" of $14,500 from mail-order interests while serving in the Congress; federal judge Otto Kerner, a former governor of Illinois and long a political ally of Chicago's Mayor Richard Daley, convicted and sentenced on several charges; Hugh J. Addonizio, former mayor of Newark, New Jersey, serving a ten-year prison term after conviction in a million-dollar extortion case that involved purchases for the city.

Other officials in New Jersey have been convicted or indicted or are facing trial. Former Mayor David Kennedy of Miami and two Dade County judges are under indictment on bribery-conspiracy counts. In New York, former Attorney General Mitchell and former Secretary of Commerce Stans were indicted on charges of obstructing justice and perjury.

Thomas Mackell, district attorney in New York City, was indicted on a charge of obstructing prosecution in a criminal case, and a similar indictment was served on the chief investigator in the Baltimore state's attorney's office. Ted Gross, former aide to New York Mayor Lindsay, pleaded guilty to taking bribes while in office.

The litany of major cases can continue with Cornelius Gallagher, former congressman, who pleaded guilty to charges of tax evasion; Thomas Dodd, late senator, censured for diverting campaign funds to personal use; Representative John Dowdy, convicted on counts of bribery, conspiracy, and perjury; the late Representative Adam Clayton Powell, fined by the House for misuse of official funds. In New Orleans, District Attorney J. Garrison was indicted on charges of conspiracy to commit bribery and to evade income taxes.

In 1971 several Texas politicians, including the speaker of the house, were convicted on bribery-conspiracy charges. Two state legislators, a fire chief in Houston, and a county judge also were convicted in Texas scandals. In Arkansas two state senators were found guilty of income tax evasion. Even a Vice-President of the United States, Spiro Agnew, was driven from office and entered a plea equivalent to one of guilty in the wake of revelations of corrupt practices.

Public officials, of course, account for many more instances of misconduct because innumerable channels of venality are open to them. Some of the more subtle but equally insidious forms of corruption are the invasion of partisan politics into every public enterprise; favoritism to the rich, a form of corporate welfarism; and the corruption of power, which takes the form of arrogance and misleads the incumbent to forget that he is a public servant accountable to the people.

The Watergate affair, with its explosive revelations, shows how far political corruption can go in its manifold ramifications. This country's official policy in recent years has been law-and-order. "[I]t is this kind of high-level concession to massive criminal activity which undermines the moral fiber of the nation, which makes its prestigious and powerful forces subject to profound suspicion, and which in the end contributes to an aura of lawlessness" (Ahern 1972 p. 165).

The National Advisory Commission on Criminal Justice Standards and Goals (1973a), set up by Attorney General Mitchell in 1971, says in its report, *Community Crime Prevention*, that corruption of public officials

... stands as a serious impediment to the task of reducing criminality in America. The existence of corruption breeds further crime by providing the citizen a model of official lawlessness that undermines any acceptable rule of law. ... As long as official corruption exists, the war against crime will be perceived by many as a war of the powerful against the powerless; "law and order" will be just a hypocritical rallying cry, and "equal justice under law" will be an empty phrase. [P. 207]

Calling the direct costs of corruption "incalculable," the report mentions the wry comment of an unnamed Justice Department official: "When we finally stop payoffs to public officials at all levels in this country, we will have found the cure to inflation." The report adds:

Other, perhaps greater, indirect costs of public corruption lie in its stimulus to further criminality. It does not deny the enormous effect of poverty, mental disease, racial discrimination, and inadequate education as root causes of crime to suggest the role official corruption plays in fostering other criminal acts. Public corruption makes an especially sinister contribution to criminality by providing an excuse and rationalization for its existence among those who commit crime. ... Simply put, official corruption breeds disrespect for the law. [P. 207]

The Commission urges states to require public officials to disclose their financial holdings and professional interests, to adopt for public officials an ethics code administered by an ethics board, to enact stringent campaign finance disclosure laws, and to define as crimes certain conflicts of interest.

The Commission also urges states to define as felonies the following practices:

An official's use of confidential information for his own or any other person's gain during his term and for two years afterward.

An official's representation of another person before a court or government agency when the client is claiming rights against the government.

An official's or his firm's acceptance of a government contract during his term and one year afterward unless the contract is awarded through competitive bidding with adequate public notice.

An official's or candidate's failure to file disclosure statement or his filing of one that is false. [P. 221]

Detection and Investigation of White-Collar Crime

White-collar crime generally is detected by one of three methods—victim complaint, informants, and affirmative search. Victim complaint does not initiate most investigations into white-collar crime. Often the victim does not realize that he has been victimized, or if he does it is long after the fact. When the victim realizes his victimization, complaining to the authorities may become bitterly frustrating. Learning to whom the alleged offense should be reported often is not easy. Ambiguities in laws and impersonality of government and business structures are sufficient to deter a victim from complaint. In addition, many victims feel that nothing concrete will result from the complaint (Hood & Sparks 1970).

Informants may play a valuable role in the detection of certain types of white-collar crime. They are most useful in Securities and Exchange Commission and banking violations, custom and tariff violations, black market operations, frauds against the government, counterfeiting, and tax evasions. Informants are not so effective in areas of white-collar criminal activity that are surrounded by private or secretive circumstances (Edelhertz 1970).

Affirmative search by regulatory or law enforcement agencies has been successful in both detection and deterrence of certain types of business crimes. Affirmative searches include financial and tax audits, food and drug qualitative and quantitative examinations, and premises inspections. While these activities have nonprosecutive objectives, such as tax collection or maintenance of safe, edible foods and drugs, each has the ultimate sanction of criminal prosecution.

Investigations of white-collar crimes proceed in much the same way as those for conventional crimes. Because of the multijurisdictional nature of white-collar crime, however, coordination of government efforts is essential but sometimes difficult because many corporations also maintain investigative units to combat such activities as employees' theft, industrial espionage, and credit fraud. Often, though, company units have done creditable investigative work (Edelhertz 1970).

In certain white-collar business crimes the threat of suspension of a license or other operating authority or the regulating agency's use of special investigative subpoenas can force answers or produce questioned records. Modern scientific methods of investigation are necessary in cases that involve mislabeling, forgery, falsification, and counterfeit products (Kwan et al. 1972).

A major problem in fighting white-collar crime is the victims' frequent reluctance to provide evidence or even to admit they have been taken. A conspiracy of silence also exists among honorable businessmen and professionals who suffer badly from illegal conduct in their ranks.

The success of white-collar criminals is laid to careless security procedures in business institutions, too. While Senator Henry Jackson, chairman of the Subcommittee on Investigations, is recommending that the Justice Department establish "a separate, centralized prosecutive and investigative arm" to deal with the problem, prosecutors around the country are calling for tougher sentences. In too many instances hundreds of thousands or millions of dollars have been stolen in investor and consumer fraud, illegal manipulation of the stock market, or income tax cheating, and only token punishments are meted out.

For instance, a Georgia bank president convicted of embezzling $4.6 million could have received as much as three hundred years in prison and a fine of $300,000. He was sentenced to ten years in prison. In Arkansas two state senators convicted of income tax evasion were mildly fined and retained their seats in the legislature. One of the noisiest cases in the annals of political history involved James Curley, former governor of Massachusetts, four times elected to Congress, and a four-term mayor of Boston. While he served a prison term for fraud he continued to draw his salary as mayor. An executive clemency order promptly freed him from prison, and he went back undisturbed to his mayoral office.

Reports for the last three months of 1972 show a wide range of punishments for persons convicted of federal income tax violations. The proportion of convictions in which prison terms were given varied from a low of 33 percent in the mid-Atlantic area to a high of 54 percent in the Southwest.

Besides asking that more tax violators be sent to jail on conviction, many also demand that new approaches be taken in large-scale corporate audits so that examinations have more depth and scope than they have had. Some persons want the appropriate federal agencies, such as the Federal Trade Commission or the Food and Drug Administration, and their local counterparts to play a more vigorous role in discovering and prosecuting frauds and in assisting the consumer. Still others suggest that local law enforcement agencies and fire and construction inspectors become more active in enforcing housing, sanitation, environmental, and pure food laws, or that they be so empowered where they lack authority. Some think this method would be an excellent means for improving police-community relations.

Certainly, "you can't beat an honest man." But the complexities of modern life and the distance of most producers from consumers also make it imperative that the government and its agencies continue to exert authority to protect potential victims of white-collar crimes.

Organized Crime and the American Way of Life

"Crime, in many ways, is a . . . mirror, caricaturing the morals and manners of a society," according to Daniel Bell (1963, p. 128).

> The jungle quality of the American business community, particularly at the turn of the century, was reflected in the mode of "business" practiced by the coarse gangster elements, most of them from new immigrant families, who were "getting ahead," just as Horatio Alger had urged. [P. 128]

The American hero was the man with the gun—hunter, frontiersman, soldier, naval hero, and in the urban slums, gangster.

> [T]he whole question of organized crime in America cannot be understood unless one appreciates (1) the distinctive role of organized gambling as a function of a mass-consumption economy; (2) the specific role of various immigrant groups as they, one after another, became involved in marginal business and crime; and (3) the relation of crime to the changing character of the urban political machines. [Bell 1962, p. 129]

Thus organized crime in America is the result of an evolutionary process. In the early part of the nineteenth century the street gangs were social organizations that practiced violence and intimidation—muscle—for fun and profit. In the cities they became useful tools in conducting the business of gambling, prostitution, and politics. On the Western frontier they became organized bands of outlaws who sold their guns to social and business groups in conflict and often became involved in train holdups, bank robberies, and gambling. At the beginning of the twentieth century gangs began to use their muscle to organize industries. For example, "in a highly chaotic and cutthroat industry such as clothing, the racketeer, paradoxically, played a stabilizing role by regulating competition and fixing prices" (Bell 1962, p. 131).

Prohibition gave racketeers the golden opportunity to use large amounts of unaccountable funds and the right political and police connections in organizing a large bootlegging operation with nationwide and often international contacts.

Before Prohibition, criminals with Irish and Jewish roots dominated organized crime in America, especially in the urban areas; those of Italian extraction entered during the dry period.

When the Volstead Act was repealed organized crime turned to industry, labor, and real estate, paying particular attention to transportation (waterfront, market, and trucking), where it levied tribute on manufacturers and retailers alike. In labor disputes a service—violence—was provided. Ironically, at times criminals that employers lured to break a strike and those unions hired to protect pickets were working for the same man under different names. Organized crime also penetrated and took over the unions that had rich treasuries and little pressure for accountability. Teamsters union leader James Hoffa's conviction revealed how firm the grip of organized crime remained in some labor organizations.

By the end of the 1930s organized crime was involved in many forms of racketeering. At the lowest level the old street gang still provided the violence and intimidation used to extort money from business, beat up labor, deliver votes to the politicians, or discipline a dissenter within the rising structure of the syndicate. At the next level were the illegitimate businesses—narcotics, gambling, and prostitution. Higher still, organized crime was beginning to manage trade associations and unions. At the highest level it was setting up businesses, investing in legitimate concerns, and controlling politics.

In the 1950s,

> ... *crime shifted its emphasis from production to consumption.* The focus of crime became the direct exploitation of the citizen as consumer, largely through gambling. And while the protection of these huge revenues was inextricably linked to politics, the relation between gambling and "the mobs" became more complicated. [Bell 1962, pp. 131–32]
>
> While Americans made gambling illegal, they did not in their hearts think of it as wicked—even the churches benefited from the bingo and lottery crazes. So they gambled—and gamblers flourished. [P. 136]

Racketeers, who justified their activity as satisfying a basic American urge for sport, viewed their businesses with no great sense of guilt.

Another area of activity, narcotics, also opened up with the prospect of enormous profits. The importation and distribution of illegal narcotics required foreign connections, skillful smuggling operations on a large scale, and a well-organized distribution setup. The syndicate was experienced and well qualified to meet these requirements. The gangster instrumental in establishing narcotics in America was the late Charles "Lucky" Luciano, second only to Capone in organizational genius. Like American business, industry, and finance, crime became organized under Luciano's leadership (Anderson 1966).

Structure of Organized Crime

The terms so often used to name organized crime in America are Mafia, Cosa Nostra, Syndicate, The Outfit, and The Organization. Cressey (1967) prefers the term Confederation because it best describes the loosely knit, Italian-dominated conspiracy of organized criminals, which operates on a nationwide basis and represents the most sophisticated and powerful group in organized crime. Today the core of organized crime in America consists of twenty-four or twenty-six "families" that operate as criminal cartels in large cities across the nation (Cressey 1967; Gage 1972).

The wealthiest and most influential families operate in New

York, New Jersey, Illinois, Florida, Louisiana, Nevada, Michigan, and Rhode Island. Their estimated strength is believed to be five thousand, with two thousand concentrated in the New York metropolitan area alone. According to Cressey (1967), the hierarchical structure of the families closely parallels that of Mafia groups that operated in Sicily. As in Sicily, the American Mafia is headed by a boss whose primary functions are maintaining order and seeking profit. Beneath each boss is an underboss, who collects information for the boss, relays messages to the boss, and passes instructions to his underlings. On the underboss's level is the consigliere, often an older member, semiretired, whose judgment is valued. Below him are the capo regime, who serve either as buffers between top men and lower level personnel, or as chiefs of operating units.

Buffers are used to maintain insulation from police investigative procedures. All commands, information, complaints, and money flow back and forth through the buffer. Below the capo regime are the soldiers, or button men, who actually operate the illicit enterprises, using as their employees the street-level personnel of organized crime. These employees, not insulated from police action, are most often arrested, for it is they who take bets, hijack trucks, answer telephones, push narcotics, and operate the legitimate businesses.

Street employees need not be of Italian extraction. For example, in a major lottery business in a black neighborhood in Chicago, bet takers were black, the bankers were Japanese-Americans, and family members licensed the operation for a fee.

Other figures that give organized crime its unique character are the enforcer, the corrupter, and the commission. The enforcer maintains organizational integrity by arranging for the maiming and/or killing of recalcitrant members, and secures repayment of loan shark investments. The corrupter establishes relations with public officials and other influential persons whose assistance is required to conduct the organization's business. The commission rules over the families and serves as combination legislature, supreme court, board of directors, and arbitration panel. The bosses of the most powerful families serve on the commission.

It is important to remember that although Italians dominate organized crime in America, it is not an Italian monopoly. To the west and south of such Mafia-dominated cities as New York, Buffalo, and Detroit are many metropolitan areas dominated by non-Italians.

Current Activities of Organized Crime

Organized crime has never limited itself to one criminal activity, but experts agree that gambling is its greatest source of revenue. Gambling activities range from simple lotteries to bookmaking on horses and other sporting events, large dice games, and illegal casinos. Most of the nation's large slum areas have some form of lottery gambling, usually known as the numbers.

In Washington, D.C., for example, it is estimated that the numbers is a $150 million annual industry based on a probable $500,000 in bets placed each day, six days a week. The industry is supported by an apparatus that involves hundreds of numbers writers and runners, most of them black, working on a full-time basis. Police say they have direct knowledge of more than fifty top writers in the city, each booking up to $5,000 a day and employing ten or more runners, or lower-level writers (*Washington Post*, March 5, 1972).

Profits from gambling are obtained through an operation called skimming. At some point during each twenty-four hours, before the day's receipts are recorded in the official set of books, a substantial percentage in cash is removed. This money eventually may go to a foreign country, such as Switzerland, and subsequently be used to purchase interests in legitimate businesses, and the source or the investor is never revealed. This legitimization of illegal money, known as laundering, is made possible— that is, legal—under the law of the foreign country.

Loan sharking is the lending of money at rates higher than the legally prescribed limit. Although the gross revenue from organized loan sharking has not been reliably determined, law enforcement officials estimate that loan sharking is second only to gambling as a source of revenue for organized crime. Gambling profits, of course, provide most of the capital for loan sharking.

This business is organized in a hierarchical structure similar to that in narcotics. At the head of the enterprise is the boss, who lends large sums of cash to trusted lieutenants, usually at the rate of 1 percent a week. Below the lieutenants are the street-level lenders, who deal directly with the debtors. The interest rate varies from 1 to 150 percent a week, according to the relationship between the lender and the borrower, the size of the loan, intended use of the money, and repayment potential. The six-for-five dollar loan, or 20 percent a week, is common among small borrowers. The loan shark organization also includes steerers, who come into contact with large numbers of people who need money. These possible borrowers are directed to the loan sharks.

Finally, the enforcer assures that the loans are repaid with interest. Loan shark customers come from many segments of American society. Most of them are unable to obtain legitimate credit because of the high-risk nature of their businesses or because they lack the credentials that legitimate lending institutions require. Repayment is often compelled by force, and sometimes the debtors are pressed into such criminal services as embezzlement. Law enforcement in loan sharking is severely handicapped, since no records are kept and the victims, who fear for their lives, are not apt to bear witness.

According to the *Task Force Report on Organized Crime* (1967), the sale of narcotics—largely heroin—is conducted like a legitimate importing-wholesaling-retailing business, which at the time of the report grossed $350 million annually. Some estimates run as high as $2 to $4 billion annually.

According to a District of Columbia Corrections Department estimate, addicts pay $109.5 million annually for their heroin supply. The "stuff," after it reaches Wasington from New York and other sources, is distributed through at least eight to ten levels of dealers and pushers before it finally settles into the hands of the addict in the street. Each dealer gets his cut, either in money or in the drug itself if he is a user. It is estimated that an average middleman can gross $4,000 a day and keep about $2,000 for himself. Of course, on some days he gets little or no money at all. According to the general observation of police, heroin apparently is increasingly becoming a medium of barter throughout the underworld.

Labor racketeering entails control of the labor supply and labor management through manipulation of labor unions. Control of the unions provides the opportunity to steal from union funds and to extort by threatening labor strife. Bribery, shakedowns, and violence have been used to keep unions and industry under the thumb of organized crime. Great profits also have been gained from the manipulation of welfare and pension funds as well as insurance contracts. Trucking, construction, and waterfront businessmen have been pressured for the sake of labor peace to put up with gambling, loan sharking, pilferage, and narcotics smuggling in their respective areas.

Clearly organized crime is a part of the American private profit economy. It is a large-scale business that provides goods and services to satisfy the demands of a large segment of the American public—drugs, alcohol, gambling, sexual pleasure, high risk loans, abortion, stolen goods. Most of these goods and services are illegal because of the official American value system that allows no compromise with supposed evil but insists that laws reflect the highest ideals, even if they are unenforceable.

The line between organized crime and legitimate business is very thin. Presumably respectable businessmen purchase stolen goods. Washington, D.C., alone, supports one hundred to one hundred and fifty full-time operators, each of whom sells and distributes stolen goods received from a cadre of twenty to twenty-five burglars employed on a full- or part-time basis. The annual volume of traffic in stolen goods is inestimable, but it is widely believed that a large number of legitimate businesses could not survive without the services of fences.

Other respectable businessmen have been known to hire labor boss racketeers to call strikes on competitors in order to gain a more favorable trade advantage. In addition, organized crime's infiltration of labor unions has resulted in sweetheart contracts—that is, labor contracts favorable to management at the expense of union members. The dispute between the Teamsters' Union and the United Farm Workers' Union in California prompted strong accusations that such transactions were involved.

Corruption Breeds Crime

Experts believe it fair to say that without the cooperation and connivance of many political and law enforcement officials organized crime could not thrive so successfully as it has in the United States. From Prohibition to the present various investigative committees, on all levels of government, have revealed that such conditions exist.

Simply the expense of gaining political office makes politicians vulnerable to offers of special interest groups, among which the underworld is prominent. Disclosures on campaign practices during the 1972 Presidential election reveal that business, labor, and special interests frequently laundered campaign contributions earmarked for particular candidates so that voters could not recognize them. These contributions were in violation of the new campaign law aimed at allowing voters to determine the actual financial backers of each candidate.

Investigations have revealed that the bribes, votes, fixes, and payoffs that organized crime gives to public officials permit it to operate with comparative immunity (Heard 1960; R. F. Kennedy 1963). At various times organized crime has been the dominant political force in Chicago, New York, Miami, Boston, Baltimore, and other major American cities. As noted, the interdependence of organized crime and the criminal justice process operates on several levels. A survey of the literature reveals that the numbers racket, other illegal forms of gambling, and large-scale narcotics smuggling could not possibly exist without the actual connivance of law enforcement officials.

> In the 1890s the Reverend Dr. Charles Parkhurst, shocked at the open police protection afforded New York's bordellos, demanded a state inquiry. In the Lexow investigation that followed, . . . a set of public hearings [were staged] that created sensation after sensation. . . . Captain Schmittberger, the "collector" for the "Tenderloin precincts"—Broadway's fabulous concentration of hotels, theaters, restaurants, gaming houses, and saloons—related in detail how protection money was distributed among the police force. Crooks, policemen, public officials, businessmen, all paraded across the stage, each adding his chapter to a sordid story of corruption and crime. The upshot of these revelations was reform. . . .
>
> It did not last, of course, just as previous reform victories had not lasted. Yet the ritual drama was re-enacted. [In the 1920s] the Seabury investigation in New York uncovered the tin-box brigade and the thirty-three little McQuades. . . . Tom Dewey became district

attorney, broke the industrial rackets, sent Lucky Luciano to jail, and went to the governor's chair in Albany. Then reform was again swallowed up in the insatiable maw of corruption until in 1950 Kefauver and his committee counsel Rudolph Halley threw a new beam of light into the seemingly bottomless pit. [Bell 1962, p. 127]

The sensational revelations of the Knapp Commission in the 1970s revealed that the ties between crime and law enforcement were stronger than ever, and since then numerous mayors and district attorneys have had friendly relations with criminal elements. How does one explain and break this repetitive cycle? Daniel Bell (1963) explains:

Americans have ... an extraordinary talent for compromise in politics and extremism in morality. The most shameless political deals (and "steals") have been rationalized as expedient and realistically necessary. Yet in no other country have there been such spectacular attempts to curb human appetites and brand them as illicit, and nowhere else such glaring failures. From the start America was at one and the same time a frontier community where "everything goes," and the fair country of the Blue Laws. [P. 95]

Thus in many respects organized crime reflects society's failure to overcome its own inherent weaknesses, which are revealed in its halfhearted attempt to proscribe certain life-styles as it looks at the same time for ways to taste them surreptitiously. Organized crime also reflects the myopic approach of the criminal justice system to the war on crime. The current tendency is to view criminality mostly in terms of individual maladjustment rather than as a consequence of individual participation in social systems. Cressey (1967) has stressed that American law enforcement is largely designed for the control of individuals, not organizations. Police and other investigative agencies are more concerned with collecting evidence that will lead to the prosecution of individuals than with securing evidence of the relationship between criminals and the structure and operations of illicit business organizations.

This view affects the way that data on crime are compiled and published; the emphasis is on criminal acts rather than on the criminal career. Such individualistic bias has created legal loopholes through which leaders of organized crime are able to escape arrest, prosecution, and imprisonment. Many Americans cannot view organized crime as a serious social problem, because even though they fear the act—"crime in the streets"—they do not hesitate to place a bet with the individual—"the nice old man at the corner newsstand." They do not see the bookmaker as a link to a far-reaching organization that channels and pools thousands of bets to finance a professional murder, to corrupt public servants, or to fund the takeover of a legitimate business. Particular crimes committed under the influence of passion, drunkenness, poverty, ignorance, have frightened or incensed many people, who have demanded stern action. A concentrated effort to investigate and eventually dismantle the empire of organized crime, though, has begun only recently.

Interagency bickering has been a stumbling block. The Federal Bureau of Investigation, for example, has been active in urging standardization of recording and reporting of individual crimes. Yet even with former Attorney General Kennedy's prodding it was reluctant to enter the area of organized crime, partly because such investigation entailed work with other agencies concerned with taxes, narcotics, smuggling, and such nonfederal crimes as murder (Marshall 1973).

In addition to federal and state jurisdictions the United States has about forty thousand different police agencies, each insisting on local autonomy. Investigation and court action are delegated to separate agencies, further divided into federal, state, and local levels. Organized crime activities, however, cut across political and geographical boundaries, spanning several states.

Many legislatures and state officers are concluding that people will not stop gambling, and so it might as well be made legal, placed under state control, and the profits shared. This attitude represents a reversal in previous moral thinking—a reversal prompted mostly by an urgently felt need for new sources of revenue. Legislators also hope the change in attitude may, as a Massachusetts official said, "knock the props from under organized crime, and ... dry up the source of funds which finance major crimes of all sorts" (*U.S. News & World Report*, July 23, 1973, p. 22).

Now eight states operate a lottery, and at least twenty-eight states permit pari-mutuel betting at horse and dog tracks. Since

April 1971 New York City has permitted off-track betting on horse races in direct competition with illegal bookmakers. State-run lotteries, however, seem to appeal to a type of clientele different from those who use the services of criminal organizations. Lottery players are mostly affluent and respectable middle class citizens; the less affluent still flock to the street bookie, who charges less per ticket, provides a more attractive payout, and gives credit to his customers. The Syndicate, experts agree, will feel some real impact only when all states are involved in off-track betting, sports-pool betting, and numbers.

With past instances of cozy relationships between organized crime and politicians, the major question still remains: "How long will it take the Syndicate to muscle in on a state gambling operation?" The issues organized crime raises are serious and the implications far-reaching. Public morality, public safety, and respect for the law are at stake. But what about the individual police officer's role in relation to organized crime? Primarily, it is that of observer and, where appropriate, investigator. The policeman supplies information that constitutes the prosecutor's raw material. Although the information a single police officer supplies may not make a case, when combined with that of other patrolmen it could supply the missing link. Hence the advice, "When in doubt, report it."

CHAPTER 6

The Quality of Life

Pursuit of Happiness, an Elusive Goal

In an era of increasing affluence and more leisure time Americans are finding happiness more elusive than ever before. On the surface their well-being far exceeds whatever the nation's founders might have had in mind in 1776 when they proclaimed the pursuit of happiness to be an inalienable right. Never before have so many people in any society, past or present, achieved lifetime dreams once limited to the few—their own homes, travel, education, improved diet. Never have so many spent so much money on recreation and leisure activities. Yet what could be described as the best of all times is beginning to look like the worst of times.

Technology produces an abundance of goods, but it also creates such new miseries as massive air and water pollution, power blackouts and brownouts, traffic congestion, reduced supplies of energy, and a strong inflationary spiral. Mental depression is epidemic in the United States; the odds are that at some time one out of every eight Americans will receive professional treatment for depression. Between 1965 and 1971 the numbers of youth under eighteen in psychiatric treatment at established mental health facilities rose by nearly two-thirds. Increasing family stress, uncertainty about values and the meaning of life, the more automated and less personal character of our society are often mentioned as the causes of such disorders.

Overall suicide rates increased during the past decade, particularly among women and the young. Neurotics Anonymous, founded in 1964, now has chapters in more than two hundred cities. The Age of Aquarius, extolling harmony and a return to brotherhood and nature, has faded away. The headlines now read: "Why Inflation Just Won't Quit"; "What Would Gas Rationing Mean to Commuters?"; "Does Separation of Powers Apply to Criminal Cases?"; "Why Is Rape on the Rise?"; "How Can We Curb Terror in Our Schools?"; "1974: A Year of Shortages"; "Should You Consider Marriage Insurance?"; "Why Hypertension Is on the Rise"; "What Does the World Think of Watergate?"

Answers to such questions are not easy. Many feel that we cannot answer them all. Some Americans' disillusionment with their society moves them to look elsewhere for elusive happiness. The number of American citizens approved for immigration into Australia has increased tremendously in recent years. The United States also has surpassed England in number of immigrants into Canada. Those who remain are paying a high price for the affluence they supposedly enjoy.

Newspapers, magazines, and the medical literature have widely publicized the case of Roseto, a community of Italian-Americans located in eastern Pennsylvania. Medical researchers in 1961 discovered that for several years nobody in Roseto under fifty had suffered a fatal heart attack. Moreover, heart-attack deaths were below the national average. A follow-up study in 1971 found not only that the overall rate of death from heart attack had sharply increased but also that some people under fifty were included. Why? After much research the reason could be summarized in a short sentence: the town had become American-ized. Greed and need had forced men to find work elsewhere and to become commuters; the strong family ties had disappeared; the pace of living had stepped up; the richer American diet had been substituted for the Italian one. Roseto had joined America, with all its problems.

Historians, such as Arthur Schlesinger, Sr., and Daniel Boor-stin, have stressed that the Founding Fathers considered the pursuit of happiness not an individual and selfish chase after pleasures but the practice and cultivation of material prosperity, well-being, and survival. It is easily understandable that even before 1776 the riches and opportunities of the New World gave settlers grounds for believing that happiness was indeed a God-given, inseparable part of the American destiny.

Several Utopias in search of the perfect society have developed since then. Theories of happiness have always been quite popular in this country, too, from the Don't Worry and Gospel of Relaxation movements of the nineteenth century to contemporary theories expounded in such bestsellers as *The Power of Positive Thinking* or *I'm O.K.—You're O.K.*

Today happiness and its pursuit are chiefly exploited in the marketplace. Television commercials tell Americans of the car manufacturers' desire to "make you happy"; of easy ways to avoid unhappiness by taking a pill; of all the happiness that will overwhelm the purchaser of a detergent, the user of a new hair color, or the traveler who goes on a certain airline. A recent radio commercial has attempted to convince Americans that happiness is indeed concealed in juicy steaks: "Return to beef . . . and to the good life."

Although the quest for happiness as a birthright is distinctively an American phenomenon, humans have long pondered such questions as: "What is happiness?"; "How does one attain it?"; "Why are people unhappy?" Epicureans, Stoics, and Hedonists debated such issues in Greece. The Hebrew prophets cited obedi-ence to the laws of Jahve as a way to happiness. In the Sermon on the Mount, Christ identified as blessed (happy) the humble, the meek, the poor in spirit, and those persecuted for a just cause, among others.

During the Middle Ages several religious movements sought

happiness in a life of poverty (a voluntary detachment from worldly goods), chastity, and obedience. Protestantism in its most rigid forms saw happiness as the by-product of godliness and hard work. In Classical and Renaissance times, however, happiness was equated with tranquility, *otium*, sheltered from mundane worries and cares.

Today, in the midst of technological explosion, many think of happiness nostalgically as a return to more traditional values and the simple life. Bluegrass, country and western music, square dancing, and quilts suddenly are becoming popular again. The approaching bicentennial celebrations are spurring the publication of books, pictorial histories, and other materials that depict past American history as a happy, glorious period, as a resounding success.

Still such novels as *Moby Dick*, plays such as *Death of a Salesman*, photographs of tenements and sweatshops, the laments of spirituals, the statistics on infant mortality, the accounts of violence and struggle—all witness that failure and discontent are part of America's past.

Using photographs, newspaper stories, novels, madhouse records, and recollections, *Wisconsin Death Trip* (Lesy 1973) constructs a scenario of suicide, arson, insanity, murder, financial catastrophe, and other woes in small Black River Falls from 1890 to 1910. Underneath Americans' incessant rush toward power and riches and the exuberant self-assurance that success is within reach is a current of frustration, at times bordering on despair, and a constant awareness that the goal may never be attained.

Today, environmental problems, scarcity of key resources, overpopulation, soaring food prices, poor quality, and the ever-present high rate of crime threaten the American Dream just as the droughts, the Depression, and other disasters did in the past. Most of these formidable problems arise from the relentless drive for riches and happiness and constant support of technological progress that so characterize America.

Historical Roots of the Ecological Crisis

What people do about their environment depends on what they think about themselves in relation to their surroundings.

Man's view of himself in relation to nature is, in its own turn, deeply conditioned by beliefs about human nature and destiny— in other words, by religion.

Westerners, regardless of actual creed, have lived for the past two thousand years very much by Christian axioms. Christianity in its Western form is a highly man-centered religion. Man is created in the image of God. He is superior to all animals and nature because of his special relationship with God, first established when God shaped Adam, and then reestablished when Christ, the second Adam, was incarnated. This special relationship is symbolized in the immortal soul every human possesses. If humans share God's transcendence of nature, then it is in God's design that humans exploit nature for their own ends. Thus Christianity, in contrast to ancient paganism and almost all Asian religions, established a dualism of man and nature (and within man, of body and soul) and provided the justification for man to believe that nature exists for him to use as he sees fit.

So was born the Western idea of man against nature, conquering the environment, shaping nature to fit any of his needs. According to Max Weber (1922, 1947), this specific motive power made possible modern capitalism. In other words, economic conditions are not enough to ensure the rise of capitalism as a system of profit-making enterprises bound together in market relations. At least one other condition is necessary, one that belongs to man's inner world: the psychological readiness to accept values and ideas favorable to such a system. Weber believed—and supported his belief with detailed comparative study—that Christianity uniquely provided this condition.

St. Francis of Assisi was the only major figure in Western Christianity who unsuccessfully attempted to depose humans from monarchy over creation and set up a democracy of all God's creatures. Darwin and Freud undermined faith in man's special place in nature. However, the idea of the human's limitless rule of creation was, and still is, firmly entrenched. Our present science and technology find their justification in it, and we shall continue to have a worsening ecological crisis until we reject the idea.

Since the roots of our trouble are so largely religious, the remedy must also be essentially religious, whether we call it that or not (White 1969). Someone has said, quite aptly, "America needs more from her politicians than new legislation on lead paint. Both leaders and led alike need to experience a change of heart so far-reaching that we begin to work without fear or favor for what is right rather than for what seems expedient." In other words, not only must man view himself as a functional part of the ecosystem—that is, like any other animal he must eat, eliminate, sleep, reproduce—but he must also feel himself a part of his environment (Deevey 1969; Shepard & McKinley 1969).

A major problem inherited from the past is the lack of a developed land or environmental ethic. For any Western man land means property and may be treated as such. Animals and plants, water and minerals on such property automatically become the property of their human owner who can, in turn, do what he wants with them and to them.

In times past even other human beings would fall under this concept of total domain. The bloody history of colonies and settlements worldwide is filled with instances of hunting parties, of settlers killing "savages" who, unfortunately, lived on their own ancestral land. The entire aboriginal population of the island of Tasmania was destroyed in this way. Settlers guided by the same principle massacred American Indians. And more than one state in the Union still grants an owner the right of unlimited use of force against trespassers on his property, with no need to consider whether they are birdwatchers or cattle rustlers.

In other words, property carries rights but almost no obligations. Moreover, property is valuable not because of its place in the environment but because of its income or development potential. Americans prefer to believe that the sins of Manifest Destiny are buried in the past, that the slaughter of Indians and the extinction of the buffalo are but regretful memories, the stuff of history. Still most people would feel perfectly justified in using their tract of land or body of water as they wanted, regardless of the impact of such action on nature. For example, in the Washington, D.C., metropolitan area only a long, bitter, and expensive fight saved a tract of wilderness, including a marsh, from bulldozing and landfill operations. The tract is essential for the survival of some specimens of the rapidly disappearing bald eagle, the nation's symbol. The developer wanted to asphalt it for use as a private airport. Such examples abound (Rodgers 1973).

The fiercest ecological battle has been fought and lost to oil interests in Alaska. In Alaska we see vividly compressed the past beauty—Texas fifty years ago or California before the turn of the century—and the present devastation of the entire American environment. The oil empire's arrival in Alaska brings with it the vast support operations of railroads, airlines, communications networks, new towns, urban growth, and the like. Yet, even as the pipeline is almost a reality, no central agency is charged with assessing and acting on the pipeline's impact. Thousands of outsiders will flock to the state, creating a major strain on such services as schools, sewers, housing, and police protection. The potential for massive increases in crime, prostitution, gambling, and the other accouterments of a fast-booming frontier economy is tremendous.

Already housing is composed almost entirely of imported prefabricated units or trailers. A ticky-tacky frontier bar atmosphere permeates every Alaskan town. The headlong rush of Alaskan development is part of a momentum that completely contradicts our knowledge of earth's capacity to support us—namely, that the resources of the earth are fixed, that rather than continuous growth merely to accommodate the increasingly false consumptive needs of an increasing number of people, growth must be directed to achieve specific public priorities (Weisberg 1970). Alaska is the biggest recent example of man's disregard for his environment in the name of profit and may well represent another giant step of greedy humans toward their own destruction.

Water: It Looks Bad, Tastes Bad, Is Bad

From coast to coast, in big cities and small towns, purity of drinking water is proving doubtful. In Miami Beach, in March 1973, residents and visitors had to boil tap water before drinking because levels of dangerous bacteria were too high. In New York City, water from the Croton aqueduct system became so infested with tiny insects and tasted so bad that emergency measures had to be taken. The vulnerability of modern water systems to equipment failures and chemical shortages was underlined when chlorine was in short supply at the Water District of Southern California. Dangers may even be more serious in smaller communities. The Environmental Protection Agency released the following findings in 1973:

1. 36 percent of tap-water samples taken in a survey of almost 1,000 community water systems contained an excess of bacterial or chemical pollutants.

2. 56 percent of the water systems were either faulty in design or construction, or were not properly maintained.

3. 77 percent of the plant operators did not have adequate training in microbiology, the basic science of their job.

4. 79 percent of the water systems had not been inspected by state or county officials in a year or more.

The Environmental Protection Agency report states that dirty drinking water is known to be responsible for at least four thousand cases of illness every year. The dark figure, however, may be ten times greater. Records of the Public Health Service show that between 1961 and 1970, 130 outbreaks of waterborne disease occurred in the United States. At least forty-six thousand persons were sick enough to report their illnesses; at least twenty died of the diseases.

Water represents festering environmental problems in modern society because we flush our body wastes into the public water supply and then spend billions in futile attempts to restore it to its original condition. The official price tag on the task of cleaning up the nation's waters is $121 billion over the next ten years. Much of the money is slated for sewage treatment plants.

Americans drink water that already has been used at least once. In theory, such water is cleaned at least twice—once by the original user before it is returned to the body of water it came from, again by the community that uses it next. Techniques for safely reusing water for drinking are well established. But although it is scientifically possible to restore drinking water to its original condition once it has been used to transport body wastes, it is just not practical.

Even well-managed treatment plants are subject to power failures, equipment breakdowns, employee strikes, and by-passing during high water. Any of these conditions may send millions of gallons of raw sewage downstream, effectively eliminating the original user's first cleaning. Even in normal operating conditions discharge of raw sewage into rivers is all too common because plants are overloaded.

For instance, in Washington an estimated thirty million gallons of sewage at least are dumped into the Potomac River daily with only primary treatment—the simplest form of sewage processing, which merely removes the larger solid matter from waste water. The Potomac River's resultant heavy load includes large amounts of typhoid, paratyphoid, and salmonella bacteria, as well as of the virus that causes infectious hepatitis. Since discharges of raw sewage into the river take place above drinking water intake points, the difficulty of properly safeguarding drinking water quality is readily understandable. Even if water treatment plants were working with full efficiency the quality of drinking water would not necessarily be assured. With present technology waterworks successfully kill the bacteria that flow into their intakes from cities higher on the watershed, but killing viruses is less certain. So the danger of hepatitis and other waterborne diseases will remain, even if billions of dollars are spent, and standards become more strict and inspection and monitoring more frequent. Recent discoveries of a connection between viruses and cancer, for example, imply that even a small amount of sewage in a water supply may be more serious than many realize. Besides, to say that water is safe to drink does not necessarily mean that it is palatable. Above and beyond safety, merely the thought of taking in water that has already passed through three or four toilets or has been used to wash hospital linens or slaughterhouse floors is not so pleasant.

Sludge disposal, too, is becoming an almost unmanageable problem. Rural residents near large cities do not smile at receiving the growing waste loads. Hence, house, office building, and factory construction is coming to a halt in several metropolitan areas because sanitation authorities refuse to extend sewer lines that drain into already overburdened treatment plants.

A constant flow of sewage, mercury, pesticides, and other toxic materials have heavily polluted most natural reserves of fresh water such as the Great Lakes. A drive to rid the Great Lakes of pollution was launched with great fanfare in 1972, but little actually has been done.

Another problem lies at the other end of this cycle—water supply. Most toilet flushes use from five to seven gallons of drinking water, which adds up to nearly half of domestic water consumption. Unlike the use of water for sprinkling lawns and washing, this part of domestic water use cannot be reduced much during droughts. If a widespread drought of several years' duration occurred now, it would be far more serious than the great drought of the 1930s.

All these factors lead clearly to the conclusion that present methods of human and industrial waste disposal are almost obsolete. Yet some professionals claim that no insurmountable water shortage exists, and the convenient system of gravity sewers that transport body and industrial wastes has no substitute. But more sewers for more people, more billions for more treatment plants, and more expensive treatment methods do not prevent outflows from damaging water quality downstream. Waste loads from municipal systems are expected to nearly quadruple over the next fifty years; the need to examine alternative approaches to pollution control is immediate. The basic question is: Can modern technology devise a method of sewage disposal better than that of using scarce and expensive drinking water to transport waste from the bathroom to the river and the treatment plant? Many maintain that the answer is yes.

Several devices for waterless disposal of human waste have been successfully tested and installed not only in vacation but also in year-round dwellings, especially in Australia, Japan, and Scandinavia. Thus the argument is between central treatment of a concentration of sewage from thousands of houses versus a point-of-origin approach in which each house or larger building disposes of its own wastes without a sewer connection. A society that has spent billions for space travel and related disposal problems surely can afford a few million for intensified research into waterless methods of human waste disposal (Leich 1973).

A National Forecast: Smog

Most of us are familiar with smog and its effect on our own lives. We breathe, and after a while deep breaths become more difficult. Our chests hurt; sometimes our eyes tear. Smog that shrouded Washington, D.C., for thirteen days during the summer of 1973 was so heavy that familiar monuments and the Capitol itself were barely visible at times. Undispersed by the wind, the atmospheric garbage hung over greater Washington as a gray, noxious blanket. Other cities from Richmond to New York felt the stinging effects of the acrid fumes. In the West emergencies were declared in Riverside and Perris, California, and an alert sounded in Los Angeles. Meanwhile, the Environmental Protection Agency proposed stringent controls for Baltimore, among other cities. That city was described as ranking with Los Angeles and New York-Northern New Jersey as the worst air-pollution areas in the country.

Air pollution is widely believed to contribute to the incidence of lung cancer, which kills sixty thousand Americans a year. The respiratory disease emphysema is the nation's fastest growing cause of death. Studies reveal that breathing New York air is to the average person equivalent to smoking thirty-eight cigarettes per day, perhaps even more (Rienow & Rienow 1969). In the opinion of Kenneth Watt, University of California zoology professor:

> It is now clear that air pollution concentrations are rising in California at a rate such that mass mortality incidents can be expected in specific areas, such as Long Beach, by the 1975–76 winter. The proportion of the population which will die in these incidents will at first equal, then exceed, that for the 1952 [British] smog disaster. [Weisberg 1970, pp. 69–70]

Nearly twenty-five hundred Londoners died from the effects of smog during the 1952 Christmas season.

The accumulating evidence and the increasing number of air alerts in various parts of the country heighten alarm among a handful of informed and concerned citizens, but the most widespread public reaction generally is apathy. When an emergency is declared most people complain of the inconvenience and ignore it; they keep driving. Public indifference, markedly in contrast to public concern about snowfalls that paralyze a city, may stem from the inability of medical and environmental experts to state precisely the risks.

Experts lack long-term records and studies of the kind that

recently established the correlation between smoking and lung cancer. Doctors hesitate to name air pollution as a contributory cause of death; so the real impact on the sick and the elderly is difficult to measure. Public officials are reluctant to release figures on increases of deaths during alerts, allegedly in order not to create public alarm. It is doubtful, anyway, that even confronted with an array of hard statistics many would really stop and listen. That the Surgeon General determined that smoking is hazardous to health has not deterred many veteran smokers from continuing the habit. The difference, of course, is that smokers at least have a choice; victims of pollution do not.

The 1970 Clean Air Act, designed to clean up cities by 1975, ordered the setting of pollutant limits on the basis of scientist-determined harm-to-health standards. From the hundreds of pollutants, six critical ones have been selected: sulfur dioxide, hydrocarbons, carbon monoxide, photochemical oxidants, nitrogen oxide, and fragments of solid waste called particulate matter.

No one doubts that air pollution stems from the chemistry of combustion and that it can be traced to the assembly lines in Detroit. To produce photochemical smog, nitrogen dioxide and hydrocarbons are necessary. The automobile produces surpluses of both. Although the hydrocarbons themselves are said not to imperil health, they are a constituent of smog. Chemical interchanges begun in the combustion chambers of cars in conditions of bright sunlight end with the creation of the gas ozone. Ozone then combines with the hydrocarbons to make smog, a complex aerosol blend of acids, alcohols, aldehydes, and ketones. The entire process takes about four hours.

Many tend to blame pollution on the absence of wind, which is not entirely correct. The wind performs the same function that water streams perform in relation to sewage; it carries away atmospheric garbage. When the air is still we are dramatically reminded of how much atmospheric waste we produce every day. As we inhale these gases and particles we are degenerating various parts of the respiratory system and increasing the deposition of bacteria, viruses, and possibly cancer-producing elements that will remain for the rest of our lives. Animal research has shown that low levels of air pollution cause grave and lasting damage. Extreme levels of carbon monoxide can cause death, but experiments have shown that even at such relatively low levels as sixty parts per million, drivers suffer impaired judgment and are more likely to have accidents. Pollutants also increase demands on the heart's performance, at times beyond its capacity. Thus although a death may appear to be due to heart failure, such failure may have occurred because of air pollution.

Atmospheric pollution also affects the amount of sunlight that reaches the earth's surface. On a smoggy day less sunlight penetrates, which has a serious impact on the weather and also is a determinant as to which animals and plants will survive. Damage to the ecosystem is caused when air pollution destroys the photosynthesis process, and trees and plants wither and die. Plants are an important link in the creation of oxygen, essential to survival, and in the production of food, either directly by way of fruits and vegetables or indirectly by way of feed for animals.

Notwithstanding the evidence that air pollution is affecting health and that more serious crises are ahead if the right weather conditions exist, the Clean Air Act has come under severe pressure. The automobile and oil industries among others have lobbied intensively for a relaxation of standards, for exceptions, and for a postponement of target dates. Even if the administration and Congress were to hold fast and oblige the automobile and other affected industries to comply with stringent air standards, many people feel that the increase in cars, miles traveled, and population are outstripping the benefits of the gradually tightening controls. Some gigantic improvements in pollution control and radical changes in travel habits—revitalized public transport, more car pools, reduced parking availability—will be necessary if attempts to clean the air and save energy are to succeed. A commercial notes, "It's a matter of life and breath" (Saar 1973; Gliner 1973).

Out of Sight, Out of Mind, But Not Out of Nature

The national throwaway binge is continuing virtually unchecked. Rough estimates list 71 billion cans, 38 billion bottles, 7 million cars, 35 million tons of paper—in all more than 5 billion tons of garbage—piled up in 1972. That pile is growing twice as fast as the Gross National Product. When people first gained some degree of environmental consciousness a predictable response followed: confusion, then a flurry of activity in both public and private sectors, then business as usual. Still no comprehensive federal legislation governs garbage. Still no serious legislation attacks the roots of the problem. Industry simply has no incentive to engage in the resource recovery that environmentalists suggest as a rational way of handling the mounting mass of garbage that surrounds us and of using fewer raw materials.

Because of such factors as publicly subsidized low rail freight rates it is cheaper, for example, to mine iron ore or cut virgin timber than to use scrap steel or recycled paper. As a result, despite official pledges and massive public relations campaigns that depict industry as dedicated to environmental protection, the share of secondary materials used in the production process has actually decreased. Markets for reclaimed materials are virtually nonexistent.

Only a few states have translated words into some action by passing legislation to regulate garbage. Oregon requires retailers to pay refunds on all empty beer and soft-drink cans and bottles. Vermont taxes all nonreturnable beverage containers. Most states and cities, however, continue to effectively ignore the problem. Their solutions still rely on newer, bigger, and more malodorous dump sites where 84 percent of garbage is sent, on sanitary landfills, on incineration and composting. Labor, collection, and transportation costs have skyrocketed; hence the price tag of municipal solid waste disposal, now estimated to be at $6.6 billion a year, will continue to increase.

Technological means for disposing of garbage more rationally have already been developed and are being tested. For example, several methods have been developed for extracting fuel from garbage. In St. Louis about a third of the daily garbage collection is shredded, trucked to a power plant, pulverized, mixed with coal, and used to fire the utility's boilers. San Diego County is using a process developed to convert tons of garbage into fuel—garb-oil—which is then sold to the local utilities company. Results have been encouraging. Since the annual municipal and industrial solid waste load could meet much of the nation's energy requirements, these experiments represent an important breakthrough. Processes to reclaim glass, metal, and paper fiber also are being perfected.

Certainly, though, few recycling operations are self-sustaining financially. Concerned environmentalists would like the federal government to grant the recycling industry the same types of incentives extended to industries that use virgin material, from direct construction grants and operating subsidies to such indirect support as loan guarantees and tax credits. Others propose that a sales tax be levied on every product, part of which would be credited to the manufacturer if his products could be easily recycled. A measure being considered would repeal freight rates that discriminate against secondary materials; another would provide tax benefits for companies that use recycled wastes in their production processes. More radical proposals would reduce or eliminate such benefits as depletion allowance, which is an effective incentive for industry to keep tapping virgin resources. At the same time many experts point out that even if recycling centers operated at a loss, a net gain would result, since the cost of garbage disposal would be lower.

Revulsion at the unsightly mess of garbage that scars urban centers and the countryside, national parks, and seashores is not the primary reason for concern about waste disposal; it is, rather, a matter of survival. The earth's resources are not inexhaustible. The total volume of workable mineral deposits is an insignificant fraction of 1 percent of the earth's crust. If scientists are correct in predicting that demands for minerals will increase exponentially for the next fifty to seventy-five years as more countries become industrialized and the world population increases, deposits of currently commercial grade will inevitably be exhausted (Lovering 1969).

Mineral exhaustion will occur even faster in the industrial countries where high-grade deposits have been, or are being, extensively mined. As industrial nations use up the cheap supplies in their own countries they become more and more dependent on foreign sources for raw materials. All industrial countries now, with the possible exception of the Soviet Union, are net importers of most of the minerals and ores they use. For example, the United States, historically blessed with some resource self-sufficiency, is experiencing a growing dependence on imported minerals. Of the thirteen basic raw materials a modern economy requires, the United States in 1970 was dependent on imports for more than half of its supplies of six. A projection for 1985 shows import dependence for nine of the thirteen basic raw materials, including three major ones—bauxite, iron ore, and tin (Brown 1973).

As dependence increases, industrialized countries will become more vulnerable to military, political, and economic action. A review of history shows that nations have risen and fallen according to shifts in sources of supply. The Arab cutoff of oil supplies to the United States for political reasons has put the well-being of this country in serious jeopardy. A research group, Data Resources, Inc., has determined that production shortages will dominate the U.S. economy in 1974 even if the oil embargo is lifted by March 1974. The greater vulnerability of industrialized nations in times of both peace and war indicates the imprudence of assuming unlimited access to the raw materials essential for survival and military power.

Many people like to think great empires in the past declined and fell to more vigorous aggressors because of moral laxity and deviant cultures, but history more realistically and more accurately relates their passing to their unwise use of available raw materials. So, too, the throwaway mentality in America now is sheer folly. The United States is on a suicide course, particularly if one keeps in mind that with 7 percent of the world population it currently accounts for 30 percent of the world's consumption of raw materials. In 1968 the United States, Canada, Europe, Russia, Japan, and Australia consumed over 90 percent of both the energy and the steel produced in the world (Ehrlich & Ehrlich 1972). From the political as well as the supply point of view, obviously such consumption cannot continue indefinitely as it constantly increases in amount.

> . . . [T]he old myth that continued growth increases the control of our environment is now simply false. We are losing control. We are destroying the air we breathe, the water we drink, and the land we walk upon. And this is not an accident. It is rooted in the fundamental attitudes and practices of advanced industrial society. It is in part the logic of capitalism, but it is more than that; it is the very relationship we assume toward the natural world.

The talk about shifting from an economy of affluence, obsolescence, redundancy and waste to an economy that recognizes scarcity must yield practical proposals for a new economics. And these proposals must include the mandatory re-cycling of all natural resources; the mandatory production of only re-cyclable containers; the rationing of all natural resources—rationing to provide for sane limits on the amounts of consumption as well as to equalize mechanisms for distribution.

Industrial processes must be rationed as to the amount of oxygen, water, or minerals they consume in production. These are no small matters, but they are only the basic parameters for what would be a truly democratic policy for our life support systems. The "economy of death" must be replaced by an economy of life. [Weisberg 1970, pp. 70–71]

Food Scare in a Land of Plenty

The recent food scare in this country, which has long fed much of the world, was a first for many Americans. The news included items about the likelihood of food shortages, an incipient black market in foodstuffs, and spiraling prices. The disruption in the food production process was real, and many still feel insecure about future availability of food. What Americans experienced was analogous to a mild earth tremor as opposed to the strong earthquakes in distant places.

While America reaps record harvests, tens of millions of people around the world are malnourished or near starvation. The President's Committee on the World Food Supply estimated in 1967 that 20 percent of the people in the underdeveloped countries (two-thirds of the world population) were undernourished—not receiving enough calories per day—and 60 percent were malnourished—seriously lacking in one or more essential nutrients, most commonly protein. Hence, as many as 1.5 billion people were either undernourished or malnourished. This estimate, now conservative, does not include the hungry and malnourished millions in the lower economic strata of developed countries, such as the United States, or the innumerable people who can afford to eat properly but are malnourished because of their ignorance of nutrition. The absolute number of people involved is simply staggering, almost unbelievable. Our unawareness of them, even when they live in our midst, is not only a sign of our prosperity but also a measure of our isolation from the rest of the world. Today's hungry multitudes are quite aware of how well the affluent few eat, and because they want to be as well fed the situation is sure to have serious political implications for the future.

This grim state results from the vagaries of the weather, the constant growth in the world population by at least seventy-five million a year, the failure of poor countries to tend adequately to their own agriculture, and the rising affluence of the world's haves. Affluence has enabled some countries to syphon off the market enormous quantities of food, thereby placing it beyond the economic reach of the poor. The most important purchases recently were those of the Soviet Union in 1972—about thirty million tons of grain, enough to provide a subsistence diet for a year for perhaps 120 to 150 million people. The depletion of reserves in the United States, which has served as the world's major granary, triggered rapid increases in the prices of wheat, corn, and soybeans, and, in turn, higher prices for all foods and a soaring inflation rate.

A cause of great debate among food experts is the issue of whether the current shortfall represents merely a down in a continuing cycle of ups and downs or is a fundamentally new condition of indefinite global scarcity. The issue is important because if the shortfall is, in fact, temporary only some improvement in the weather is necessary; if the shortfall really is more serious, far more difficult and complicated steps are needed among both the food-short and the food-surplus nations (Borgstrom 1973).

The United States government apparently sees the scarcity as short term. From this view flows its policy of selling commercially as much food as possible and providing only the leftovers for relief. Actually, almost no leftovers exist; programs such as Food for Peace are practically dead. Thus only good weather in crop-producing countries stands in the way of widespread famine in large areas of the world, such as southern Asia or the sub-Saharan countries. The United States, indeed, appears to have no comprehensive policy to guide it in this area. It is no better prepared in food than it is in oil.

The condition of world food scarcity is too new and tentative.

Everyone agrees that the situation requires a high measure of international cooperation. Many advocate serious consideration of the United Nations Food and Agriculture Organization proposal for an internationally managed world food bank to maintain some semblance of order and stability in the world food economy. A world reserve could be built up in times of relative abundance and used in times of acute scarcity. Not many countries are eager to join, though. Americans, oriented toward a free market, have traditionally resisted the idea of world commodities agreements but have managed to increase distrust and suspicion among their own paying customers and allies. After years of massive efforts to convince Europe and Japan to open up as markets for American agricultural products, an overnight embargo for a while stopped such major export items as soybeans

The world food crisis is so serious that major confrontations may occur sooner than expected; instances of such conflicts are already abundant. Under the pressures of competition to loot the sea, Soviet fishing ships sometimes penetrate waters off both coasts of the United States and Canada. They have even been accused of interfering with American lobstermen and destroying their equipment. Between 1961 and 1971 the Peruvian government seized thirty American tuna fishing boats and Ecuador took seventy others in disputes over the limits of territorial waters. The aggressive activities of the far-ranging Japanese fleets have aroused antagonism in Mexico, and Cuban fishing boats have been captured in Florida waters. A recent serious confrontation took place between Iceland and Britain, when Iceland claimed extensive territorial limits. The list of conflicts undoubtedly will grow as the competition becomes more fierce when stocks dwindle from overexploitation and oceanic pollution.

General food shortages have caused many to see the oceans of the world as virtually limitless sources of food. However, marine biologist J. H. Ryther aptly states:

The open sea—90 percent of the ocean and nearly three-fourths of the earth's surface—is essentially a biological desert. It produces a negligible fraction of the world's fish catch at present and has little or no potential for yielding more in the future. [Ehrlich & Ehrlich 1972, p. 125]

What about farming the sea? Farming the sea presents an array of formidable problems, especially in the areas of fertilizing and harvesting. Even when these problems are solved, pollution may well have so increased as to make farming impossible. Pollution, in fact, leads many experts to believe that the sea may not be able to support even the limited yield we now extract from it. The dramatic drop in yield, which began in 1969, may be in a most serious way the beginning of the end. Since only a few percent of the world's calories come from the sea some might conclude that a reduction in ocean yield is not so important. Unfortunately, it is extremely serious (Ehrlich & Ehrlich 1972). A major factor in the recent food crisis and spiraling inflation was the failure of anchovy fisheries off the coast of Peru to produce anything near normal supplies of what has been, until now, a basic source of the world's protein feed meal.

Thus, Japan and the Soviet Union, which have traditionally turned to the sea for their animal protein supplies, are facing a grim future and must turn to world grain markets to offset the fish decline. Their problems undoubtedly will spark among the Japanese, the Russians, and the West European countries some very keen competition for available food exports. Consequently, a cooperative global approach to the management of oceanic fisheries must be developed, or the world will suffer a continuing depletion of stocks, a reduction in catch, and soaring seafood prices that will make those of the early 1970s seem modest in comparison.

This situation may well be advantageous to the United States as a major food producer, but its repercussions on the domestic market may not always be advantageous to the average citizen. To fully exploit any competitive advantage in agricultural exports Americans probably would have to limit their intake of certain types of food, or would have to buy lower grades of certain items because the higher grades would be reserved for export. The cycle is quite simple. If Americans want to maintain their high standard of living, which also means a high level of waste, they must continue to import raw and strategic material from other countries that are stiffening their bargaining positions.

In order to maintain the balance of payments the United States must use its best weapon—food exportation. Not even the agricultural potential of this country is limitless, though. Rapid expansion of the beef supply to accommodate both domestic demand (117 pounds per capita in 1972) and foreign needs will be quite difficult. A commercially satisfactory way of getting more than one calf per beef cow per year has not yet been found. Nor can most ranchers significantly increase the number of beef cows because not enough unused cattle range and pastureland are available. Soybeans, another key food, have frustrated scientists' attempts to achieve a breakthrough in yield per acre. The fourfold increase of soybean production in the United States since 1950 has been achieved almost entirely by expanding acreage at the expense of other crops. Such expansion, of course, cannot continue indefinitely.

Thus, Americans face a dilemma: to maintain the good life that technology makes possible they must either tighten their belts or experience at least periodical food shortages, increased food prices, and lower quality supplies. The impact of this situation on the domestic poor will be quite serious. Substantial poverty exists in every section of the United States but is most widespread in the South, where nearly 50 percent of all families are poor, and almost 70 percent are either poor or have very low standards of living. The Appalachian region alone, much of it in the South, has five million poor out of fifteen million people (Horton & Leslie 1970; Kahn 1973). Altogether, the Senate Select Committee on Nutrition and Human Needs says, twenty-five to twenty-seven million people in this country "lack the resources needed to purchase a nutritionally adequate diet." Of them only twelve million are being helped through the food stamp program, which provides a maximum of $116 a month for a family of four.

While millions of Americans need food because they are poor, many of the affluent are malnourished because of their ignorance of nutrition, or because the food industry is deliberately misleading them. According to the industry, snack foods alone accounted for $3.4 billion in 1971, and the projection is for a 6 percent annual growth rate. Such items as Nestle Vee-Kreme, Cheezo Nuggets, Captain Jimmy's Cosmic Color Poppers, Temptein Pepperoni, Likwifier, Bioiron, and Pringle's Potato Chips are staging a real invasion of the supermarket.

Many experts feel that in creating and intensively advertising such pleasure foods the industry has destroyed in America the concept of good nutrition. They claim that several thousand Americans die prematurely each year because of the food they eat. Sugared foods keep dentists busy. Surprisingly, even a former president of the Institute of Food Technologists, George F. Stewart, now at the University of California, was so overcome by the bizarre sights at a food convention that he commented:

> I worry about it. I think it's awful. I don't know where it is taking us. There's a lot of stuff put on the market that's not food. I worry whether my kids and I will be able to get good food. We may be losing a social and cultural good. But I'm in the minority. [In McCarthy 1973]

Eater's Digest aptly adds:

> The industry says of its so-called pleasure foods, that we are only giving what the public demands. ... If the public wants something that industry scientists know contributes to a bad diet and to some of the most serious illnesses, should industry try to sell as much of it as fast as it can? If your kids come home and want to borrow ten bucks to buy some marijuana or heroin, would you respond as readily to that consumer demand? [In McCarthy 1973]

These comments are similar to those of Dr. Morris E. Chafetz, director of the National Institute on Alcohol Abuse and Alcoholism, at the Sixteenth Annual Institute of Alcohol Studies of the Texas Commission on Alcoholism:

> When I see fast-action commercials targeted at inexperienced drinkers who, by the way, are also inexperienced drivers; when I see alcoholic pop wines advertised as though they were soda pop; when I see the Nation's most devastating drug being handled in this way; then I think we have to ask some hard questions: Has our concern with profit become greater than our concern with people? Have producers been neglecting their social consciences? And have purveyors been unaware or unconcerned with the drug implications of what they are doing? If these are truly responsible people ... then I believe they must do some serious self-examination and take some positive action for themselves before they are compelled to do so by society. [*Alcohol and Health Notes*, October 1973]

Although Dr. Chafetz correctly stresses industry's responsibility in producing and advertising imitation foods or alcoholic beverages, we should not forget that we are also part of the problem. Though large corporations may produce these worthless and unhealthy materials, we purchase them; we even welcome them when they relieve us of the task of properly feeding ourselves and our children. It is indeed sad that modern man is so easily duped by a label stating that vitamins have been added to a product of indefinite composition even as he overlooks foods that nature has fortified with vitamins and minerals.

Conclusion

We have not discussed many other important areas concerned with the quality of life: how society treats its weaker members; widespread discontent with the seemingly meaningless tasks workers must perform (blue-collar blues); the increased amount of leisure time available to many who do not know how to or cannot afford to use it satisfactorily; statistics that show that large numbers of Americans retire in poverty, destitution, and poor health; the loss of belonging to a community of shared purposes and values (see Hamalian & Karl 1970; Lapp 1973; Morgan 1973; Turk et al. 1972; Illich 1973).

The most serious menace to the quality of life is the rape of the land, the air, and the waters for commercial profit. Here, too, only major issues were discussed. Important topics left out include: the growing threat of atomic waste pollution, pesticides and related compounds, noise pollution, and heavy metals pollution; issues related to birth control, family planning, and population control.

It is difficult to convincingly show the gravity of the situation and to arouse people to some sort of action. Most people see no immediate personal, life-and-death crisis, for no one appears to have been wiped out by smog, pesticides, or junk food. A snowstorm, a hurricane, an impending flood elicit higher levels of response and more feverish activity than does a "hazardous" reading on the air quality scale or news of heavy mercury pollution of edible fish. The only difference in actual danger is that in the long run the effects of environmental pollution are in what is accumulated, but they are not any less real. What is the difference between the loss of life in flood waters and death over months or years, perhaps after a long, lingering illness, because of cancer, emphysema, or hepatitis?

Modern man likes to look with disdain and compassion on earlier man, who at times called for an orgiastic enjoyment of life because the life span was so short and brutal. But not much has actually changed. Modern man follows his technologically less equipped ancestors in an orgy of consumption and waste, as if there were no tomorrow, as if no future generations would inherit spaceship Earth. The high rate of cancer deaths in advanced societies has been quite aptly compared to the bubonic plague epidemics that ravaged medieval Europe. Just as then, the dead are buried and hastily forgotten, but the survivors continue to commit the same irreparable errors, frantically trying to enjoy life as they wait for the fatal telling signs to appear on their bodies. The apprehension and actual terror in the contemporary person who discovers a lump in a vulnerable part of the body differs little from our ancestors' fear.

Have we really progressed? No doubt the environmental crisis cannot be dealt with effectively unless we change our general value framework and relearn how to live ecologically with other people and with the land, to see ourselves as part of an interlocking collective unit (Gliner 1973). A massive conversion to a new religion may be required. Domination through growth has indeed held the American mind for so long that to many any suggestion of curtailing growth is unthinkable—heretical. To yank modern man away from his destructive pattern of life will require a total emotional purging. In other words, the major survival crisis that man today faces is not overpopulation, environmental pollution, energy shortages, or even unjust social relations *as single problems.* Rather, it is their common denominator: man's unwillingness or inability to change his values, beliefs, attitudes, behaviors, and institutions. The answer to the anguished question, "Can man do anything about his society before it is too late?" hinges on whether or not man can develop in time a meaningful and responsive method for changing his behavior and his social institutions.

Part III

Deviance and Personality Problems

CHAPTER 7

Ours Is a Violent History

Violence in America

On September 26, 1872, three mounted bandits rode to the gate of the Kansas City fair, where a crowd of ten thousand had gathered. They shot at the ticket seller, by mistake hit a small girl in the leg, and made off for the woods with less than $1,000. In reporting the incident the Kansas City *Times* called the robbery "so diabolically daring and so utterly in contempt of fear that we are bound to admire it and revere its perpetrators." Two days later the *Times* compared the outlaws with the knights of King Arthur's Round Table. This incident and many others show how deeply engrained in American life is the tradition, even the love, of violence (Herbers 1970).

American culture is interlaced with threads of violence, and many leisure activities thrive on it—prizefighting, wrestling, hockey, football, roller derbies. Some American pastimes contain an element of latent violence—automobile and motorcycle racing, for instance, which often involve wrecks, injuries, and fiery death. Many individual pursuits are to different extents potentially violent—hunting, deepsea sport fishing, shooting river rapids, car wrecking.

America's literary tradition, oral and written, is replete with death, danger, and violence. The cruel practical jokes and bloodthirsty tall tales of frontier humorists tell us much about life on the cutting edge of a wilderness. The burning cities of Ignatius Donnelly's *Caesar's Column*, Jack London's *The Iron Heel*, and other turn-of-the-century social novels reflect in their flames the revolutionary discontent of farmers and industrial workers in the 1890s. Mark Twain's *Pudd'nhead Wilson*, Melville's "Benito Cereno," and Richard Wright's *Native Son* measure the racial hostility that black and white Americans have been struggling with since the seventeenth century. The war novels of Crane, Hemingway, and Dos Passos express experiences with violence (Lynn 1970). Movies, plays, poems, novels, and paintings exalt and embody war and violence. Some of the most popular television programs fictionalize working law enforcement officials, detectives, bounty hunters, and gangsters. The classic American art form, the Western saga, stands as a unique monument to the individual's use of force and violence to achieve justice (Bryant 1971).

Although the cult of violence is not limited to American culture, many unique aspects of the society and politics have contributed to individual and collective violence here. Among them are the psychological residues of slavery, the coexistence of mass consumption with pockets and strata of sullen poverty, and the conflict among competing ethics that leaves many people without clear guidelines for daily living. Other sources of violence in America's national life are inheritances from its past: praise of violent acts for good causes, committed by revolutionaries, frontiersmen, and vigilantes; immigrant expectations of an earthly paradise only partially realized; and the unresolved tensions of rapid and unregulated urban and industrial growth (Graham & Gurr 1970).

A Definition of Violence

We look at violence from perspectives affected by our beliefs and cultural experiences. Commonly the term is negative—used to categorize and condemn acts of which one disapproves. If one is sympathetic with the reasons that underlie violence, especially collective violence, one may call it protest. When public individuals, such as police and soldiers, use the term violence it is typically referred to as legitimate force. Violence, force, protest, legality, legitimacy are emotion-laden words.

Violence is defined here as behavior designed to inflict physical injury to people or damage to property. Specific acts of violence may be regarded as good, bad, or neutral, depending on who engages in them and against whom the action is directed. Force, a more general concept, is the actual or threatened use of violence to compel others to do what they might not otherwise do. Thus force and violence are closely linked concepts. Force involves the threat, if not the actuality, of violence; violence is forceful if it is used with the intent to change others' actions. Protest does not necessarily imply force or violence but is an expression of dissatisfaction with other people's actions, and can take individual or collective, verbal or physical, peaceful or violent forms. Many Americans are most concerned with collective and physical forms of protest, but these forms do not necessarily include the use of force or violence, nor do public protesters use them frequently (Graham & Gurr 1970).

Legality and legitimacy are words used to pass judgment on the desirability of violence, force, and protest, as well as other acts. Formal community decision-making procedures determine the legality of actions. Acts are legitimate if enough community members regard them as desirable or justifiable. In an ideal, perfect society the two terms "legal" and "legitimate" would be interchangeable: the community would regard as legitimate all acts judged legal; all illegal acts would be illegitimate. In reality, when violence, force, and protest are or have been involved, no such clear-cut distinction holds in the United States or elsewhere. Most northerners and most southerners thought the competing causes of the Civil War to be both legal and legitimate. Americans deplored the assassination of President Kennedy; yet we wonder how many would have applauded an attempt on the life of, say, Fidel Castro.

The vigilante movement has been a strong current in American culture. Private citizens' violent acts were technically illegal but popularly approved as legitimate. The complexity of the American conflict between legitimacy and legality of actions would be apparent in an analysis of the 1960s demonstrations and riots. Some demonstrations were legal; others were not because municipal, state, or federal authorities proscribed them. In some American cities they might all have been either approved or ruled illegal. Most demonstrators regarded their actions as legitimate, regardless of their legality; many Americans regarded demonstrations as illegitimate and at times even as a form of treason, whatever their legality. These distinctions are not just an idle academic exercise. They demonstrate that Americans historically have not agreed, and do not now agree, on the propriety of different kinds of force, violence, and protest.

Historical Patterns of Violence

Historically Americans have used violence in order to accomplish their goals. Considerable violence has been connected with most events in American history, even with the most noble chapters. Again and again violence was used with approval when it was a means to a widely accepted end. We can identify the following major historical patterns of American violence (Brown 1970).

1. *Criminal Violence.* Organized interstate gangs of criminals can be traced well back into the eighteenth century. First engaged in horse theft and counterfeiting, after the Civil War such gangs specialized in train and bank robberies. The modern era of big-city organized crime, involving police and politics, began to emerge in the twentieth century. America's attitude toward criminals has always been ambiguous—officially condemning and proscribing, but at times openly admiring and praising. The Robin Hood symbol represents society's view of the bandit as hero rather than enemy.

2. *Feud Violence.* Although it generally has been associated with the hillbilly of the southern Appalachians, the feud also has

been prevalent in Texas and the Southwest, triggered at times by animosities generated by the Civil War.

3. *Lynch Mob Violence.* Lynch law initially meant the infliction of corporal punishment, but by the middle of the nineteenth century it became synonymous with hanging or killing by illegal group action. Frequently used in all sections of the country against whites as well as blacks, lynching became in the postwar era predominantly the fate of southern blacks.

4. *Violence Inspired by Racial, Ethnic, and Religious Prejudice.* Racial conflict between whites and blacks has persisted throughout the history of American violence, and in the last hundred years the Ku Klux Klan has been a most consistent and visible practitioner. A score of other racial, ethnic, and religious movements have paralleled the Klan: protestant anti-Catholic crusades, anti-Chinese agitation in the West, murderous anti-Italian mobs in the South, bloody clashes between old-stock Americans and the newly arrived southeastern Europeans.

5. *Urban Riots.* Urban disturbances date to colonial times. Later, in the 1830s, 1840s, and 1850s, urban rioting was the result of slum conditions and severe ethnic and religious differences in the cities of the Northeast. The modern police system, in fact, was created in response to those riots, and the National Guard was formed in reaction to the widespread labor uprisings in 1877. Most people identify riots with urban race riots. From 1900 to 1949, thirty-three major interracial disturbances occurred in the United States. With the exception of the Harlem riots (1935 and 1943), whites were the main aggressors, and most of the casualties were blacks. The rioting in 1964 (Harlem, Rochester) and 1965 (Los Angeles' Watts) introduced the present pattern of black initiative aimed at property destruction.

6. *Freelance Multiple Murders.* Numerous freelance murders were committed during frontier times. Contemporary Americans suddenly became aware of this kind of violent behavior when, first, in Chicago Richard Speck murdered eight student nurses and, later, Charles Whitman displayed his unerring marksmanship from the top of the University of Texas tower. Since then several other instances of multiple murder have occurred.

7. *Political Assassination.* Between 1865 and 1965 four

presidents (Lincoln, Garfield, McKinley, and Kennedy) were assassinated. Other presidents have been intended targets in attempts that failed. Robert Kennedy, Martin Luther King, Jr., Medgar Evers, and Malcolm X are among other victims of political assassinations.

8. *Police Violence.* Undue violence in the course of enforcing the law has long been a matter of concern. In earlier generations the public worried about the use of the third degree to obtain confessions; currently the concern is with police brutality, chiefly against blacks and other minorities. Occurrences during the Democratic National Convention in Chicago in 1968 and May Day in Washington, D.C., in 1971 have been identified as police riots, where the excessive use of force created a situation of "order without law" (Lipsky 1970). Related to police use of violence has been the large amount of violence associated with the incarceration of suspects and convicts (Murton 1972).

9. *Revolutionary Violence.* America was conceived and born in violence—violence instigated by the Sons of Liberty and the patriots of American port cities during the 1760s and 1770s. Tarring and feathering was widely used to uproot Toryism. Aside from regular military clashes, guerrilla strife occurred from the Hudson to the Savannah and included much pillage and mayhem. The position that the end justifies the means became the keystone of revolutionary ideology. The Revolution was successful; therefore it was immediately enshrined in America's tradition and history. Consequently Americans have never shied from using violence in the interest of any cause declared to be a good one. Decades of violence, mischief, and fratricide followed the Civil War and the Reconstruction era. The Indian Wars, begun in Virginia in 1607, continued nearly three hundred years until the final massacre at Wounded Knee, South Dakota.

10. *Vigilante Violence.* Vigilantism seems to thrive on American soil. Taking the law into one's own hands, as vigilantism is defined, is repugnant to British legal tradition. The action was initiated to bring needed law and order to the frontier regions, where no effective governmental presence existed. When the United States became less rural and more urban, vigilantism did not disappear but switched goals. Instead of horse thieves and counterfeiters, vigilantes chose as their targets immigrants,

blacks, radicals, nonconformists, civil libertarians, and labor leaders, to name a few. Aggressive vigilantism has been a recurrent response of middle and working class Americans to perceived threats from outsiders or classes beneath their status, security, and cultural integrity. Vigilantism as a spontaneous group reaction of witnesses to a crime in progress or as a concerted effort to apprehend a suspect has reappeared, especially in ethnic neighborhoods of large urban areas such as New York City.

11. *Agrarian Uprisings.* Both colonial and national American history record frequent agrarian uprisings accompanied, of course, by violence. Shays's Rebellion, the Whisky Rebellion, the Fries Rebellion, the Western Claim Clubs' tactics and the Night Riders' raids are among the best known instances of violent reactions among populist and land reform activists as well as their opponents. Interestingly, farmers repeatedly used the principles that sparked the American Revolution to justify their violent and destructive actions.

12. *Labor Violence.* On May 16, 1973, an association that represented fifty-five hundred firms, mainly nonunion building contractors, filed one of the largest cases ever to come before the National Labor Relations Board. The complaint: attacks on open-shop construction projects and employees are costing more than $5 million annually in damages to nonunion operators. In 1972 alone more than one hundred seventy acts of violence were reported. The labor movement reveals the same mixture of good ends and bad means—violence—that characterized the agrarian movement; hence many refer to the late nineteenth and early twentieth centuries as the dynamite period in American labor relations. Taft (1964) has demonstrated that most labor violence in American history was not a deliberate tactic of working-class organization but a result of forceful employer resistance to worker organization and demand. Companies resorted to violent strikebreaking tactics and coercive and terroristic acts against union organizers. Employers' violence often provided a model and impetus for workers' counterviolence. The Black Hole of Ludlow and the anarchy and unrestrained class warfare that ensued symbolize the violent character of most American labor transactions. Today labor-management relations have become

more civilized, but at times greed and the American way of life still lead to violent confrontations.

13. *School Violence.* School officials across the country must cope with violence and crime, which usually occur as children strike out against other children, teachers, and school property. Junior high schools appear to be the most dangerous battle-grounds. The problems, which are worst in central-city schools, are the same as those in adult society: murder, rape, drug ped-dling, armed robbery, arson, vandalism, and wanton destruction. Often racial tensions are a factor. School violence is relatively new in the United States, particularly at the elementary school level. It differs from the campus unrest of the sixties in that it has no political or protest motives.

What, then, shall we conclude? Is or is not America a violent country? If yes, in relationship to what? A task force of the National Commission on the Causes and Prevention of Violence (1970) concludes the following in its report on *Violence in America:*

Whether the United States is now a "violent society" can be an-swered not in the abstract, but only by comparison, either with the American past or with other nations. The historical evidence sug-gests that we were somewhat more violent toward one another in this decade [1960s] than we have been in most others, but probably less violent in total magnitude of civil strife than in the latter nineteenth century, when the turmoil of Reconstruction was followed by mas-sive racial and labor violence. Even so, in contemporary comparison with other nations, acts of collective violence by private citizens of the United States in the last twenty years have been extraordinarily numerous. . . . In numbers of political assassinations, riots, politically relevant armed group attacks, and demonstrations, the United States since 1948 has been among the half-dozen most tumultuous nations in the world. . . . In a comparison that gives greatest weight to the frequency of violent events, the United States ranks fourteenth among 84 nations. In another comparison, based on the severity of all manifestations of political instability, violent or not violent, the United States stands 46th among 84 nations. In other words, the United States . . . had much political violence by comparison with other nations, but relative stability of its political institutions in spite of it. Paradoxically, we have been a turbulent people, but a relatively stable Republic. [Pp. 798–801]

The Sources of Violence

Are we violent by nature or by circumstance? What sets us up for violence? What could set the stage for a better society? Hobbes, a seventeenth-century philosopher, built his natural law doctrine on man's natural propensity toward unlimited self-assertion, to be *homo homini lupus*—any man is a wolf in his dealings with another man. Thus the inescapable legacy of human nature is a "life . . . [that is] solitary, poor, nasty, brutish, and short."

Ethologists give new credence to this pessimistic view in their study of animal behavior in natural habitats. They have concluded that the aggressive drive in animals is innate, along with hunger, sex, and fear (Lorenz 1966; Ardrey 1966; Storr 1968). Most social scientists, however, do not consider aggression as basically spontaneous or instinctive; the weight of the evidence at hand does not support such a view. Aggression is regarded, rather, as an emotional response to socially induced frustrations or as a learned response to specific situations. In other words, nature provides only the capacity for violence; social circumstance determines how or whether the capacity is exercised.

It is realistic, then, to envision a society in which we would so construct cultural traditions and institutions as to minimize violence. In the cultures of the Arapesh of New Guinea, the Lepchas of Sikkim, and the pygmies of the Congo rain forest, for example, a desire for such concrete physical pleasures as eating, drinking, sex, and laughter replaces the desire for aggression. Some social scientists contend that the amount of physical violence in a given society is directly proportional to the repression of pleasure in the daily environment.

That culture is a powerful determinant of the human propensity for violence is easily illustrated. For example, Manhattan Island has more murders per year than all of England and Wales; in Wichita Falls, Texas, the number of homicides per year exceeds the combined amount for the four major Italian cities. It seems fair to conclude that the human has the cultural capacity to minimize or maximize recourse to violence.

So many theories attempt to explain the causes of violence that cataloging is difficult. One general approach begins with the assumption that human frustrations over some of the material and social circumstances of life are a necessary precondition of group protest and collective violence. The more intense the discontent, the more intense collective violence is likely to be.

Certain general conditions have been identified as highly conducive to a climate of unrest and discontent. One is a pattern of rising expectations among people who are blocked because of lack of opportunity or the unyielding resistance of others. Demands of groups that have felt unjustifiably excluded from a fair share of the social, economic, and political privileges of the majority have many times provided reasons and justification for group conflict. Aspirations of blacks and of latecomers to America—Irish, Italians, Slavs, Jews—have provided repeated occasions for violence.

However, denial of just demands and the ruling class's strong resistance to change considered undesirable have been sources of equal or greater collective violence than has the resolution of rising expectations. Groups farther up the socioeconomic ladder account for innumerable instances of violence in retaliation for presumed threats from the new immigrants who got too close. Companies resorted to coercive and terroristic tactics to break strikes. Often such action was a model and an incentive for worker counterviolence which led to even more violent conflict. Aggressive vigilantism also has been used to resist change when the middle and working class believed that their status, security, and cultural integrity were being threatened. Contemporary instances of vigilantism include harassment of hippie and peacenik settlements in rural and small-town areas and the urban neovigilante organizations, white and black, for group defense.

Another element often associated with outbreaks of rebellion and revolution is a sharp deterioration of socioeconomic or political conditions after a prolonged period of steady improvement (Davies 1962). In other words, frustrated hope is much more likely to cause violence than is stark deprivation.

Remember, however, that discontent is only the background condition for collective violence. Popular attitudes and cultural values will determine whether and how actual violence will occur. Even given extreme frustration and an immediate cue, violence will not necessarily erupt unless a third factor is present—low inhibitions. Moreover, certain group dynamics and other conditions are necessary. They have been identified as follows (Dancey 1968):

1. A group of associates socially accepts and justifies violence for the purposes concerned.
2. There is a prospect of gaining something or some advantage by means of violence.
3. It is considered unlikely that it could be gained without violence.
4. One can probably get away with it. The risks appear to be small.

An ecological factor often is associated with violence: overcrowding of human populations may lead to aggressiveness. Ethologists and other social scientists have explored the concepts of territory and defensible space as important variables to be considered in attempts to understand urban violence. The physical form of housing (number of stories, bigness) apparently has some influence and impact on the presence or absence of violence and crime (Newman 1973; Jeffery 1971).

According to psychological theories and findings, violence is part of each individual's adjustment pattern for living in a society; that is, it may be the result of faltering and unsuccessful attempts to function in society. For instance, a child may find attempts to socialize him confusing and conflicting, and he will react with violent tantrums or other forms of open hostility. An immigrant, seeking to learn a new role in a new culture, will at times strike at what frustrates him, at what he fails to understand, in an attempt to rearrange or remove the condition.

Violence also may be the result of an impulse. Thus it is neither the result of internal maladjustment nor necessarily a planned, purposeful activity. According to this view, an aggressive cue—a fight word, for example—often is at work. If cultural values sanction the cue, the individual then will strike out violently (Taylor & Soady 1972; Berkowitz 1968).

Do not forget, however, that much human aggressive behavior has nothing to do with feelings. The trigger man for Murder Inc. or the bombardier on a mission over a hostile country may feel no animosity toward his victims. He kills not because he is angry but because he is rewarded. Thus violent behavior quite possibly is the result of a complex web of factors, biological, physiological, learned, and environmental. Since aggressive behavior is the greatest human problem, further research is imperative in order to achieve control before an advanced technology of destruction solves the problem (Moyer 1973).

How Successful Is Violence?

Throughout history, violence seems to have been the chief means for social reform. Followers of the doctrines of Frantz Fanon and Che Guevara assert that if those who engage in such acts are sufficiently dedicated, revolution can always be accomplished. A Rand Corporation Research Study concluded, similarly, that "for revolution to win, it *need not* initially have the spontaneous support, sympathy, or loyalty of the people . . . revolution can make substantial progress *without* substantial popular endorsement" (Leites & Wolf 1970, p. 149). Many law-and-order advocates and counterinsurgency experts hold essentially the same point of view in regard to governmental use of force.

To what extent do theory and historical evidence support this view on the effectiveness of force for modifying others' behavior? Psychological and ethological evidence on human and animal aggression show that the two most fundamental responses to the use of force are to flee or to fight. Force threatens and angers humans, particularly if they believe it to be illegitimate and unjust. Threatened, they will defend themselves if they can and flee if they can't. Angered, they would like to retaliate in kind. Thus humans who fear assault arm themselves and are psychologically ready to react violently to the slightest provocation, even though it may exist only in their minds.

Governments react in the same way with the allocation of apparently extraordinary amounts of money for arms stockpiles to counteract both internal and external threats. The wisdom of such measures, which invite a similar counterreaction from the opponent, has been widely debated. Escalating spirals of force and counterforce have only two inherent limitations: one side's exhaustion of resources for force or one side's attainment of a capacity for genocidal victory. Many explain the current detente between East and West as an effect of a mutual realization that the vicious cycle will exhaust both sides' available resources. Some attribute the diversion of Black Panther activities into more peaceful pursuits to their realization that the government was using its capacity for genocidal victory to overcome the challenge of militancy.

Other limitations presuppose a tacit bond between opponents: one side's acceptance of the other's ultimate authority, a neutral's arbitration of the conflict, recognition of mutual interest that makes bargaining possible, perception that acquiescence to a powerful opponent will have effects less harmful than those in resisting to a certain death. If one of these bases for cooperation does not exist, the conflict probably will be savagely destructive. Violence succeeds when one group so overpowers its opponents that their only choice, short of death, is submission. History records many such instances, most of them governmental successes. The only shortcoming is that overpowering violence succeeds only in the short run if the opponents have not been completely exterminated. For example, the Russian government successfully quelled the 1905 revolution only to be overthrown a few years later. In the United States, the North's success in the Civil War generated years of vigilante violence.

Graham and Gurr (1970) note that three conditions are necessary for governmental success in maintaining law and order: public belief that governmental use of force is legitimate, consistent use of force, and remedial action for the grievances that incite private violence. Fulfillment of these three conditions accounted for the decline of working-class violence in nineteenth-century England. In Cuba the Batista government's response to private violence was inconsistent and terroristic, and lacked any significant attempt to reduce grievances. That the government fell was no surprise to the informed observer.

Thus, the best indicator of success of violence is the resolution of grievances that aroused protest. Measurement of success in every case is obviously difficult; at times it is doubtful that any success has been achieved. The final outcome of the Vietnam war is in that way uncertain. Politically a successful revolution ends the worst abuses and inefficiencies and settles for a time the most serious conflicts, but any accurate measurement of its permanent effects on the average human's values and belief system is much more difficult. Crane Brinton (1965) states:

> In our Western society men have continued to hold certain senti-
> ments and to conform to certain set ways of doing things even after
> they have changed what they say about these sentiments and these
> acts. Our revolutions seem to have changed men's minds more com-
> pletely than they changed men's habits. This is by no means to say
> that they changed nothing at all, that what men think is of no impor-
> tance. [P. 247]

In other words, most humans basically are establishmentari-
ans. Although they may readily accept a certain amount of
change, excessive demands may backfire. For example, the tragic
fall of Salvador Allende's freely elected Chilean government has
been attributed to his too fast and too demanding introduction
of long overdue social changes.

Violence can also serve as a catalyst, that is, it can create a
sense of solidarity within a community (Coser 1967). This unin-
tended effect is not limited to private violence; law enforcement
agents also may induce a sense of solidarity against their behavior. Sheriffs and other law officers used violent methods to crush
protest activities and voter registration drives in the South during
the 1960s, thereby arousing public revulsion and prompting federal legislation. Thus, ironically, violence aimed at maintaining
a repressive caste system—"keep them in their places"—became
the most effective argument in favor of measures to abolish that
system. The use of violence actually may be suicidal.

Violence can be a successful mechanism for conflict resolution.
Its positive or negative effects depend on innumerable historical,
economic, circumstantial, and other variables.

Alternatives to Violence

Responses of government officials to threats of or actual collective violence can be either a strengthening of existing systems of
social control by means of force or relief of unsettling conditions
by means of public and private efforts. History shows that primary reliance on force has, at best, an indeterminate outcome.
Public force will contain specific outbursts of violence, but is

unlikely to prevent recurrence (perhaps modified) of the violence. If not popularly supported, public force will so alienate the people that dissidents will have little difficulty in seriously challenging or overthrowing the regime. Comparative studies show that a government must be cautious in its reliance on force as a means to maintain order, consistent in exercising the amount of force it chooses to use, and equipped with well-trained and highly disciplined police forces.

Even though efforts to eliminate the conditions that lead to collective violence may tax the society's resources, they pose fewer problems than does increased reliance on force, and they are the best possibility for completely defusing the situation and solving it equitably. Government and management in the United States have learned this lesson in relation to labor violence. In the past twenty-five years American labor violence has been greatly mitigated because employers have recognized unions and will negotiate rather than retaliate. In both the United States and England, as well as in other countries, the long-range fruits of compromise, often branded as displays of weakness, were decreases, not increases, in violent conflict (National Commission on the Causes and Prevention of Violence, 1970). A society that wants fewer violent outbursts, then, should reduce the general level of frustration by judiciously using governmental, economic, and political reform, and by means of institutional development among society's aggrieved classes. Recourse to legalized violence should be kept to a minimum as a temporary, emergency measure if long-lasting civil peace is the goal.

CHAPTER 8

Crime in America

The Study of Crime

The study of crime can be fascinating, for criminal activity often arouses intense passions. A mixture of fear, enmity, admiration, and envy excites an impelling sense of curiosity about the roots of a criminal offense and the forces that led victim and offender to their fates. In its more sensational forms, crime can greatly heighten the population's feelings of morbid excitement.

Mass media coverage of criminal activity opens up for public scrutiny intimate areas in the lives of the law violator and the victim. Such news vicariously involves millions of viewers and provides otherwise taboo information about the ways some people live.

In the United States stories of violent brutality, well-planned robbery, and clever swindles constantly entertain the public imagination. These stories are assured a prominent place in social conversations, front-page lines in dailies and periodicals, and primary coverage on radio and television. In addition to these real-life situations, mystery and detective fiction is extremely popular, both as reading and as television material (Bloch & Geis 1970).

Crime is by no means a recent phenomenon. On the contrary, prerevolutionary criminal activity was extensive; train and bank robbers roamed the Old West; bootlegging and gangsterism were rampant in the roaring twenties; gang murders were common in rural areas and in ethnic ghettoes; and many other crimes, including burglary, rape, larceny, have abounded. The change has been in geographical distribution and prevalence of certain crimes. New crimes are occurring: airliner hijacking, computer- and industry-related crimes, crimes related to businessman-consumer transactions, and crimes that affect the environment and ecology. Crime allegedly is now spilling over into the previously safe suburban neighborhoods. Drug use and addiction, once limited to ghetto and slum, now are equally widespread among the middle and upper classes.

Thus besides appealing to the public imagination crime is understandably the object of much concern, distaste, and horror. In the early part of the nineteenth century, for instance, many Americans were troubled about what they believed to be an epidemic of immorality and criminality and what some crime watchers believed to be a sign of impending social chaos and destruction. In particular, the middle classes were convinced that the newly created classes—industrial workers and industrial poor —were increasingly living with crime and depravity. Urban riots, the militancy of the labor movement, and growing revolutionary ideas with populist overtones convinced many people that these were indeed dangerous classes.

Recent presidential elections indicate that Americans now are just as concerned about questions of crime, social order, and justice. The dangerous classes are, of course, new: urban blacks, Puerto Ricans, Chicanos. In their midst the new revolutionary movements have developed. Just as in the nineteenth century, when poor immigrant groups were confined to the slums, impending doom, chaos, and societal destruction are predicted.

Partly because they have shared the average human's anxiety, partly because of their own philosophical and social concerns, intellectuals during the last century or so have undertaken an intensive reconsideration of the causes, nature, and distribution of crime. They have further begun to study relationships between legal institutions and crime, and the nature of justice (Douglas 1971). The people who pioneered the development of modern criminology not only reflected their cultural epochs but also left the indelible stamp of their own personalities on criminological thought. Most of the notable persons included in *Pioneers in Criminology* (Mannheim 1960) were Europeans, especially Italian and English. Many were lawyers: Cesare Beccaria, Jeremy Bentham, Enrico Ferri, Raffaele Garofalo, Gabriel Tarde, Hans Gross, Charles Doe, and Pedro Montero. Others were physicians: Cesare Lombroso, Isaac Ray, Henry Haudsley, Charles Goring, and Gustav Aschaffenburg. Criminology evolved early into two major schools: the classical, based on Beccaria, and the positivist, led by Lombroso. C. Ray Jeffery (1960) has succinctly drawn the distinction between the two schools:

> The Classical School defined crime in legal terms; the Positive School rejected the legal definition of crime. The Classical School focused attention on crime as a legal entity; the Positive School focused attention on the act as a psychological entity. The Classical School emphasized free will; the Positive School emphasized determinism. The Classical School theorized that punishment had a deterrent effect; the Positive School said that punishment should be replaced by a scientific treatment of criminals calculated to protect society. [P. 366]

Since then several theoretical approaches in criminology have been developed. Neo-Lombrosians stress the significance of bodily factors in criminality; others favor a psychological frame of reference, emphasizing, for instance, defective intelligence or Freudian concepts; still others center on economic and environmental factors, such as poor housing, poverty, and disrupted family life. These views need not be antagonistic; they can be complementary.

Contemporary Public Concern About Crime

In recent years crime has become a matter of intense public concern. In March 1965 President Johnson told Congress that "Crime has become a malignant enemy in America's midst." He also noted that crime "will not yield to quick and easy answers," but that " we must identify and eliminate the causes of criminal activity whether they lie in the environment around us or deep in the nature of individual men. We must arrest and reverse the trend toward lawlessness" (*New York Times*, March 9, 1965). To accomplish this goal he appointed a Commission on Law Enforcement and the Administration of Justice.

The Commission's nine-volume report, 2,248 double-columned pages long, appeared in 1967. The report reviewed what was known or suspected about crime, contributed new information, and explored such previously neglected issues as the amount and kinds of unreported crime. The Commission offered diverse explanations of crime and advanced different insights into its problems. "The causes of crime are numerous and mysterious and intertwined. Each single crime is a response to a specific situation by a person with an infinitely complicated psychological and emotional makeup subjected to infinitely complicated external pressures" (President's Commission on Law Enforcement and the Administration of Justice 1967 *b*, pp. 1–2).

Unfortunately, action programs that the Commission suggested were poorly received in Congress. The 1968 Omnibus Crime Control and Safe Streets Act was passed more in response to public fears than to sober research. Many of its provisions ran directly counter to the Commission's recommendations. Other investigations in areas related to crime and delinquency included those of the National Commission on Civil Disorders, which looked into the causes of riots and lootings; the National Commission on the Causes and Prevention of Violence, which examined the role of force and brutality in American life; the Joint Commission on Correctional Manpower and Training, which studied methods for handling offenders; and the National Advisory Commission on Criminal Justice Standards and Goals, appointed in 1971, which formulated national criminal justice standards and goals for crime reduction and prevention at state and local levels. These commissions on crime and its treatment have gathered more information than ever before in the history of criminology. It is true that governmental inquiries into crime do not dwell long on basic theoretical issues, but since they mostly aim at the solution of a specific problem they have greatly contributed to better comprehension of crime-related issues (Bloch & Geis 1970).

The Definition of Crime

The word *crime* is used so frequently and heard so often that many people assume that its meaning is the same in every instance. Yet definitions of crime vary widely. To administrators of justice and to lawyers a crime is an illegal act. From a religious perspective crime equals sinful behavior. Some social scientists equate crime with deviation from the accepted norms of a culture; others call crime those acts that are injurious to society. Many now categorize as criminal those acts that deviate from norms of behavior that dominant segments of the society value highly.

The term *crime* is legally defined in the penal code of every state in the United States. A typical code definition is the following:

> A crime or public offense is an intentional act committed or omitted in violation of a law forbidding or commanding it, and to which is annexed either of the following punishments: death, imprisonment, fine, removal from office; or disqualification to hold or enjoy any office of honor, trust, or profit in this state. [*West's California Codes* 1968, secs. 15–20]

Most codes also provide that in every crime a union or joint operation of act and intent or criminal negligence must exist (Haskell & Yablonsky 1970).

Although crime is, first, a legal concept—human behavior punishable under the criminal law—many contend that it is much more than just a legal phenomenon. The frontiers of criminology would not be so difficult to define if so many doubts about the meaning of its fundamental concept did not exist.

It has been argued, for example, that the notion of crime as covering everything punishable under the criminal law has become too broad. Federal law alone, for instance, defines twenty-eight hundred offenses. State laws and local ordinances proscribe even more misdemeanor or felony violations, prohibitions against harming another person, stealing, violations of public morals or public order, infringement of government revenue provisions, and participation in activities defined as hazardous to the public. Also, the exact content of the law and the penalties to be inflicted for violations vary among jurisdictions.

Criminal law seldom follows an integrated or coherent pattern in any country. Some laws represent universal prohibitions; others are the clear creation of vested-interest groups. Francis A. Allen (1964*a*) said:

> It is more than poetic metaphor to suggest that the system of criminal justice may be viewed as a weary Atlas upon whose shoulders we have heaped a crushing burden of responsibilities relating to public policy in its various aspects. This we have done thoughtlessly without inquiring whether the burden can be effectively borne.

The difference between crime and civil wrongs, or torts, is far from clear because the two often overlap. Most serious crimes, such as murder, arson, rape, and robbery, are at the same time torts that entitle the victim to claim civil damages. Moreover, the idea that the legislator can and should treat crime and tort as alternatives, with administrative action as a third possibility, has been playing an increasing part in public policy (Mannheim 1965; Davis 1969).

This notion heightens the controversy that surrounds the distinction between *mala in se* (acts wrong by nature) and *mala prohibita* (acts wrong only because of a man-made law, by convention). The distinction between *mala in se* and *mala prohibita* has been popular in English law at least since the Middle Ages. Fornication, for example, belonged to the first, and coining was assigned to the second.

The existence of wrongs by nature was based on the idea of a body of law founded on the nature of man, which is independent of time and place and of man-made laws. This theory has been discredited in many circles siince the eighteenth century, but the Nazi experience and some issues related to the Vietnam conflict have led to a reconsideration of the position. The idea that the legal definition of crime is the only one is refuted in the opinion that law is nothing but one system of norms among other systems that order human' thoughts and behavior. When the law fails to provide the answer or when the answer it offers seems unsatisfactory, an alternative may be found in religion, custom, morality, or another more specialized value system or code that operates in a given culture.

What, then, is one to conclude? A few points can be established. First, the term *crime* should be used technically only to refer to conduct that is legally crime. Second, such conduct if fully proved is crime regardless of whether it actually leads to a conviction before a criminal court, is dealt with in other agencies, or is dealt with at all.

Third, scientific investigation in criminology is not limited in scope to what is legally crime in a given country at a given time but is free to use its own classifications. In order to reach a workable definition of crime, any purely formal, and eventually inadequate, definition can be supplemented by referring to other, nonlegal forces for social control of human behavior. For instance, crime is not identical with conduct that violates the norms of religion or custom, but the two often have been closely related to legal norms, either as they inspire the lawmaker or as, in their turn, they are influenced by that person.

Last, law and morality are intrinsically different. The law emphasizes the external, morality more the internal side of human behavior; the law stresses the need not to commit disapproved acts, morality expects us not only to refrain but also to act; the law requires a certain amount of standardization, precision, and predictability—values less vital in morality.

Thus many forms of human behavior are criminal without being immoral, many are immoral but not illegal, and some are both immoral and illegal (Mannheim 1965). Although the gap between law and morality should not be too wide or too conspicuous (otherwise the law would lose one of its strongest supports), legislators must judiciously determine immoral behavior that also should be declared illegal.

Dependence on criminal law to enforce morals creates acute strains in modern society, leading to inefficient law enforcement and thereby lessening the actual realization of justice. Part of the modern crime problem, many believe, is a product of this over-dependence on law as a means for bringing about desired behavioral responses (Kadish 1967). Despite the inadequacies, sociologists and criminologists usually use the exclusively legal definition of crime, mostly because crime statistics are derived from law violations known to the police, offenses cleared by arrest, court records, and data obtained about persons on probation, in prison, or on parole.

How Much Crime?

Anyone who tries to uncover facts and figures about crime and criminals quickly learns that there are many figures but few facts. Yet the importance of crime statistics in shaping attitudes and policies is unquestionable. Numbers tend to generate confidence; figures and percentages lend a quite substantial, even magical quality. Policymakers and the public are quite attentive and responsive to such announcements as "Crime has increased by X%" or "Crime has decreased by Y%." Albert Biderman (1966) confirms this statement:

1. Crime rates are a much used indicator of basic social problems in the nation.

2. They have been subject to great attention in recent public discussion.

3. They illustrate the special kind of difficulties that occur where the data are developed by, or from, agencies directly involved with the phenomenon measured.

4. They constitute an illustration of the possibility of an indicator being poorly adapted to reflect the nature and significance of social change. [P. 112]

The Uniform Crime Reports, for example, contain data on willful homicide, forcible rape, aggravated assault, robbery, burglary, larceny of $50 and over, and automobile theft—seven crimes that, taken as a group, are described as an "index of serious crime" in America. The Federal Bureau of Investigation claims that the seven classifications establish an "index to measure the trend and distribution of crime" (UCR, August 1969), but most researchers are critical of the index and of other crime statistics. Lloyd Ohlin (*New York Times,* February 4, 1968) called the UCR index "almost worthless," and Thorsten Sellin said that the United States "has the worst crime statistics of any major country in the Western world" (U.S. National Commission on the Causes and Prevention of Violence 1969, p. 372).

The UCR and other police data are most frequently criticized as being misleading because, first, in standardizing data by age and sex they fail to consider that the most crime-prone age group has increased disproportionately. In other words, a crime rise does not necessarily mean that people are getting worse but simply that the proportion of people in the most crime-prone age group (fifteen to twenty-four) has increased.

For example, in Washington, D.C., the number of persons aged fifteen to twenty-four increased by 33 percent between 1960 and 1970, while Washington's overall population declined slightly. In the same ten years the rate of serious crime in the District of Columbia rose by about 350 percent. But between 1950 and 1960, when the proportion of the fifteen to twenty-four-year-olds in the city population remained steady, crime rose by only 11 percent.

Another criticism of crime figures is that joyriding does not belong in the serious crime category (nine out of ten stolen cars are returned to their owners). Nor is the definition of grand larceny as "theft of more than $50" in keeping with the increase in prosperity and inflationary trends (Robison 1966; Schumach 1965). Some writers also contend that the UCR and other police figures are open to abuse for political and other purposes (Sparks 1965).

More precise and probably different kinds of definitions are needed to identify serious crimes and to distinguish them from less serious ones. The categories currently used are not exhaustive, not mutually exclusive, and not uniformly applied among cities or precincts. The FBI crime clocks, which yearly show a progressively smaller period between crimes, create an even more flagrant distortion. When a population grows by almost three million persons every year, the interval between crimes is necessarily smaller this year than it was last year even if the crime rate is not larger. It has been suggested that the FBI could better serve the public by stating, for example, that the average citizen's chance of becoming a victim of any crime of violence is 1 in 146,000 per day (Clark 1970).

A more important criticism of the UCR crime index is that it treats all seven crimes as equally serious criminal events and thus is not an index at all. For example, the UCR shows a crime rate of 1,654 for Massachusetts, where the homicide rate was 2.4 in 1966, but for Mississippi, where the homicide rate was 9.7, the crime rate was only 587. The unwary reader surely would conclude that he would be safer in Mississippi than in Massachusetts —a possibly dangerous conclusion.

Sellin and Wolfgang (1964) have developed a system of weighting crimes according to the degree of seriousness. Their scale gives a weight of one point for the crimes assessed least serious—breaking and entering and larceny of under $10—and a weight of twenty-six points for the crime assessed most serious —murder or willful homicide. One problem that such an index cannot adequately deal with is the difference between society's and the victim's view of a crime.

Until agreement is reached on measures that bring together items into a useful index, criminal statistics must continue to provide basic data broken down into component parts. Then persons who advocate various viewpoints may select and deal with data they consider significant. Any index of crime should be regarded as premature, at least for the time being.

The Unreported Crime: The Dark Figure

The President's Commission on Law Enforcement and the Administration of Justice sponsored the first intensive attempt in the United States to use sample surveys of the general population for estimating the incidence of crime.

The Commission concluded that "the actual amount of crime in the United States today is several times that reported" in national tabulations of crime rates.

In a National Opinion Research Center survey of a national sample of ten thousand householders, each person was questioned about whether he or anyone living with him had been a victim of a crime during the twelve preceding months. The survey estimated the rate of personal crimes as double that of reported figures and more than double for crimes against property. Forcible rapes were more than three and a half times the reported rate, burglaries three times more, aggravated assaults and larcenies of $50 and over were more than double, and robberies were 50 percent greater. Only vehicle thefts were reported to be lower. Perhaps people report a car stolen but then find the car either because they misplaced it or because somebody borrowed it (Ennis 1967).

An even larger deviation was discovered in a Bureau of Social Science Research survey conducted in high and medium crime rate precincts in the District of Columbia. The survey rates for various offenses were three to ten times greater than the reported rates (Biderman 1967).

Although victimization surveys represent a major methodological breakthrough in estimating the dark figure of crime, the actual number of crimes committed will always be unknown. First, people simply will not report participation in illegal activities, such as violation of gambling, game, or liquor laws, abortion, or the use of narcotics. Crimes such as carrying concealed weapons, sexual offenses committed privately and by mutual agreement, and individual narcotics transactions, always will be beyond the range of tabulation (Bloch & Geis 1970).

Why Is a Crime Unreported Or Unrecorded?

Even crimes considered to be the most serious (robbery, aggravated assault, and burglary) are for several reasons substantially underrepresented in criminal statistics. The victim or other witnesses may not perceive the behavior as crime. Even if the victim realizes that a crime has been committed, he may not report it because of sympathy for the offender, dislike or distrust of the police and the courts, fear of reprisal, fear of exposure of his own deviant activity, and other reasons. A major reason for failure to notify police about a crime is skepticism about the effectiveness of police action. In the National Opinion Research Center study, all the victims who reported an offense were asked how the police reacted and how far the case proceeded through the courts. The process was simplified as follows (Ennis 1967):

1. Given a real victimization, the police were or were not notified.

2. Once notified, the police either came to the scene of the victimization (or in some other way acknowledged the event) or failed to do so.

3. Once they arrived, the police did or did not regard the incident as a crime.

4. Regarding the matter as a crime, the police did or did not make an arrest.

5. Once an arrest was made, there was or was not a trial (including a plea of guilty).

6. The outcome of the trial was to free the suspect, to punish him "too leniently," or to find him guilty and give him the "proper" punishment.

Figure 8.1 shows that a large shrinkage occurred because police either did not come when called or failed to regard the incident as a crime and consequently did not record it. In Washington, D.C., an analysis of unpublished police statistics revealed that 35 to 40 percent of all patrol car runs on serious crime complaints during a thirteen-month period in 1971–72 did not result in written reports and thus were not reflected in the department's official crime figures (*Washington Post*, December 1973). Similarly, in Boston and Chicago the number of crimes allegedly reported was two to three times greater than the number found in police statistics (Hood & Sparks 1970). Understandably a crime wave can easily be made to appear or disappear at will with changes in the reporting system.

Crime: What of the Future?

The President's Commission on Law Enforcement and the Administration of Justice (1967a) noted, "If it is true, as Commission surveys tend to indicate, that society has not yet found fully reliable methods for measuring the volume of crime, it is even more true that it has failed to find such methods for measuring the trend of crime" (p. 23). Nevertheless, the Commission did predict an upward spiral in crime rates in the near future. It also suggested remedies for the situation:

The Commission believes that age, urbanization, and other shifts in population already under way will likely operate over the next five

FIGURE 8.1 The 'shrinkage' of crimes from victim's action to conviction according to survey respondents. It should be noted that, from the fourth circle on, the victim may simply have been ill-informed.

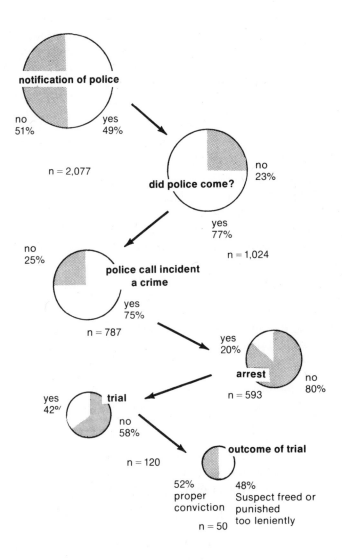

notification of police

no
51%

yes
49%

n = 2,077

did police come?

no
23%

yes
77%

n = 1,024

no
25%

police call incident
a crime

yes
75%

n = 787

yes
20%

arrest

no
80%

n = 593

yes
42°/

trial

no
58%

n = 120

outcome of trial

52%
proper
conviction

48%
Suspect freed or
punished
too leniently

n = 50

to ten years to increase the volume of offenses faster than population growth. Further dipping into reservoirs of unreported crime will likely combine with this real increase in crime to produce even greater increases in reported crime rates. Many of the basic social forces that tend to increase the amount of real crime are already taking effect and are for the most part irreversible. If society is to be successful in its desire to reduce the amount of real crime, it must find new ways to create the kinds of conditions and inducements—social, environmental, and psychological—that will bring about a greater commitment to law-abiding conduct on the part of all Americans and a better understanding of the great stake that all men have in being able to trust in the honesty and integrity of their fellow citizens. [P. 31]

In particular, the Commission predicted:

1. There is likely to be a continued proliferation in the number of acts defined as crimes during future years.

2. There is likely to be a continued increase in the number of crimes reported to the authorities.

3. There is apt to be a continuing rise in crime rates with the continuation of economic affluence in the United States.

4. Further development of "professionalization" of personnel in law enforcement work is apt to produce an increase in reported and recorded crime.

5. There is apt to be a considerable growth in female crime rates as social conditions further blur the distinction between the roles and the activities of men and women in the United States. [Pp. 30–31]

The constantly increasing crime rates in recent years confirmed the Commission's predictions. Between 1955 and 1971 the number of crimes multiplied more than fourfold. In 1968 the annual rise was 17 percent; in 1969 and 1970 it was 11 percent; in 1971, 6 percent. In 1972 crime as measured by the crime index offenses declined 3 percent over 1971. However, violent crimes were still increasing: forcible rape up 11 percent; aggravated assault, 6 percent; and murder, 4 percent. Property crimes decreased 3 percent as a group. Remember that while crime in the cities decreased, it increased in suburban and rural areas. Therefore it seems premature to infer, as government officials did, that the figures are "signs that the worst of the long crime wave is over [and that] a milestone has been achieved"

(*U.S. News and World Report,* April 9, 1973, p. 26). With a large unknown element in the data base, according to statisticians, it is impossible to say now whether crime is increasing, decreasing, or holding steady.

A Climate of Fear

Despite the recent glad tidings from the Justice Department that crime in America went down in 1972, fear of crime seems to be at an all-time high. Urban fear, which has some racial overtones, is greater because residents are confused and highly mobile, and crime is constantly publicized. Such fear often generates a fortress mentality that alters the way people see themselves and the way they live. Its manifestations are all too familiar: four locks on apartment doors; evening social gatherings abandoned or held before sunset; cabs, buses, and gas stations that no longer make change; armed guards inside high schools; and for almost everyone a constant feeling of vulnerability.

Ironically, fear helps to create the ideal conditions for criminal activity: deserted streets, an atmosphere of suspicion, a withdrawal into minding one's own business, loss of confidence in police. Crime, once concentrated in the ghetto, has pushed out into middle class residential neighborhoods and the suburbs, often following the spread of the drug problem to which it is so closely tied.

All these conditions continue despite what is probably the most comprehensive and costly assault ever launched against street crime. With millions of dollars in grants from the federal Law Enforcement Assistance Administration, police departments across America are increasing their ranks and experimenting with helicopters, computers, and improved patrol techniques. Businessmen and homeowners have spawned a flourishing private security industry. The army of private guards grows steadily, and the use of electronic devices to detect crime is rapidly increasing in stores, offices, and factories. Citizens are banding together for self-protection, patrolling their own apartment houses, blocks, and residential neighborhoods.

The police have matched the stepped-up volunteer effort. Police forces have increased in size through new hiring, scheduling

changes, and the use of civilian workers to free desk-bound policemen for duty in the streets. In several localities police are
fielding squads in plainclothes and disguises to increase actual
arrest rates. Installation of high-intensity sodium lighting on
main thoroughfares, restoration of foot patrols, and more mounted patrols are among the measures adopted to combat crime.

The United States is paying a high price for all this security.
Barred windows on city streets, identification checks in school
and apartment houses, police helicopters hovering at night with
searchlights, sodium lights casting a harsh, prison yard glare on
city streets—these are hardly the makings of an open society.
Even more damaging is the growing psychic toll. Suspicion of
every strange face, withdrawal into defensible space, shrinking of
social contacts, and feelings of isolation and helplessness characterize life today. Some experts claim that the fear is disproportionate to the actual probability of being victimized, but
Americans ironically are imprisoning themselves and appear
ready to surrender some of their individual human rights to increased state power in order to fight crime.

Among the tools President Nixon sought to "turn the tide of
crime in America" were laws to restore the death penalty for
certain crimes and to stiffen penalties for trafficking in hard drugs
—heroin and morphine. Some disagree, pointing out that stronger law enforcement and a punitive approach are stopgap, short-
term measures. Emphasis on criminal apprehension instead of on
attacks against the roots of the problems through social action
programs, they claim, is unfair to everyone and to the criminal
justice system in particular. A police captain said recently, "If
law enforcement catches more criminals, the prisons fill up,
criminals are paroled sooner, then probation officers are flooded,
and the criminal gets back into trouble" (*Newsweek,* December
18, 1972, p. 36).

The root causes of crime should be a central concern if a
long-term solution is desired. But such a solution will demand a
national commitment far greater in time and money than most
Americans are ready to accept. The commitment would be in
jobs, educational opportunities, housing, rehabilitation, treatment, court and prison reforms, residential and community treat-

ment centers for offenders, better pay for law enforcement officers, and more just social and economic policies.

Above all, citizens must become concerned with crime as a civic problem that requires a long-term solution, eventually demanding major social changes. Too many people are interested in, or worried about, crime only when it affects them personally, and then they seek only temporary solutions, mostly in the form of containment. In other words, they want crime to go away without the need to surrender anything in their lives or to introduce any changes in society. The National Commission on the Causes and Prevention of Violence (1970) insisted that it is essential to prevent "further social fragmentation of the urban environment." Noting that "the fear of being victimized by criminal attack has touched us all in some way," the Commission warns: "The fragile sense of community that enables us to live and work peaceably together in common institutions is in danger. . . . We must act now if the trend is to be reversed." That warning was written over four years ago!

CHAPTER 9

Juvenile Delinquency and Youth Crime

Problems of Definition

Recently, a therapist (Walker 1972) who works daily with delinquents and their families soberly reported, "Working with delinquents and their families is like walking uphill in a mudslide. The problems abound. There are personal problems, interpersonal problems, community problems, social problems, and cultural problems" (p. 20). The implication, of course, is that society has been waging a losing battle against youthful deviants—those labeled delinquents. The truth of this statement cannot be determined, because we are not certain about exactly what delinquency is—that is, how it should be defined, what causes such deviancy, how much delinquency exists, or how best to deal with it. A direct, factual, and simple definition is possible, but the many legal, clinical, administrative, judicial, and behavioral definitions lead only to greater confusion rather than to clarity. Korn and McCorkle (1959) suggest that for two reasons delinquency, from a legal point of view, is treated more broadly and vaguely than is the legal concept of crime:

> (1) It covers many behaviors that would not be considered criminal if committed by adults, and (2) the juridical definition of these behaviors (e.g., "incorrigibility") is frequently much more general than would be constitutionally tolerated in criminal statutes (for adults), which require precise descriptions of the activities as illegal. [P. 183]

Statutes vary among jurisdictions in the United States. Each defines for itself what delinquency means, and each stipulates who among the young shall be subject to juvenile court jurisdiction. The juvenile code usually defines as delinquent an extremely broad range of behaviors. Thus a court can label a youth as delinquent for: committing a felonious act, such as murder, rape, or burglary; engaging in what would otherwise be called misdemeanors, such as shoplifting or simple assault; and/or acting in a way not consistent with societal norms, such as being incorrigible or beyond parental supervision.

Juvenile courts, which for the past seventy-five years have been the official agencies for social control of delinquents, have also dealt with matters other than delinquency that affect juveniles, such as dependency and neglect. Quite generally children who come under juvenile court jurisdiction may be classified into two categories: (1) those who have engaged in behavior that would be criminal if committed by adults; (2) those who have not committed such offenses. The second group may be further classified into two distinct categories composed of youths who have violated specific ordinances applicable only to children, such as curfew or truancy, and those who have broken no law but are designated beyond control, ungovernable, incorrigible, minors in need of supervision (MINS), or persons in need of supervision (PINS). Sheridan (1967) says:

> With few exceptions, the same dispositions are permitted in the case of these children that are authorized for youngsters who have committed acts that would be crimes if committed by an adult. In other

words, children who have not indulged in criminal conduct find themselves thrown into the correctional system. [P. 27]

The Juvenile Court

Platt (1969 *b*) explains the dual responsibility of the juvenile court as not simply a historical accident. As the child-saving movement developed momentum at the turn of the century, reformists and altruists sought both to control youthful deviance and to assist the young in redirecting their lives. Consequently, they brought attention to, and thus "invented," new categories of youthful misbehavior that previously had not been viewed as important (pp. 21–38).

The juvenile court system was part of a general movement to remove youths, particularly adolescents, from the adult criminal law process and to create special programs and processes for dealing with delinquent, dependent, and neglected children. Considered "an integral part of total welfare planning," the juvenile court also was viewed as "one of the greatest advances in child welfare that has ever occurred" (Chute 1949, p. 7).

The first juvenile court was established in 1899 in Chicago. It and others subsequently created became statute-established tribunals to determine the legal status of children and adolescents who came within their purview. Underlying the juvenile court movement was the concept of *parens patriae,* by which the courts were authorized to handle with wide discretion the problems of "its least fortunate junior citizens" (Schramm 1949, p. 31).

According to Platt (1969 *a*):

The administration of juvenile justice differed in many important respects from the criminal court process. A child was not accused of a crime but offered assistance and guidance; intervention in his life was not supposed to carry the stigma of a criminal record; judicial records were not generally available to the press or public, and hearings were conducted in relative privacy; proceedings were informal and due process safeguards were not applicable due to the court's civil jurisdiction. [Pp. 137–38]

Platt (1969 *b*) later discusses the intent of the child savers, particularly their concern for the welfare of children:

The juvenile court was not perceived by its supporters as a revolutionary experiment but rather as a culmination of traditionally valued practices. The child-saving movement was "antilegal" in the sense that it derogated civil rights and procedural formalties while relying heavily on extralegal techniques. The judges of the new court were empowered to investigate the character and social life of predelinquent as well as delinquent children; they examined motivation rather than intent, seeking to identify the moral reputation of problematic children. The requirements of preventive penology and child-saving further justified the court's intervention in cases where no offense had actually been committed but where, for example, a child was posing problems for some person in authority, such as a parent or teacher or social worker. [P. 18]

Approaches to Delinquency

The historical development of the juvenile court as a result of the child savers' concern for the health and welfare of children and adolescents aids in understanding the difficulty in forming a definition of delinquency. If Tappan (1949) is correct, however, recognition of two distinct views—the legal view and the casework approach—can help to solve the definitional problem. He argues that concepts of delinquency have been derived largely from these two views, and they in turn tend to reflect the two main phases of juvenile court work—the adjudication of cases and probation supervision.

In the legal approach to misconduct, according to Tappan, the description of offenses and penalties in specific terms is customary in order to protect the citizen from arbitrary or unjust acts of police and judicial authority and, at the same time, to protect the community from dangerous persons. A legal approach in adult courts demands the following requirements:

> ... (1) that a specific charge be alleged against the defendant, (2) that it be defined in definite terms by law, (3) that the offense be proved rather conclusively, (4) that protection be given the accused during trial against conviction by false, misleading, prejudicial, irrelevant, or immaterial evidence. [P. 4]

Tappan then says that in a legalistic approach to dealing with delinquents:

The full rigors of the criminal law are mitigated by reason of the offender's youth, but the judicial view would preserve in the hearings of children's courts a real test of the individual's status as a delinquent before applying to him the modern and individualized method of treatment. *The child is not a delinquent unless the court has found him so.* [P. 5] [Emphasis added]

In contrast to the formalism of the legal approach, the casework model presupposes that the delinquent is "sick" and in need of therapeutic attention. Theoretically, the worker attempts to define the personal and situational problems that affect the juvenile, including his home, family, and community, and then proceeds to develop a nonmoralistic and nonpunitive treatment plan. He behaves in informal and frequently extralegal ways in order to provide "what is best" for the child.

In describing the casework approach while tracing the history of the juvenile court movement and the process of dealing with offenders as sick persons, Cohen and Short (1966) assert:

The manifest function of the juvenile court ... is usually phrased in the statutes in some such words as these: to secure for each child within its jurisdiction such care, custody, and treatment as should have been provided by the child's natural parents. It is not to punish but to "help children in trouble," to do what is in the best interest of the child and the state to "rehabilitate." [Pp. 84–85]

Rehabilitative Ideal

The attempt to understand and cure offenders, especially juveniles, has been approached with zeal and often with sophisticated correctional programs—with what Allen (1964 *b*) has called the "rehabilitative ideal":

The rehabilitative ideal is itself a complex of ideas which, perhaps, defies an exact definition. The essential points, however, can be identified. It is assumed, first, that human behavior is the product of antecedent causes. These causes can be identified as part of the physical universe.... Knowledge of the antecedents of human behavior makes possible an approach to the scientific control of human behavior. Finally ... it is assumed that measures employed to treat the convicted offender should serve as a therapeutic function; that such measures should be designed to effect changes in the behavior of the convicted person and in the interest of his own happiness, health, and satisfactions and in the interest of social defense. [P. 26]

The nature of the casework approach was to avoid the stigmatizing effects of labeling a child as delinquent. Constitutional safeguards inherent in the criminal justice process, particularly that of due process, were minimized because if the unfortunate child was to receive expert attention, court personnel needed every effort and opportunity to do what was "best for the child." Since normal rules of evidence were minimized, a child was always at the mercy of the court and adults who would decide what was in his best interest. We shall see later that stigmatizing was not avoided.

The *Gault* decision (*In re Gault*, May 15, 1967) drastically changed in theory and practice the idea that constitutional safeguards could forever be minimized. In this historic Supreme Court decision, the justices state that in many ways a juvenile court hearing is similar to a criminal proceeding, and as such a juvenile is entitled to due process of law. In their opinion they quoted a 1953 observation of the late Arthur P. Vanderbilt (1967), chief justice of the Supreme Court of New Jersey:

> In their zeal to care for children neither juvenile judges nor welfare workers can be permitted to violate the Constitution, especially the constitutional provisions as to due process that are involved in moving a child from its home. The indispensable elements of due process are: first, a tribunal with jurisdiction; second, notice of a hearing to the proper parties; and, finally, a fair hearing. All three must be present if we are to treat the child as an individual human being and not to revert, in spite of good intentions, to the more primitive days when he was treated as a chattel. [P. 61]

The *Gault* decision, handed down in 1967, has had a dramatic impact on the nature of juvenile court structure and processes. In effect it forced a blending of the casework and legal approaches to handling juveniles into a sociological approach in which the rights of the child and his needs are simultaneously considered.

The *Gault* decision did not remove the wide discretionary latitude of the juvenile court in adjudication and treatment processes. Almost every conceivable act, criminal and noncriminal, that a juvenile commits still falls within the purview of the court.

It still permits intervention on the basis of rather vague measures of societal standards and norms. The decision only assures fairer hearings.

Thus a child whose behavior shows no specific and serious law violation can still be treated preventively if found to suffer from problems of social or psychological maladjustment. Courts continue to deal with dependent and neglected, as well as delinquent, children in administrative or legal fashion, even though some constraints on dispositional alternatives exist now.

Juvenile Code

The Code of the State of Maryland illustrates contemporary attitudes toward dealing with children. In its latest code, for example, nondelinquent children who are in need of supervision may not be committed to a juvenile training institution. However, the court still retains authority to institutionalize such a child if it believes confinement is in the child's best interests and welfare. Article 52A, Section 5, Paragraph (c) of the Maryland Annotated Code reads as follows:

> *Commitment of delinquent, mentally handicapped, dependent or neglected child or child in need of supervision.* ... Any juvenile court judge may commit: (1) any delinquent child that has been so adjudicated by said judge to the custody of the Secretary of Health and Mental Hygiene or to any public or private institution or agency other than the Department of Health and Mental Hygiene, or to the custody of a person selected by said judge; (2) any child in need of supervision that has been so adjudicated by said judge to the custody of the Secretary of Health and Mental Hygiene, or to any public or private institution or agency other than the Department of Health and Mental Hygiene or to the custody of a person selected by said judge; (3) any mentally handicapped child that has been so adjudicated by said judge to the custody of the Secretary of Health and Mental Hygiene; (4) any dependent child that has been so adjudicated by said judge to the local social services department, or to any other public or private agency which provides facilities for dependent children, or to the custody of a person selected by said judge; (5) any neglected child that has been so adjudicated by said judge to the local social services department or to any public or private agency that provides facilities or services for neglected children. ... Any child

who has been determined in need of care or treatment within the provisions (of this Article) ... shall remain under the continuing jurisdiction of the court in which his case was heard until that court finally determines jurisdiction.

Thus every child in the state, depending on the label the court affixes, can be institutionalized for care and treatment, even though the child may not have committed an adult proscribed deviant act. Maryland is rather unusual in that it provides to juveniles on a statewide basis both probation and aftercare services, not in a youth commission or some similar agency but in a Department of Health and Mental Hygiene. Nonetheless, the state defines the various categories of children who potentially come within the purview of its juvenile courts (Article 26, Section 70–1, Paragraph 1, 1973 Cumulative Supplement):

(b) *"Minor"* means a person who has not reached his 18th birthday.

(g) *"Delinquent Act"* means an act which is in violation of 66½ of this Code (traffic), any other traffic violation, or an act which would be a crime if done by a person who is not a child.

(h) *"Delinquent Child "* means a child who commits a delinquent act and who requires supervision, treatment, or rehabilitation.

(i) *"Child in Need of Supervision"* means a child:

(1) Subject to compulsory school attendance who is habitually and without justification truant from school;

(2) Without substantial fault on the part of his parents, guardian, or other custodian, who is habitually disobedient, ungovernable, and beyond their control;

(3) Who so deports himself as to injure or endanger himself or others; or

(4) Who has committed an offense applicable only to children; and

(5) Requires guidance, treatment, or rehabilitation.

Dependent children are described as those who have been deprived of adequate support, neglected children as those who require the aid of the court. However, all of these children, and delinquents as well, can be institutionalized or placed in facilities other than their homes by court action and according to rather vaguely defined statutes. Maryland may be unique, as indicated earlier, in that dependent and neglected children are institutionalized in facilities different from those to which delinquent children are committed. But children nonetheless can be taken away from their homes and families, and almost universally for indeterminate periods of time.

An examination of other statutes and codes related to the definitions of delinquency, dependency, and neglect suggests that the general terms of juvenile delinquency statutes permit courts to take hold in rather broadly and somewhat imprecisely defined circumstances of conduct, attitude, or social situation. Further, even though due process is supposedly assured to youngsters and their families, juvenile courts do in fact widely and increasingly exercise their discretion to deal with cases deemed either presently delinquent or in danger of becoming so—say, dependent and neglected children.

Noncriminal cases that frequently come to the attention of other social agencies do not have attached the same kinds of stigmas that are present in juvenile courts. Since agencies other than courts (family service and private counseling groups) frequently deal with youths who behave in deviant and disruptive but not necessarily criminal ways, delinquency may have little specific behavior content, either in law or in fact, other than the provision that acts that would otherwise be crimes are defined for the juvenile as delinquency (Shireman 1962).

Delinquency Defined and Measured

Now we can return to the earlier discussion of the problem in defining delinquency and perhaps even resolve the issue, however indefinitely and without complete satisfaction. Tappan (1949) concludes the following:

> *The juvenile delinquent is a person who has been adjudicated as such by a court of proper jurisdiction* though he may be no different, up until the time of court contact and adjudication at any rate, from masses of children who are not delinquent. *Delinquency is any act, course of conduct, or situation which might be brought before a court and adjudicated* whether in fact it comes to be treated there or by some other resource or indeed remains untreated. It will be noted that under these definitions adjudicable conduct may be defined as delinquent in the abstract, but it cannot be measured as delinquency until a court has found the facts of delinquency to exist. [P. 30]

Tappan's position is somewhat legalistic in that he insists that no delinquency exists unless and until a court officially says it exists. But we know, and Tappan admits, that some delinquent acts do not come to the court's attention. Police constantly deal with youthful deviancy. Just because the acts are not cleared does not mean that they have not occurred; only the official label is missing because the court cannot act unless and until someone brings an alleged delinquent to its attention. Consequently, whatever the definitional problems, we still have the reality of behavior that, although youth committed, is nonetheless violative or against social norms as spelled out in juvenile codes and adult criminal statutes.

How do we know how much delinquency exists or how many children are delinquents? If we cannot label as delinquent acts those behaviors that do not officially come before the court, what do we call them? And if children are diverted from the court, as they are with increasing frequency today, do we still call them delinquents because they would have come before the court had they not been diverted, even if an official police and/or court program diverts them? These and other questions further complicate efforts to define delinquency and determine who indeed is a delinquent. Thus an answer to the question, Can delinquency be measured?, must with few qualifications be answered no!

Data on arrest rates and formal referrals to juvenile courts are available from the police and especially from the *Uniform Crime Reports*. Considerable data also are associated with juvenile court processing of delinquents and the populations of training schools as well as other institutions to which delinquents are committed. These data provide a partial measure of the extent and distribution of official acts of delinquency and populations of children who are adjudicated delinquents, but precisely how much delinquency occurs throughout the country is unknown. The extent of crime has been discussed in greater detail (chap. 8); so it is sufficient to repeat here that the difficulty in defining crime and delinquency (that is, differing definitions based on codes and statutes in various jurisdictions) is coupled with the ways in which delinquency statistics are reported and summarized, if they are reported at all, to cloud the issue.

The *Uniform Crime Reports* allow at least some approximate

notion of the numbers of children reported to be arrested and the specific charges involved. However, court data are fragmentary, incomplete, and beyond comparison, primarily because of definitional problems. For example, incorrigibility may mean in one jurisdiction "beyond the control of parents"; in another it may cover home and school truancy. In contrast, adult crime, such as murder, grand larceny, and rape, is precisely defined quite similarly regardless of jurisdiction.

Rising Rates of Delinquency

The President's Crime Commission estimated in 1967 that one in every nine children was referred to juvenile court for an act of delinquency before the eighteenth birthday—the usual cutoff point that separates delinquents from adult criminals. According to these statistics, for the male population the ratio rose to one in six. Whether delinquency is now on the rise is a debatable issue, for current arrest records indicate only that more delinquents are officially taken into custody than had been in previous years. In question is whether law enforcement agencies are more diligent in arresting youthful offenders, police departments have more manpower and thus are better able to arrest, or more delinquent acts are being reported to the police. The only certainty is that young adults under age eighteen are being arrested for serious as well as minor offenses.

From 1960 to 1965, according to the Crime Commission, arrests for serious crimes among persons under age eighteen increased 47 percent, while the population increase in that age bracket was only 17 percent. According to the 1972 *Uniform Crime Reports* (FBI 1972, p. 34) this rate may have decreased significantly, for during the period 1967–72 police arrests of persons under age eighteen for all offenses except traffic were up only 28 percent. For crime index offenses the rate of increase was 36 percent.

Of all 1972 crime index offenses solved, 27 percent involved persons under age eighteen; persons ten to seventeen years of age accounted for only 16 percent of the total United States population (FBI 1972, p. 31). The FBI (1972) states that with 6,195 law enforcement agencies reporting (on an estimated United States population of 160,416,000 persons), 9.5 percent of all persons arrested were under age fifteen (665,887 youths); 25.6 percent of persons arrested were under age eighteen (1,793,984 youths).

Numerous agencies and resources, including families, schools, churches, welfare agencies, and police departments, refer youths to juvenile courts. Police, though, probably constitute the largest single referral source and, compared to the court, dispose of more cases of alleged delinquency and deviant behavior than any other agency in the country. A comparison of dispositional patterns for handling juvenile offenders between 1968 and 1972 shows remarkable consistency (Table 9.1). Analysis of the data reveals that police agencies that report arrest and dispositional data cover only approximately half of the United States population; therefore, it is impossible to gather complete data on actual activities throughout the entire country. How much the data are biased in favor of small communities or large cities is not known.

The data that are reported, however, indicate (if the two-year comparison is reasonably accurate) that police departments dispose of almost half of all cases that involve youths arrested without ever officially sending them to juvenile courts. These data cover only official arrests; no set of baseline data can reveal how many youths policemen stop, interrogate, interview, or otherwise deal with informally throughout the year. It seems reasonable to assume, however, that if reporting police departments officially handle over 1.25 million dispositions annually, they probably deal unofficially with at least twice as many cases.

Police Intervention

From the managerial and social problem points of view, juvenile delinquency and deviancy are formidable, irrespective of whether or not the problem is growing. Police problems in handling juveniles require attention, time, money, and considerable understanding of adolescent culture and community values and programs. A particular concern, then, is the policeman's role in dealing *unofficially* with juveniles, and especially the alternatives available to him.

In recent years, for example, a new program development known as the Youth Service Bureau (YSB) has served as an

TABLE 9.1

**Percentages of Police Dispositions of Juvenile Offenders
Taken into Custody: 1968 and 1972**

| | *Total** | | *Handled within
PD & Released* | | *Referred to
Juvenile Court* | |
|---|---|---|---|---|---|---|
| Years | 68 | 72 | 68 | 72 | 68 | 72 |
| Percentage | 100.0 | 100.0 | 46.3 | 45.0 | 48.8 | 50.8 |

| | *Referred to
Welfare Agency* | | *Referred to
Other Police Agency* | | *Referred to Criminal
or Adult Court* | |
|---|---|---|---|---|---|---|
| Years | 68 | 72 | 68 | 72 | 68 | 72 |
| Percentage | 1.6 | 1.3 | 2.3 | 1.6 | 1.0 | 1.3 |

SOURCE: Uniform Crime Reports 1968, p. 106; and 1972, p. 116

*For 1968 the data reflect activities of 3,751 reporting police agencies, covering a total population of 104,585,000, and represent a total of 1,245,763 actual dispositions.

For 1972 the data reflect activities of 4,269 reporting police agencies, covering a total population of 103,320,000, and represent a total of 1,270,860 actual dispositions.

official community resource for diverting youthful offenders. YSBs, which are increasing in number throughout the country, combine services and programs to deal with troubled youth and to prevent delinquency (see, e.g., Norman 1972). YSBs are either administratively attached to or otherwise closely related to police departments. Together with other kinds of diversion and prevention activities, the bureaus suggest that police departments more than ever before are dynamically involved in preventive as well as law enforcement efforts. More than in adult crime, police are increasingly called on to provide welfare and rehabilitative efforts for juveniles, and they consequently spend considerable time in such activities.

Historically, models for dealing with known delinquents have been based on theories of causation. Not that efforts to control or prevent delinquency have always been based on scientific procedure; it is only a gross simplification to describe the motivations and intentions of persons who organize programs. In the positive criminological tradition, which, for example, holds the belief that poverty is a primary cause of delinquency, efforts to eradicate poverty have carried the hope that delinquency would be reduced. Recreational, vocational, and academic programs are other examples of activities that have been developed in an effort to reduce delinquency. All are based on the belief that the provision of essential programs and services in these areas will have a direct impact on the delinquency problem.

That no single cause or combination of causes has been discovered has not deterred social planners from attempting to prevent and control delinquency. Also, regardless of philosophy, juvenile courts and correctional agencies abound in almost every jurisdiction. Juveniles continue to commit offenses; both police and juvenile courts continue to deal with them officially and unofficially; and all states have some kind of institutional program for the detection and treatment of the juvenile offender.

Yet criminologists, social scientists, and behavioral scientists, individually and collectively, agree that no perfect model is now known for effectively dealing with the delinquency problem. No acceptable method, model, or program effectively relieves the problem. We know neither the causes of delinquency nor the best ways to deal with it.

In a report on the nature and extent of crime and delinquency in the District of Columbia, researchers point out the high rate of recidivism among youthful offenders. They indicate, in fact, that almost 61 percent of those arrested had one or more prior referrals to the juvenile court. In discussing these data they add, "Although such statistics highlight only the failures of the system and none of the successes, they underscore the dimensions of the problem confronting this city" (*Report of the President's Commission on Crime in the District of Columbia 1966*, p. 656).

State of Knowledge

Several persons have examined the state of knowledge about causation (see, e.g., Knight 1972; Matza 1964; Sellin & Wolfgang 1969). Others have also examined processes of delinquency prevention and treatment (see, e.g., Schur 1973; Lerman 1970; Cohn 1973). Theorists are unable to agree on what causes delinquency, and practitioners similarly conclude that no known model is available for its prevention or control. In fact, those who have studied processes of delinquency control, prevention, and treatment have reached the almost inescapable conclusion that the criminal justice system has failed to deal with the problem adequately or effectively. Lerman (1970) adds both a caveat and a warning:

The consistent finding that treatment programs have not yet been proved to have an appreciable impact on failure rates should not be misinterpreted. For even though institutions for delinquents are probably not highly successful—regardless of treatment type—there is no reason to go back to harsher methods of child handling. It can be argued, rather, that even when boys are kept for only four months and treated with trust ... there is no evidence that this "coddling" will yield greater failure rates.... The need for a humanitarian approach needs to be divorced from any specific mode of treatment. [P. 326]

Schur (1973) is willing to go further. He argues that the delinquency problem may possibly be reduced by taking two profound, albeit unpopular, steps. First, he argues that many offenses that bring juveniles to the official attention of police and courts ought to be wiped off the books or decriminalized. For instance, he says that such offenses as incorrigibility and truancy have no justification. Second, he suggests that where "official" delinquency exists, agencies and agents of formal control ought not to intervene. He believes that rates of success would be higher if more youths were left alone and allowed an opportunity to mature and grow up spontaneously. As the book title indicates, this is "radical non-intervention." Schur concludes, "Our young people deserve something better than being 'processed.' Hopefully, we are beginning to realize this" (p. 171).

Future Directions

Amid the struggle between theoreticians and practitioners on how best to deal with the juvenile delinquent some responsible people are suggesting that a way to cope with the problem does exist. They do not agree completely with Schur that "we should leave them alone," nor do they argue for a hard-line approach. Instead, they look at some basic realities and attempt to place them in proper perspective.

In the report of the National Advisory Commission on Criminal Justice Standards and Goals, *Corrections* (1973 b), it is pointed out that the juvenile recidivist rather than the first offender poses the more serious dilemma for society, especially since the recidivist usually tends to commit the most serious offenses:

Because most youngsters mature out of delinquent behavior on their own and because present intervention programs are admittedly inadequate, a recent study suggests, it may be more effective to leave the first offenders alone (Wolfgang 1970, pp. 27–50). If they were disregarded, resources could be concentrated on delinquents with three or more official police contacts, who account for a high proportion of serious crime. [P. 248]

The *Corrections* report states that first offenders should not be ignored, for many indeed may need some kind of help. But, the report adds, it may be in society's as well as the youngster's best interests not to process him through the criminal justice system. Rather, he should be diverted and given the kinds of assistance most appropriate to prevent further delinquent behavior.

Even then the police will be involved in handling juveniles, but their work may be more a function of "informal police-community relations, the nature of the community, and its geographical location than observance of abstract principles of law enforcement" (Chambliss & Liell 1966, p. 310).

The juvenile court also will continue to be heavily involved in the delinquency problem, but in its final report the National Advisory Commission on Criminal Justice Standards and Goals (1973 c) redefines the role of the court, particularly with diversion in mind:

The Commission recommends that jurisdiction over juveniles be placed in a family court which should be a division of a trial court of general jurisdiction. The family court should have jurisdiction over all legal matters related to family life, including delinquency, neglect, support, adoption, custody, paternity actions, divorce, annulment, and assaults involving family members. Dependent children—those needing help through no fault of their parents—should be handled outside the court system. [P. 169]

The problem of juvenile delinquency, its understanding, control, and prevention, is serious not only for police, courts, and correctional personnel but also for society. Questions about its causation, definition, and possible increase cannot be resolved completely. However, society must not play ostrich on the issue, burying its head in the sand and hoping it will go away. Students are researching the problem; practitioners are serious about understanding its consequences. If hope exists for its future control, that hope probably lies in the cooperative efforts of both scholars and practitioners in confronting and dealing with the real issues. The police, unquestionably, have a vital stake in resolving the problem and in working with others toward that end.

CHAPTER 10

The Loss of Self:
Mental Illness and Suicide

Historical Development

Social workers, psychiatrists, psychologists, counselors, and others engaged in diagnostic and therapeutic work with persons labeled as mentally ill have long suggested a crude way of determining whether a person whose behavior appears to be deviant is indeed ill and in need of treatment: "If your problems are getting in the way of daily functioning, if you are unable to meet the normal demands of a reasonable society, then it is time to get some help."

This crude measure, of course, in no way distinguishes degrees of illness or whether, in fact, illness really exists; it merely suggests that the person and others view the behavior as requiring change. A significant difficulty, however, is that mentally ill people do not always realize that their behavior or thoughts are inappropriate. Additionally, those who must live and work with people who seem to be ill often have questionable motives for wanting them in treatment.

Even psychiatrists and psychologists are sometimes unable to diagnose mental illness or to determine when and if a person so labeled has been cured. In a recent experiment, for example, a group of professional therapists feigned illness and had themselves committed to a mental hospital. Once labeled as schizophrenic, they were unable to convince their therapists that they were cured. Because the therapists were busy, incompetent, or unable to understand what they were dealing with, or because of a combination of factors, they did not see their patients as cured and were unwilling to release them from the mental hospital (Rosenhan 1973). Mental illness is difficult to describe and define. In a sense it is nothing more than a label that one person affixes to another in describing behavior and thought processes that appear to be outside the norms of society. Mental illness from one perspective, then, is in the eye of the beholder. W. I. Thomas says that what men perceive to be real and true is real in its social consequences. (This theme is repeated in all of Thomas's works. See, e.g., Thomas 1951).

Man has almost always recognized that some of his fellow men have been unable to live in and adjust to the normal demands of society. However, methods for dealing with deviants labeled mentally ill have not always been humane, just, and according to medical principles. That is, persons now called mentally ill—as well as those called mentally incompetent, handicapped, or feeble-minded—have been seen in different lights in different periods of history.

Before written history, men drew on the sides of caves and then formed pictures on papyrus. Even then, references were made to persons considered deranged, and some mental illness was described. The Ebers Papyrus, from 1550 B.C., contains the line, "... his mind raves through something entering from above," which has been assumed to illustrate the early attribution of mental illness to evil spirits. Certainly it was an attempt at finding explanation and solution in an area where no pattern of solution existed.

Early church records often refer to the mentally ill as being possessed of the devil. Treatment, of course, was harsh, for in lieu of repentance (of which the mentally ill were incapable) the only salvation was exorcism, banishment, death, stoning, and/or other forms of physical abuse. At the very least, mentally ill persons as well as those considered feebleminded were shunned or otherwise ostracized from society. Some were seen as having been cursed; yet curiously enough, some people earlier and perhaps even now have suggested that the mentally ill are closer to God than more normal people.

Today, we tend to treat mental illness as a physical impairment or medical problem. Nevertheless, we still treat the mentally ill as a distinct group, and, surprisingly, many of the historical concerns remain. For example, we still see the deranged as dangerous even though they may be quite harmless. We are fearful of associating with them, as though we expect their disease to be contagious. Further, we still segregate them from normal society, although we now call the places of confinement hospitals.

We have now a vast body of knowledge with which to attack mental illness, not only in pharmacology but also in psychology and psychiatry as well as in sociological processes for dealing with the problems of the mentally ill and their families. For primitive man just out of caves, dealing with mental illness was not so easy.

Living on a planet he could not explain, dealing with life and death and illness, early man naturally feared and at times worshiped the sun, the wind, the moon, and the gods that he saw impinging on his life. Whenever anything unfortunate happened, an evil spirit caused it, and evil spirits probably were everywhere in the vast, baffling, lonely world that early man had to cope with.

Modern Reaction

Early modern forms of treatment for mental illness varied from making a hole in the patient's skull (trepanning) to permit the escape of the evil spirit believed to cause the behavior, to exorcism of the spirits through religious rites. Another treatment, bleeding, was applied to everyone regardless of station in life.

The early Greeks were the first to use a more scientific approach to mental disturbance. In the third century B.C., Hippocrates stated that mental disorders had natural causes and should be so treated. His thesis was a great leap forward. Hippocrates also saw brain pathology, heredity, and head injuries as causal factors in mental illness.

Plato, at approximately the same time, contended that the mentally ill were not responsible for their acts and should not be treated as criminals. Instead, he claimed, they should be given humane care in their own communities. Interestingly, this concept was not fully appreciated until the twentieth century, although the relationship of criminal responsibility and mental illness has caused a recurring debate for many centuries.

Plato's student, Aristotle, believed that reason was independent and immortal and could not be diseased. He believed that mental disorders were a reflection of organic difficulties. He said that mental illness was a physical or medical problem, not functional nor solely a product of the mind. Because Aristotle was influential, his insight into mental illness led often to more humane treatment and pleasant surroundings and a beginning form of occupational and social rehabilitation. Cruel, crude, and harsh treatment, however, were not abandoned.

In the fifteenth and sixteenth centuries, the first asylums for the insane (institutions now called hospitals) appeared in Europe. Bethlehem Hospital, established about 1400 A.D. in London, seems fairly typical of the asylums. However, despite the intent of its founders to provide humane treatment, conditions there became deplorable:

> Its popular name, "Bedlam," added a new connotation to a word in the English language (pandemonium became "sheer Bedlam"). Violent patients were exhibited to the public for a fee, and the harmless were sent into the streets to beg. Beatings, chains, and other physical means of restraint were common. The quarters habitually were unspeakable. Yet—even so—in England and in other countries more enlightened, sensitive persons were making their voices heard: a faint cry in the wilderness at first, finally reaching a crescendo. [National Institute of Mental Health 1970, p. 3]

In the United States the move toward therapeutic and humanitarian treatment for the mentally ill was slow. The colonists were trying to subdue a tough and resistant continent. Their first order of business was survival; so they had little time for dealing with the deranged. Schools and churches were built first, then hospitals, but these were primarily for the medically ill.

Settlers here brought some European ideas about witches and demonical possession. Because few were medically trained, later and better trends in European thought about madness were unknown. Therefore, harsh treatment methods were the only ones available, and even those were available only rarely.

The mentally ill and feebleminded usually were merely locked up and fed occasionally. Well-to-do families tended to conceal mentally disturbed persons in their households, frequently in boarded-up attics or in cellars. The poor either were left to wander about as beggars and misfits or were put in jails, stockades, almshouses (poorhouses), kennels, or cages. Some were driven out of town so that the community would not have to support them or be reminded of their derangement. By the late 1600s, though, some were housed with private families at either public or church expense.

Hospitalization

In 1756 Benjamin Franklin, campaigning for proper care of the mentally ill, was instrumental in opening Pennsylvania Hospital in Philadelphia to care for the mentally as well as medically ill. But not until 1773 was the first hospital devoted exclusively to the care of the mentally ill opened in Williamsburg, Virginia. Albert Deutsch, who wrote *The Mentally Ill in America*, gives a vivid description of the services in this hospital and concludes that although the program was of doubtful benefit it was the best available at the time.

Just before the end of the eighteenth century Dr. Benjamin Rush began to advocate better and kinder care for the mentally ill. He struck at the hearsay, superstitions, and ignorance that surrounded mental illness, and for the first time in the United States he raised its study to a scientific level. Although he used the then-customary methods of bleeding, restraint, and cold showers, his treatment was free of the brutality and cruelty that for centuries had characterized much of the care of the disturbed.

Dr. Rush introduced occupational therapy, amusements, and exercise for the patients, and saw to it that they had decent quarters. His systematic treatise on psychiatry was the first significant contribution to American research, and he organized the first course in psychiatry in the United States.

While some advances were being made here, two humanitarian reformers were wielding influence in Europe—Dr. Philippe Pinel in France and William Tuke in England. In 1792, Pinel changed the worst asylum in Paris from a custodial, repressive institution, where patients were tacitly assumed to be incurable and hence received no therapeutic treatment, to a progressive, psychiatrically oriented hospital. His "moral treatment" excluded chains and bleeding and was devoted exclusively to the "mind."

In 1796, William Tuke founded the York Retreat, a Quaker institution where patients were treated as guests in a family environment with religious overtones. Here harsh treatment of any kind was forbidden. At most, and in rare cases, straitjacket or solitary confinement was permitted.

Program Reform

The examples of Pinel and Tuke eventually were followed in the United States. Sweeping reforms were instituted, and new facilities were built and administered according to the revised pattern. Unfortunately, this system tended to care only for persons from affluent families. Few facilities were available to the poor. Communities dealt with the aged, orphaned, and insane poor as "paupers," and gave them minimal aid or attention. At times they were sent to almshouses, where at least they had a place to sleep and eat. Many of the poor unfortunates were jailed, not as punishment but simply to get them off the streets and away from the eyes of respectable citizens.

Dorothea Lynde Dix, perhaps America's greatest early reformer in promoting care for the mentally ill, saw a jail of this kind and was so horrified that she began a life-work of crusading for intelligent and humane care and treatment. She visited institutions, alerted and worked with the press, made countless talks to galvanize public opinion, and sent memorials (petitions asking that something be done) to state legislatures.

In 1845, Dorothea Dix (1967) wrote *Remarks on Prisons and Prison Discipline in the United States.* She said:

> Insanity is sometimes developed in this, as in all other prisons, but so also is it in communities; and I consider neither the "silent" nor "separate" systems as specially disposing convicts to insanity; but the want of pure air in the lodging-cells is, I doubt not, one of the many exciting causes of this malady in all prisons, and in all institutions in which ventilation is defective. . . . Great, very great inconvenience is experienced from this unhappy class of prisoners in all prisons; they cannot receive from the prison-officers that appropriate and peculiar care their condition demands. [Pp. 42–43]

Her activities culminated in a large state mental hospital that was, at that time, seen as an advance. Today, of course, huge hospitals are anachronisms. Dix is further recognized as the founder of Saint Elizabeth's Hospital in the District of Columbia. She lobbied through Congress a bill to set aside 12.25 million acres of federally owned land for the "indigent insane." The bill was passed in both houses in 1854, but President Franklin Pierce's landmark veto denied its fulfillment. President Pierce, fiercely opposed to encroaching federalism, rejected the bill on the grounds that it would be a recognition of federal responsibility for the ill, the poor, and the incompetent.

> Miss Dix then turned to Scotland, England, and Europe where she brought about revolutionary changes in their systems. In sum total, she was responsible for the founding or enlarging of 32 mental hospitals in the United States or abroad, though lack of vigilance by others after her initial work allowed many to deteriorate. Transfer of the poor insane from jails to mental hospitas—though appropriate—brought on much overcrowding. [NIMH 1970, p. 5]

In 1890, passage of a law requiring state provisions of institutionalization and treatment for the insane triggered advances in many states. Some organized programs and centralized administrative authority were instituted. Many adopted the pleasing "cottage system," in which patients were housed in separate, homelike cottages instead of massive buildings. Many of these cottages as well as the massive institutional structures still exist throughout the United States and can be observed in tours of various mental hospital grounds.

One unfortunate side effect of this thrust toward the construction of mental hospital facilities, still known at that time as asylums, was a neglect of research and methods of treatment. Medicine was concerned with physical disabilities and diseases; it tended to minimize the psychological importance of studying the mentally ill. In 1844, thirteen eminent psychiatrists expressed their collective concern about this neglect and consequently founded a group that was the predecessor of the American Psychiatric Association. Its basic purpose was to study mental illness and exchange ideas and experiences.

Research and Prevention

Systematic research began near the end of the nineteenth century. Medical practitioners became interested in the problems of cause and treatment of mental illness, and the new profession of social casework began to deal with the problems of the mentally ill and their families. Mary Richmond (1917), credited with the founding of modern social work, summarized the role and responsibilities of the caseworker in alleviating all kinds of human misery, including mental illness, and discussed the relationship between social casework and social reform:

> New methods of social treatment have been developed by the charity organization campaigns for better housing and for the prevention of tuberculosis; by the long struggle of another group of social reformers to secure diagnosis and care of the feebleminded; by child labor reform, by industrial legislation, by the recreation movement, the mental hygiene movement, and a host of other social reforms. The significance of these reforms here is that, after they had achieved a measure of success, case work treatment had at its command more varied resources, adaptable to individual situations, and that therefore the diagnosis of those situations assumed fresh importance. [P. 32]

As charity and social workers became involved with the problems of the mentally ill, particularly in relation to cultural and environmental causes, physicians (especially psychiatrists) investigated organic causes. Simultaneously, hospitals were developed to sort out patients through observation and short-term treatment before commitment to general mental hospitals. These hospitals also provided training, education, and research facilities for psychiatrists and medical students. A short time later, after-care programs and outpatient clinics were established.

Professional competition between neurologists and psychiatrists had the fortunate effect of a more medically oriented approach within the institutions. That is, the idea that mental illness indicated demoniacal possession was discarded, and the illness was seen finally as a medical problem. Then, of course, because it was a medical problem, it was potentially capable of cure.

Mental disorders came to be defined and classified into two groups: those caused by organic brain disturbance, and those with no apparent physical cause (psychogenic). Persons concerned with nomenclature devised further subclassifications and proceeded to label every conceivable kind of mental aberrance, primarily by cause.

Medical Problem

As the idea of mental illness as a medical problem gained acceptance, several schools of thought about causes emerged. Psychiatric research produced the organicists, who believed that brain pathology was the primary key to causes and that an organic base existed for all mental disturbances. This school preceded the school that today finds causes in chemical or metabolic irregularities within the body as well as in brain damage.

A second school saw the causes as primarily psychological; that is, consequences of life-styles or environmental or sociocultural influences. Sigmund Freud, who developed psychoanalysis at the turn of the century, was in the vanguard of this group. In fact, Freud raised a significant stir in medical circles, and eventually among laymen, when he theorized that the primary cause for mental illness could be related to psychosexual development. He distinguished among persons who were neurotic, or unable to adjust to societal demands, persons who acted out their problems, and persons who were psychotic, or so unable to adjust that they literally retreated or withdrew from reality.

Some investigators asserted that mental illness was a hereditary disease, perhaps aggravated by environmental factors, but nonetheless passed on through generations:

> But if we were seriously minded to check the increase or lessen the production of, insanity, it would be necessary to begin even farther back, and to lay down rules to prevent the propagation of a disease which is one of the most hereditary of diseases. Although it cannot, like smallpox or fever, be communicated from individual to individual . . . unhappily it is a disease which, having existed in the parent, may entail upon the child a predisposition more or less strong to a like disease. . . . It would scarcely be an exaggeration to say that few persons go mad, save from palpable physical causes, who do not show more or less by their gait, manner, gestures, habits of thought, feeling and action, that they have a sort of predestination to madness. [Maudsley 1878, pp. 275–76]

Contemporary research suggests the inadequacy of the organic and psychological theories taken alone. The thought now is that the two theories need to be merged, since no single cause, or theory, explains all mental illness, and since research reveals that most mental illness has organic as well as psychological roots. Although this multicausal estimation tends to prevail, the central concept has many subdivisions. Researchers now work in such areas as psychology, analytical psychology, and biosocial psychology, but unlike earlier researchers, adherents of different schools of thought now tend to work together and integrate their data with those from related fields such as genetics, anatomy, neurology, and sociology. One recent and excellent example of the ways in which representatives of several disciplines can work together on mental health is reported in *Interdisciplinary Team Research: Methods and Problems* (Luszki 1958). This type of research, however, is not without difficulty, especially in the area of definitions. For example, Luszki (1958) states:

> The meaning attached to mental health is a major determining factor in the kind of research set up. If it is oriented toward mental illness, it is generally hospital centered, and emphasis tends to be placed on the psychiatrist-psychologist-physiologist team, with the psychiatrist as key person in the research. The sociologist and the anthropologist are often peripheral in spite of the fact that family and cultural problems are involved. [P. 7]

Mental Hygiene Movement

The work of Dix, Richmond, Freud, and others initiated the mental hygiene movement during the early years of the twentieth century. The impetus came largely from the untiring work of Clifford W. Beers, who wrote *A Mind That Found Itself.* In this autobiographical book, Beers described the three years he spent in mental institutions and detailed the lack of patient therapy, the harsh treatment, and the generally deplorable conditions of the hospitals. The conditions Beers described were no better than those that had aroused Dorothea Dix a half-century earlier.

Beers, who apparently recovered from both his illness and his three-year institutionalization, devoted his life to developing a national and worldwide mental hygiene program. In 1909, when Freud's works were gaining popularity, he formed the National Committee for Mental Hygiene, forerunner of the American Mental Health Association. The National Committee had broad aims in the areas of reform in care and treatment, public education, research into causes, nature, and treatment, and creation of services for the prevention of mental breakdowns (NIMH 1970, p. 8).

Developments in the treatment and prevention of mental illness were considerable over the next few decades. Most states established a central authority for the care and treatment of the mentally ill, and private philanthropic and church groups paid more attention to relieving the causes of mental illness and providing direct services to mentally ill patients and their families.

However, not until World War II did the idea of mental illness begin to receive attention as a serious social problem in the United States. Literature about the meaning and significance of the problem came out of scholarly journals and into the mass media, including radio. Many writers suggested that the time had come to unlock the cells and back wards of mental hospitals and, in view of the educational efforts of the mental hygiene movement, to recognize that mental illness was indeed a disease none need be ashamed of.

The number of men rejected for military service because of mental and emotional disturbances (1.75 million) aroused public concern. By the end of the war and during the late 1940s, scores of organizations had volunteered their services to the mental health movement. State legislatures began to provide more meaningful support for programs of education, training in the field, and facilities. Nationally, Congress passed landmark legislation, the National Mental Health Act of 1946. The act provided for establishment of the National Institute of Mental Health, which exists today, and also granted assistance to state and private nonprofit institutions for mental health research, training, and services.

As clinical psychology, psychiatry, and social work attracted more persons, and as more hospitals, clinics, outpatient services, and facilities were developed as places for practitioners, more personnel were available to provide preventive and therapeutic services. Hospital populations increased, and civil procedures were developed for committing the mentally ill to hospitals for observation and treatment. Criminal courts became more concerned about the problem of responsibility and demanded that proper and adequate facilities be made available for care of the criminally insane. The increased involvement of the courts, in both civil and criminal proceedings, made police more concerned with mental illness as a social problem.

Congressional Action

Congress continued to express its concern for mental hygiene and established the Joint Commission on Mental Illness and Health. In 1961 the Commission published a report, *Action for Mental Health*, which revealed the results of its national survey and recommended new approaches to the social problem. The Commission's report and activities gave the United States a new awareness of the need to improve mental health services.

In 1963, the Community Mental Health Centers Act was passed. The act authorized federal aid for constructing comprehensive community mental health centers across the country. The goal was to create in every community or regional area a full and coordinated range of preventive and treatment services, available around the clock, close to home, for all in need. For the first time in the history of mental health care in this country, ways to help *prevent* mental illness and promote mental health were instituted. As with other diseases, prevention became as important as treatment.

Prevention received further attention when President Nixon appointed the President's Task Force on the Mentally Handicapped. In its final report issued in 1970, the Task Force wrestled with the problem of definitions and major social causes of mental illness:

> The reciprocal relationship between mental disability and social problems such as racism, poverty, violence, crime and delinquency, and overcrowding is real and complex. Racism is declared by many authorities to be the Nation's number one mental health problem. Substandard housing and education, which are correlates of racism and poverty, are associated with higher rates of mental retardation and mental illness. Violence, ranging from civil disorders to street crimes, from wars to assassinations, causes mental anguish. Mental instability, in certain cases, causes violence. Environmental pollution has its effects of both body and mind. Individuals impaired—physically, mentally, or emotionally—by environmental and social outrages cannot function efficiently as citizens to correct them.
>
> It is inappropriate to rest the case for improving social conditions solely on the rationale of preventing mental retardation and mental illness. Yet improvement of these conditions will help substantially to prevent mental disability. Conversely, programs directed towards preventing mental retardation and mental illness will improve social conditions. [P. 37]

Relation to Other Social Problems

The Task Force statement is rather bold, indicting other social problems as significant factors in the causes of mental disability, which remains a significant social problem in mid-twentieth-century America. Although little documentary proof or evidence is presented to back up its beliefs, the Task Force nonetheless probably represents many of the currently held beliefs of most practitioners, researchers, and theorists. The Task Force does not minimize the influence of organic processes, but it does suggest that one appropriate, even necessary, step society must take if it wants to deal constructively with the problem of mental disability is to recognize the importance of socio-environmental factors in producing the problem. Further research, of course, is needed to substantiate the conclusions.

The Task Force also deals with the difficulty of defining terms, such as deviance, criminality, and delinquency, and recognizes its inability to deal with the labels society has placed on various categories of mental disability. Its summary states the case:

> Society has always distinguished between the mentally ill and the mentally retarded: paired but distinct terms such as "madmen" and "fools," "lunatics" and "idiots" have been handed down in common parlance and legal history. . . . The main basis for the distinction was that the "idiot" was presumed to be incurable whereas the "lunatic" might be expected to recover. . . . It was also generally held that the impairment associated with retardation was present in early childhood and persisted through the individual's life whereas the symptoms of mental illness . . . usually occurred in adult life in persons who had previously functioned normally.
>
> Advances in knowledge of causation, management, and specific treatment have shown that these distinctions are far less sharp than was originally supposed. Both mental illness and mental retardation may have physiological and socio-environmental causes, or both. Also, the retarded child, struggling with his environment, may become psychotic; the psychotic child may develop grave learning problems.
>
> A system of classification of mental disability is essential for diagnosis, for epidemiological purposes, and for international communication. But because mental disability presents so few objective diagnostic criteria . . . classification is mainly based on symptoms and the little that is known of biological causes. *A serious practical disadvantage of this system is that it has led to the "labeling" of individuals in terms that only too often suggest an unmodifiable disease process or basic constitutional deficiency and therefore a discouraging end state, and to the provision of services in keeping with the label rather than with the needs of the individual.* [P. 10]

The Task Force was unable to define precisely the various terms with which it dealt in its report, and it recognized, too, that every state tends to define the terms in legal language peculiar to the state. Consequently, the Task Force decided to use the generic term "mental disability," which is described to mean a range from "people who are acutely disturbed for a brief period of time to people who are severely handicapped for their full life span" (p. 11).

Numbers and Costs

Current statistics indicate that mentally ill persons occupy about 37 percent of all hospital beds in the United States (NIMH 1970; President's Task Force 1970). In 1968, there were about 1.6 million patient care episodes (number of patients at beginning of year plus new admissions) in state, county, federal, and private mental hospitals, and in general hospitals with psychiatric services. At the end of 1969, 367,000 were patients in public mental hospitals. This number represented a decline for the fourteenth consecutive year and 192,000 fewer than in 1955, when the downward decline began. Also at this approximate time tranquilizing medication became plentiful and was prescribed for many persons who would have become hospital patients but were under control in their own homes with medication and could be treated as out-patients.

In addition to resident patients in 1968, over 1.5 million persons were served in 2,282 reporting outpatient facilities in the United States. In 1969, nearly $3 billion was spent on care and treatment of patients in public mental hospitals; the average daily cost of care per person was estimated at $12.59.

The size and scope of the mental disability problem are almost impossible to determine. While the President's Task Force estimates that some 20 million (10 percent of the total population) Americans could benefit from mental health services, only 3.5 million actually receive some kind of care. Another significant study suggests that this figure is a gross underestimation.

In the 1950s, a group of researchers studied the mental health of the Midtown section of Manhattan in New York City. In their report, *Mental Health in the Metropolis,* they assert (after carefully defining their terms) that over 23 percent of the population were impaired enough to require some kind of mental health treatment (Srole et al. 1962, p. 138).

Although figures are difficult to compute, it is estimated that mental illness costs more than $20 billion annually. This amount includes more than $4 billion from public and private agencies, governmental jurisdictions, and individuals for treatment and preventive services. It also includes approximately $16 billion in economic losses from inability to work, excessive absenteeism, and other similar factors (President's Task Force 1970, p. 8).

About 6 million Americans have been labeled mentally retarded; 215,000 are institutionalized at any given time, and 619,000 are attending special classes. The cost of mental retardation comes to about $8 billion annually. Included are $2.5 billion for residential treatment, special education, and clinical and rehabilitation services, and an estimated $5.5 billion for loss of earnings. What governments pay for such indirect costs as welfare and additional medical coverage, and the amounts individuals and private groups spend indirectly, are incalculable.

The Task Force (1970) also states that with regard to mental illness and mental retardation:

> ... losses chargeable to premature deaths, to the criminal activities of drug addicts and other disturbed individuals, and to pain, frustration, and other intangible factors that seriously reduce the quality of life, for both those with mental disabilities and those close to them, are not included. [P. 8]

Law Enforcement and Criminal Responsibility

Besides the anguish and difficulties the mentally disabled create for those closest to them, they pose serious problems for other segments of society. One significant area directly affected is law enforcement, which is concerned in at least two distinct but related areas.

Our earlier discussions about crime, delinquency, and deviance indicated that we do not know now what causes such behavior; at least we cannot point to a single causal factor. However, sufficient evidence exists to show that mental disability, whatever its causes, is a primary source of violative behavior. Thus drug addicts, alcoholics, neurotics, and psychotics, as well as the alienated and disenchanted, frequently commit acts that are in violation of criminal and juvenile codes. So the police are constantly dealing with people who are mentally disabled.

Since the neoclassical period in criminology, persons who

commit criminal acts but who are not considered mentally responsible have been excused from culpability; that is, they have legally been viewed as not having criminal responsibility (*mens rea*).

The controversy over criminal responsibility has a long record. Although very young children and the so-called feebleminded have been excused from prosecution on the grounds that they could not possibly have sufficient *intent* to commit criminal acts, the insane have not always been excused. In 1843, the English courts developed a test to determine criminal insanity. Most courts adopted the M'Naughten Rule and even today it is popularly applied in the United States. The rule essentially asks whether or not the defendant is capable of distinguishing between right and wrong:

> To establish a defense on the grounds of insanity, it must be clearly proved that at the time of committing the act, the party accused was labouring under such a defect of reason, from the disease of the mind, as not to know the nature and quality of the act he was doing, or if he did know it that he did not know he was doing what was wrong. The mode of putting the latter part of the question to the jury has been whether the accused at the time of doing the act knew the difference between right and wrong.

The so-called irresistible impulse rule was added in 1861. Continuing conflict between jurists and psychiatrists led to adoption in 1954 of a new rule to test for criminal responsibility. The Durham Rule states, "An accused is not criminally responsible if his unlawful act was the product of mental disease or defect."

Note that the test is not one of *knowledge* but of a defendant's ability to *behave* normally. It does not ask whether he knew the difference between right and wrong; it asks only if his behavior was the result of his mental illness or defect.

In 1962, after studying the issue at some length, the American Law Institute wrote a new version, which it recommended be adopted in the American courts:

> (1) A person is not responsible for criminal conduct if at the time of such conduct as a result of mental disease or defect he lacks substantial capacity either to appreciate the criminality [wrongfulness] of his conduct or to conform his conduct to the requirements of law. (2)

The terms "mental disease" or "defect" do not include an abnormality manifested only by repeated criminal or otherwise anti-social conduct.

The ALI proposal, includes the requirement of intellectual or behavioral problems and is much broader in its definition of mental illness. The controversy continues, however, because judges, psychiatrists, prosecutors, and defense attorneys are unable to agree on which rule is the best for court use.

Some persons, such as Bernard Diamond, advocate the concept of *diminished responsibility*, which in effect asks that the state try a defendant who claims to be mentally ill on a charge that reflects the defendant's level of mental ability adjustment. For example, if a person is thought to be mentally ill and has committed murder, he might be tried on the charge of manslaughter, since that is the highest level offense he is capable of planning and executing.

Others advocate that the only solution to the problem is to try the defendant on the legitimate charge but then hold a sanity hearing to determine whether, after conviction, the defendant should be imprisoned or hospitalized. While rule controversy ensues, however, the problem belongs to the courts and correctional agencies. In discharging their responsibilities for investigating and preparing evidence for possible prosecution, the police must nonetheless deal with the mentally disabled on a daily basis. Consequently, mental disability presents an almost unique social problem for which no simple solution exists.

Several recent studies (see, e.g., Webster 1970; National Institute of Law Enforcement and Criminal Justice 1970) suggest that police spend as much as 15 percent of their time in social service activities. Handling potential suicides, chasing runaway children, managing distraught parents, transporting mentally disabled persons to hospitals, searching for mental hospital escapees, and dealing with senile persons on the streets are only a few of the daily activities of a beat patrolman. How a given society, or community, chooses to deal with the problem, of course, directly affects the policeman's work, role, and image. What the laws state he can and cannot do either facilitates or complicates his daily work.

Suicide

Suicide probably is one of the most difficult problems for police, not only because of frequently changing statutes but also because suicide is so fraught with religious, moral, and emotional overtones. The problem affects every community in every society, and police frequently are called on to intervene. Many groups deal with suicide, at the theoretical as well as the practical level, and some groups organized in recent years provide preventive help. Suicide prevention bureaus, rap-type groups, hotlines, and others have set up programs to talk people out of taking their lives. How successful these groups and the police are at dissuading potential suicides, though, cannot be determined.

According to the World Health Organization (WHO 1973, p. G8), at least a thousand persons worldwide commit suicide every day, and at least ten times as many attempt it. WHO reports that at periods of major instability, as in aftermaths of wars or persecutions, suicide rates tend to reach a peak in the affected countries. A stable factor, at least in this century, is the large number of male over female suicides. In recent years suicide and attempts have increased among younger age groups, although most suicides continue to occur among the elderly.

Hungary reportedly has the highest suicide rate in the world—33.1 per 100,000 population; the United States ranks sixth—10.9 per 100,000. The WHO report indicates that one reason for increased worldwide suicide rates is reflected in changing methods of self-destruction. For example, domestic gas is easily accessible, and sedative drugs and hypnotics have become readily available for overdoses.

Other contributing factors mentioned in the WHO report, especially personal and environmental factors, include bereavement, social isolation, chronic physical illness, psychotic disturbance, alcoholism, and drug addiction. The report also states, "Indeed, drug addiction itself has been likened to a form of slow suicide when the addict is well aware that persistence in his addiction is physically harmful, and there is the added risk of accidental overdose" (p. G8).

Suicide is viewed as a denial of the human's most urgent need, self-preservation, and contradicts the valuation of human life that is implicit in democratic and social ethics. Yet recorded evidence shows that suicide occurred more than four thousand years ago, and quite possibly people may have been committing suicide since shortly after human existence on earth began. Few societies condone suicide; most condemn it.

In ancient Greece and Rome, suicide was considered a crime against the state. Throughout the Middle Ages, English practice was to drag bodies of suicides through the streets, hang them naked upside down in public view, and impale them on stakes at public crossroads—punishment really aimed at the dead person's survivors and to set an example for others. As early as the eleventh century, the custom was to censure the suicide's family, refuse burial in the church or city cemetary (a practice still common in some cultures), and confiscate the survivors' property. Most jurisdictions in the United States still prohibit suicide. The British Suicide Act, passed in 1961, makes suicide and attempted suicide noncriminal acts, but complicity in the suicide of another remains a felony (Frederick & Lague 1972, p. 2).

Suicide and Law

United States law basically is derived from the older English law, and most states still define suicide and attempted suicide as crimes. Society's other severe moral judgments are reflected in other ways. For example, the family of a suicide victim has difficulty in collecting insurance payments, and survivors frequently are so embarrassed about the act that for long periods of time they feel like social outcasts.

The approximately 24,000 suicides in the United States each year cost our states and municipalities almost $4 billion annually. This estimated amount includes primarily such expenses as emergency facilities, brief hospitalization, and loss of income. It does not reflect the costs incurred for police services or medical and psychiatric care for the survivors.

Although the American rate of suicide is 10.9 per 100,000 population, the rate for the past twenty years has remained at about 1 percent of all deaths each year. In actual numbers, suicide ranks as the tenth leading cause of death for all ages. These figures are not altogether reliable, for in many cases it is impossible to determine whether an accidental death was really an accident or was intentional. For that reason and others, vital statistics experts believe that the suicide ranking may actually be as high as fifth or sixth among the leading causes of death.

Most suicides occur in urban areas, especially among minority groups. The highest numbers tend to occur in April and May; December has the lowest rate, although the number often increases around the Christmas holidays when many people become depressed over the absence of loved ones. The records also reveal that suicide is most likely to occur on Friday or Monday, and Sunday is a strong third. Three times as many women as men attempt suicide, but three times as many men as women complete the act. Men tend to use guns or explosives; women usually use barbiturates and other less violent forms. Only 3 percent of all suicides on a national basis are a result of jumping from high places, but the rate goes up to 33 percent in New York City, where many buildings are very high (Frederick & Lague 1972, p. 5).

Increasing Rates

The suicide rate appears to be increasing significantly among blacks, American Indians, and Spanish-surnamed groups, but it is increasing most among the young. Over the last twenty-five years, suicide has risen to the fourth leading cause of death among people ten to twenty-four years of age. "Their helplessness, hopelessness, and loneliness are usually brought on by family problems, but all kinds of problems—the failure to make good grades or to be accepted into a school group, an argument with a friend—are magnified in their small world" (Frederick & Lague 1972, pp. 10–11). Additionally, drug use and abuse among the young has increased significantly, and young persons not uncommonly commit suicide by overdose or while under the influence of drugs—for example, on LSD trips.

The scope of care, management, and treatment of the mentally disabled, including those who attempt suicide, has gradually widened in the United States, but the effectiveness of some measures cannot always be determined. Psychiatry is largely responsible for the design and implementation of treatment programs, which have developed along three major lines: psychotherapy, rehabilitative therapy, and physiological and chemical methods and therapy. Electroshock and especially insulin therapy, which were the primary means of treatment only a few years ago, have largely given way to psychoactive drugs, which since the mid-1950s have brought a dramatic improvement in management of the mentally ill.

Many people have criticized the use of drugs such as tranquilizers and antidepressants because the drugs do not in themselves cure illness. They tend to modify disturbances, help to make additional therapy more effective, and frequently make possible more patient maintenance in the home and community instead of hospitals. The basic criticism is that drugs are overused in order to control patients and otherwise reduce the risk of their acting out in destructive ways against themselves and others (Henry 1973).

Effectiveness of Psychiatric Care

Several persons have criticized not only the use of drugs for control but also the overall effectiveness of psychiatry in dealing curatively with the mentally disabled. Szasz (1961) and Halleck (1971) contend that mental illness is nothing more than a label that agents of authority use to control segments of the population that are distracting, eccentric, or otherwise behaving in deviant ways.

Halleck argues that labeling persons as mentally ill has some very negative as well as self-serving consequences. "The definitions that determine who is in need of help are constantly changing: sometimes they expand the patient population; sometimes they contract it" (p. 20).

Halleck says that some segments of the population, such as blacks and the poor, receive inadequate treatment, are overdiagnosed, and usually are undertreated (pp. 110–12). He notes that psychiatrists who fail to understand the sociology and psychology of their work are failing all of their own patients and society at large, who depend on them for professional help and guidance:

Too many psychiatrists still communicate to their patients that mental illness is an affliction, something that has to be visited upon them by an external force. . . . Psychiatrists seem to assume that a clear understanding of the arbitrary basis of the mental illness role is beyond the intellectual capacity of their patients or of the public.

Psychiatry will never be able to deal with critical moral and political questions unless psychiatrists become more consistent in conceptualizing and publicizing their work. Psychiatrists must immediately stop all propaganda designed to convince the public that mental illness is "a disease just like any other disease." Instead, they should publicly acknowledge that some behavior disorders resemble physical illness and others do not. They should explain the advantages and disadvantages of the mental illness role and they should tell the public whatever they know about the causes of human suffering. [Pp. 247–48]

Mental disability, regardless of type, label, or diagnosis, represents a serious social problem in the United States. Regardless of the endless arguments over causation and methods of treatment, it does surely exist and causes considerable suffering for a sizable segment of the population. It has considerable economic impact not only in terms of prevention and treatment costs but also in such indirect costs as loss of earnings and welfare programs. Other costs are reflected in the daily activities of the criminal justice system, whose employees, whether in law enforcement, the courts, or corrections, must deal with the disabled, their families, and others on a daily, face-to-face basis.

CHAPTER 11

The Problem of Overcriminalization

Overdependence on the Law

On March 11, 1971, President Nixon addressed the following remarks to the National Conference on the Judiciary in Williamsburg, Virginia:

> What can be done now to break the logjam of justice today, to ensure the right to a speedy trial, and to enhance respect for the law? We have to find ways to clear the courts of the endless stream of what are termed "victimless crimes" that get in the way of serious consideration of serious crimes. There are more important matters for highly skilled judges and prosecutors. . . . [National Commission on Marijuana 1972, p. 145]

The former President's comments reflect a growing concern

for what has become one of the most serious problems for the criminal justice system—overcriminalization of behavior.

Simply stated, several categories of conduct presently defined as criminal appear ill-suited to law enforcement, deterrence of proscribed conduct, and maintenance of respect for the criminal justice system among significant elements of the population. Examples of statutes that create problems of overcriminalization are laws that deal with morals, such as sexual conduct and gambling, and behavior that requires social services, such as disorderly conduct, objectionable language, and vagrancy. The common characteristics of crimes in these categories are that: no victim exists in the usual sense of the word because participants in the offense are willing; the defendant himself is the victim; or the victim's interest is often so insubstantial that it does not justify imposition of the criminal sanction to protect it. Thus one of the essential reasons for imposing criminal penalties—to deter conduct clearly and significantly harmful to persons or property of others—is lacking.

In most United States jurisdictions any sexual activity other than so-called normal intercourse between married partners is a crime. Quite probably no laws are broken more often! If all violators were prosecuted and punished, a majority of the adult population in America would be imprisoned at some time. Statutes prohibit and provide for penalties for fornication between consenting unmarried adults, homosexuality, adultery, and all kinds of "abnormal" sexual conduct, even between married people. Mostly, the aim of such laws is to satisfy public conscience with strict judgments and public condemnation of immoral and irreligious behavior that, being subject to temptation, humans in private. Thurman Arnold (1935) has written:

> Most unenforced criminal laws survive in order to satisfy moral objections to established modes of conduct. They are unenforced because we want to continue our conduct, and unrepealed because we want to preserve our morals [P. 160]

However, morals have changed for more people, especially younger people, and an ever larger segment of society vociferously denies the standards embodied in these laws. A recent survey of sexual behavior and attitudes reveals that the United States is in the midst of a sexual liberation movement. Premarital sex, for example, has become both acceptable and widespread. As expected, the change is especially noteworthy in females. Also, couples have generally increased the variety of intercourse techniques, the frequency of coitus, and experimentation with extraordinary sexual practices. In other words, people are now doing things that a generation ago were unthinkable, or at least were among the best-guarded intimate secrets (Hunt 1973).

Similar to sexual conduct statutes are the morals laws that punish for the sale and purchase of prostitutes' services, large-scale gambling, and abortion. Some people maintain that these statutes are more justified than are those related to sexual conduct because they proscribe acts that have a commercial character and hence elicit more repugnance. Pandering for profit to human weakness is deemed more abhorrent than merely giving in to temptation. Some stress that these offenses carry additional harms in their wake. Thus a by-product of prostitution is making the prospective customer a victim of the so-called Murphy game and other fraudulent practices. Prostitution is also deemed offensive to respectable persons, visitors, and tourists in the neighborhoods that streetwalkers and their pimps frequent.

Another category of overcriminalization appears in statutes related to illness and conditions that require the provision of social services. For example, some laws punish intoxication and possession of addictive drugs. Many people maintain that society's interest in preventing these evils and in protecting the offender from himself is stronger than the moral statutes. For instance, arrest of alcoholics gets them off the streets where they may be harmed while drunk. In the winter arrest may contribute to their actual survival. Arrest also prevents the public drunkard from making a spectacle that is offensive to sober people.

The narcotics addict represents a more dramatic problem, for his personal destruction is more complete and his breach of society deeper. For example, to support his habit the addict is often driven to commit property-related crimes or even more serious crimes against the person, such as robbery and mugging. In arresting, prosecuting, and jailing the drug addict, society recognizes an obligation, mostly unfulfilled in reality, to provide rehabilitative and therapeutic services.

Nuisance statutes constitute the last category of overcriminalization. Ostensibly they penalize disorderly conduct and vagrancy. Disorderly conduct statutes generally deal with such matters as affrays, loud and boisterous public gatherings, swearing and profanity in public, ball games in the street, indecent proposals, causing a disturbance, and failing to move on when a police officer so orders. Vagrancy includes the offenses of leading an immoral or profligate life without evidence of lawful means of support, frequenting houses of ill fame, begging and common law vagrancy, and loitering in gambling establishments, unlicensed saloons, or places where narcotics are found.

Nuisance laws originated in feudal times to aid in keeping indentured servants and farmers from moving elsewhere and finding freedom. They were used again at the onset of the industrial revolution in Europe to keep people from leaving the impoverished existence of the countryside for life in industrial urban centers. Today nuisance laws usually are invoked to keep unwelcome persons out of better neighborhoods and protect community tranquility, and as weapons against prostitutes, gamblers, demonstrators, and others whose apprehension would otherwise be difficult (Campbell et al. 1970).

The Costs of Overcriminalization

Most of the conduct that morals, illness, and nuisance statutes prohibit is somewhat undesirable or aesthetically repugnant, but should it be prohibited by criminal statute? The criminal sanction is optimally used only when several conditions are satisfied. According to Packer (1968), the conditions include the following:

1. The conduct in question is prominent in most people's view of socially threatening behavior, and is not condoned by any significant segment of society.
2. Subjecting it to the criminal sanction is not inconsistent with the goals of punishment.
3. Suppressing it will not inhibit socially desirable conduct.
4. The conduct may be dealt with through evenhanded and nondiscriminatory enforcement.
5. Controlling it through the criminal process will not expose that process to severe qualitative or quantitative strains.

6. There are no reasonable alternatives to the criminal sanction for dealing with it. [P. 296]

Application of these criteria to nuisance statutes raises several questions about their propriety.

First, laws that punish gambling, prostitution, and drug offenses are difficult to enforce and apparently fail as effective deterrents to continued criminal conduct. We must conclude that current practices fail to keep the proscribed conduct within manageable limits and at the same time require considerable police, court, and correctional time that might be better spent on more serious offenses.

Second, policies on nuisance statutes help to diminish the sense of respect for the law, especially among poor urban residents. The laws also reflect a dual standard of justice—one for the wealthy and white, another for the poor and nonwhite. The double standard is quite evident, for example, in gambling, when the numbers runner goes to jail but the securities violator often pays only a small fine, and respectable organizations are legally permitted to operate such games of chance as bingo and raffles.

Third, organized crime thrives on victimless crimes, especially gambling and drugs, and inevitably corrupts police. The layman's belief that large-scale gambling, narcotics, and prostitution operations could not thrive without police neglect for a fee has received ample support from investigations of police corruption in New York City, Chicago, and other jurisdictions.

Fourth, enforcement difficulties related to public acceptance of this kind of illegal conduct and the way it is typically organized have driven enforcement agencies to excesses in pursuit of evidence. The adoption of such practices as no-knock entry, wiretapping, and the widespread use of informers and electronic interception has often been justified as necessary to wage an effective war against criminal activities.

Such practices in a democratic society are undesirable in themselves and existing evidence shows that they have often been misused. An eight-week *New York Times* investigation has disclosed that mistaken, violent, and illegal drug raids are not isolated occurrences, as the government has claimed, but have been carried out frequently in the past three years. In the Los Angeles area a policeman has acknowledged that such mistakes happen once or twice a month; in Miami complaints of police harassment during drug searches are reportedly so numerous that the Legal Services of Greater Miami can no longer handle the caseload. According to the *Times*, abuses of police power and no-knock laws occur on the federal, state, and local levels:

> Details of each raid vary, but generally they involve heavily armed policemen, arriving at night, often unshaven and in slovenly "undercover" attire, bashing down the doors to a private home or apartment and holding the ... residents at gun point while they ransack the house.... Sometimes the agents have warrants and identify themselves. Sometimes they do not.

These tactics have resulted in at least four deaths, including that of a policeman. Such practices have initiated considerable litigation in the courts, thereby damaging citizens' respect for and trust in the justice system.

Fifth, offenses related to drug addiction may constitute well over half of the arrests for serious crime made each year. Although the Supreme Court (*Robinson* v. *California*) has declared addiction to be an illness, conduct directly related to it, such as an addict's possession of drugs and needles, is considered criminal conduct. The number of arrests for possession of marijuana also has grown at an astronomical rate over the last few years. Thus many people now question the wisdom of attempting to cope with the narcotics problem within the framework of the criminal justice system and have called for narcotics policy reform (Washington Lawyers' Committee 1972).

Sixth, police demoralization is quite high because effective enforcement of laws related to victimless crimes is virtually impossible; yet police often are subjected to public pressure and criticism for failing to establish efficient control over the proscribed behaviors. Self-appointed morals crusaders often unnecessarily stir up public opinion, and politicians campaigning on a strict law-and-order platform sometimes commit police to performance with spectacular and quick results in a complex area of criminal activity.

Finally, the study of victimless crime reveals society's impressive inconsistency in this area. Why, for example, are some citizens allowed to gamble, with money that perhaps they can ill afford, on such risky ventures as the stock market, state lotteries, and pari-mutuel betting, while others are prohibited from betting in, say, a numbers pool? Why license the sale of some personal services, such as escort services and massage parlors, and not others, such as prostitution and bogus massage parlors? Why are such potentially harmful drugs as tobacco and alcohol sold without prescription and merely taxed, when others, such as marijuana, cocaine, and heroin, are unavailable at any price except through illicit channels? Why is paternalistic legislation defended and supported sometimes—safety helmets for motorcyclists or restrictions on school-run sex education programs—and other times ignored or opposed, as in the use of automobile safety devices or restrictions on unsavory aspects of children's television programs and general advertising?

The list of paradoxes is almost endless. The explanation, in every case, is ideological and historical, not logical. In other words, no rational theory, empirically well grounded, can justify such prohibitions, or legalizations (Bedau 1973).

Thus the overcriminalization problem is ripe for careful analysis and for recommendations on reform of present laws and practices. The evils of prostitution, gambling, and narcotics probably result more from their illegality than from their inherent harmfulness. Illegality often results in risk for both seller and buyer, as in the Murphy game. Risk may well make a situation more attractive, but it can also result in tragic deaths. Illegal abortions often are clumsily performed in unclean conditions. Prostitutes transmit venereal disease, but if they were not criminals, they would (if licensed) be required to protect their own as well as their customers' health through periodic medical examinations.

Cheating in illegal gambling, with no lawful avenue of redress, is another problem in overcriminalization. Also, because of the high cost of illegal narcotics, addicts must spend $20 to $100 per day in order to support their habits. Sources of their funds are in such activities as prostitution and violent crimes against person or property.

Moreover, the prostitution, gambling, and narcotics industries require organization. For example, the numbers writer and run-

mission members included present and former governors, judges, state and local police, and prison officials.

A similar statement came from the National Commission on Marijuana and Drug Abuse (1972):

> We believe that the criminal law is too harsh a tool to apply to personal possession even in the effort to discourage use. It implies an overwhelming indictment of the behavior which we believe is not appropriate. The actual and potential harm of the use of the drug is not great enough to justify intrusion by the criminal law into private behavior. . . . [The] government must show a compelling reason to justify invasion of the home in order to prevent personal use of marijuana. We find little in marijuana's effects or in its social impact to support such a determination. . . . The time consumed in arresting possessors is inefficiently used when contrasted with an equal amount of time invested in apprehending major dealers. . . . Most law enforcement officials, district attorneys and judges recognize the ineffectiveness of the possession penalty as a deterrent. Its perpetuation results in the making of what is commonly referred to as "cheap" cases that have little or no impact on deterring sale. . . . A final cost of the possession laws is the disrespect which the laws and their enforcement engender in the young. Our youth cannot understand why society chooses to criminalize a behavior with so little visible ill-effect or adverse social impact. [Pp. 140–45]

In other words, the Commission found that the total scheme in force in every state and at the federal level, which prohibited by law all marijuana-related behavior, failed to discourage use and inhibited effective concentration of efforts to reduce and treat irresponsible use. Thus it recommended:

> 1. Possession of marijuana for personal use should no longer be an offense, but marijuana possessed in public should remain contraband subject to summary seizure and forfeiture.
> 2. Casual distribution of small amounts of marijuana for no remuneration, or insignificant remuneration not involving profit should no longer be an offense. [P. 152]

In 1973 the American Bar Association adopted a resolution to support marijuana decriminalization. At the annual convention the association's house of delegates passed the resolutions by votes of 122–70 and 103–84. The delegates objected specifically to discriminatory enforcement patterns and excessive prosecution of users.

Oregon has led the movement to place personal, private use of the drug in a more rational context. On June 30, 1973, the Oregon State Legislature passed a bill to decriminalize marijuana by making its possession or use (up to one ounce) a violation punishable by a fine not to exceed $100.

Conversely, a New York State drug law that became effective September 1, 1973, makes possession of as little as an ounce of marijuana a felony punishable by imprisonment for up to fifteen years. The new law may appeal to millions of New Yorkers, frightened and infuriated by the crimes that the city's estimated 125,000 addicts commit. But to many critics, including professionals at every level of the criminal justice system, the law seems little more than a politically inspired measure, neither humane nor really practical.

Although the crimes addicts commit are real and numerous, society should reflect on why they are perpetrated and why people become addicts. The answer to the first question may be that society has decided to make illegal, and therefore extremely expensive, what the addicts want or need. Thus society has effectively created its own problem, just as it did during prohibition, and just as it would should tobacco become, overnight, a forbidden substance. The answer to the second question may lie in the deprivation and despair in many people's lives. Dr. Payte has said:

> Minimizing social factors (as linked to drug abuse) may be comforting to parents and social institutions, but in my opinion it is a dangerous indulgence that may further postpone the kind of national introspection and soul searching that may eventually be required to reach a real understanding of the major contributing factors of the prevalent need and/or desire to alter consciousness by chemical means to simply endure life as we know it today. [*National Drug Reporter*, August 31, 1973]

During a visit in the United States Frances Verrinder, editor of Britain's *Drugs and Society*, answered the question, Where would you spend "drug money"?

> I think the money would even be better spent trying to do something about unemployment, creating jobs for people. Why not spend

money on public housing, free medical services? What I'd also like to see is more facilities for people with problems. We don't get much support from each other. I'd like to see how we can build in social organizations those kinds of supports. . . . If I had $5 million, I'd try to find a run-down depressed community and instead of running a drug program, I'd feed the money into community-oriented activities to enrich people's lives. [*National Drug Reporter*, August 15, 1973]

In other words, the social strategy should center primarily on the deep-rooted causes or conditions of addiction, and on the most effective means of eradicating them: employment, education, decent housing, and a better quality of life. From a short-term tactical point of view, a direct attack on the price of hard drugs probably would discourage both organized and satellite crime. The obvious and most sensible course would be to permit physicians to prescribe drugs more freely to addicts but also to encourage the addict to accept treatment.

Public education not limited to illegal drugs but covering every type of drug ought also to be a primary strategy. It is well known that each year the legal drug industry unconcernedly devotes hundreds of millions of dollars to producing psychotropic drugs, including barbiturates, tranquilizers, and amphetamines, in gross excess of any conceivable legitimate medical needs. These mind drugs are easily available to almost everyone, and slick advertising campaigns are designed to persuade people of the medical and social propriety of chemically screening out all of life's daily emotional hazards (Gravel 1972). Dr. Mitchell Rosenthal, director of the Phoenix Rehabilitation Program in New York City, testified at a Senate hearing:

While everyone deplores the misuse of psychoactive drugs by young people, a major industry with practically unlimited access to the mass media has been convincing the American people, young and old alike, that drugs effect instant and significant changes, that indeed they work "miracles" such as making a "boring woman" exciting to a husband so that he proclaims her to be a "new woman."

Physicians seem to have fallen into a rut and have lost sight of alternatives to drug use. Critics point out that medical journals and meetings, which drug companies heavily subsidize, are devoid of genuine and critical debate on the use of psychotropics.

Some persons call for a governmental ban on television ads for nonprescriptive drugs, just as liquor and cigarette ads are banned. Alternatively, networks could be required to provide free air time for public service ads that present scientific evidence and philosophical arguments against the casual use of drugs. Pill ads also should be banned from children's programs.

A sane national policy to curb drug misuses of any kind should rely less on criminal law and more on a thorough reexamination of the American way of life. We must reassess the ways we help or do not help one another, and commit ourselves to ending any double standard in both the prescription and the proscription of drugs.

Enforcement of Morals: How Necessary?

Five federal laws presently prohibit distributions of obscene materials in the United States, and five federal agencies are responsible for enforcement. The Postal Service, the Customs Bureau, and the Federal Communications Commission investigate violations within their jurisdictions. The FBI investigates violations of statutes that deal with transportation and common carriers. The Department of Justice is responsible for prosecution or other judicial enforcement.

Most states have statutes that generally prohibit the distribution of obscene materials, and the statutes of forty-one states contain some special prohibition on the distribution of sexual materials to minors. None of the federal statutes define the term *obscene.* State statutes either do not define the term or incorporate the Constitutional standard established by the Supreme Court.

For many years the Supreme Court assumed that laws generally prohibiting dissemination of obscene materials were consistent with the Constitution's free speech guarantees. In 1957, in the case of *Roth* v. *United States,* the Court held that such laws were Constitutional, but it set a narrowly restrictive standard of what is obscene. *Stanley* v. *Georgia* (1969) and subsequent decisions narrowed the permissible test even further in stating that distribution could not be prohibited if the material did not meet three criteria:

1. The dominant theme of the materials, taken as a whole, must appeal to "prurient" interest in sex.

2. The material must be "patently offensive" because it affronts "contemporary community standards" regarding the depiction of sexual matters.

3. And the material must lack "redeeming social value."

In an attempt in 1973 to end years of confusion over pornography laws, the U.S. Supreme Court in a split five to four decision prescribed a new test to determine what state laws may prohibit as obscene:

The basic guidelines for the trier of fact must be:

1. Whether the average person, applying contemporary community standards, would find that the work, taken as a whole, appeals to the prurient interest.

2. Whether the work depicts or describes, in a patently offensive way, sexual conduct specifically defined by the applicable state law.

3. And whether the work, taken as a whole, lacks serious literary, artistic, political or scientific value.

The Court thus abandoned the "utterly without redeeming social value" test and the idea of a national standard for determining whether material is obscene. Some welcomed the ruling as finally ending the age of permissiveness: others saw it as a serious infringement on the nation's civil liberties.

In his dissent Justice Douglas said:

[T]he court has worked hard to define obscenity and concededly has failed . . . [because] there are no constitutional guidelines for deciding what is and what is not obscene, [so that it is a matter of] tastes and standards. . . . What shocks me may be sustenance for my neighbor.

Justice Douglas would have preferred that:

If there are to be restraints on what is obscene, then a constitutional amendment should be the way of achieving that end. . . . I do not think that we, the judges, were ever given the constitutional power to make definitions of obscenity. If it is to be defined, let the people debate and decide by a constitutional amendment what they want to ban as obscene. . . . Whatever the choice, the courts will have some guidelines. Now we have none except our predilections. [In *U.S. News & World Report*, July 2, 1973, p. 36]

In a separate dissent Justice Brennan argued that "the suppression of obscenity cannot be reconciled with the fundamental principles of the First and Fourteenth Amendments." It may be useful to recall here the words of the late Justice Hugo Black of the U.S. Supreme Court:

> It is one of the most amazing things about the ingeniousness of the times that strong arguments are made, which almost convince me, that it is very foolish of me to think "no law" means no law. But what it says is "Congress shall make no law. . . ." Then I move on to the words "abridging the freedom of speech or of the press." It says Congress shall make no law doing that. What it means, according to a current philosophy that I do not share, is that Congress shall be able to make just such a law unless we judges object too strongly. . . . It says "no law" and that is what I believe it means. . . . My view is, without deviation, without exception, without any ifs, buts, or whereases, that freedom of speech means that you shall not do something to people either for the views they have or the views they express or the words they speak or write.

Acknowledging "the inherent dangers of undertaking to regulate any forms of expression," the Court decided, however, that it is permissible to regulate "works which depict or describe sexual conduct." Good reasons should be given to justify the regulation of works in such a category; none were offered. Thus the Court delivered an opinion based not, say, on findings and conclusions about the effect of sexual materials on persons exposed to them but on the premise that obscene materials are not entitled to the protections the First and Fourteenth Amendments accord to speech. Consequently, the Court ruling seems to be an arbitrary one because it *assumes* that Constitutional guarantees can be denied to pornographic material but must be applied to, say, portrayals of violence—even those that minors view.

The Court states that concern about loss of basic freedoms is unnecessary because the prohibited material has no worth; the obscene label is limited to materials "lacking in serious literary, artistic, political or scientific value." In other words, the Court has declared Constitutional a prohibition on the manufacture and scale of material that is in bad taste, dull, or worthless from an aesthetic or instructional point of view, but only when it is related to sexual matters. It seems inequitable to proscribe poor quality in the portrayal of sex when ugliness and bad taste abound in architecture, speeches, cartoons, jokes, clothes, movies, and much printed matter. Who is the ultimate arbiter of "serious artistic, literary, political or scientific value"? Who would agree that the state has the right to proscribe something or somebody because certain standards are not met? Unfortunately, dullness and drudgery are the very texture of many people's lives.

The opinion Chief Justice Burger delivered also made abundant use of such terms as "prurient," "offensive," "patently offensive," "lewd," and "lacking in serious value," obviously subjective concepts, undefinable and existing in the minds of the beholders. The Court more or less acknowledged this subjectivity when it introduced the concept of a local community standard in place of a national standard for determining what is prurient or offensive. But then, what is or who is "the community"?

The Court should have recognized that differences also exist at the "local community" level when it said, "It is neither realistic nor constitutionally sound to read the First Amendment as requiring that the people of Maine or Mississippi accept public depiction of conduct found tolerable in Las Vegas or New York City." Different people in the same state or community may feel differently about what is obscene.

The only decision that would make sense would include recognition that each of the two hundred million Americans is a qualified judge, which is exactly what the First Amendment established once and for all.

Ironically, the new community standards criterion will damage the legitimate publisher more than the manufacturer of hard-core pornography. The legitimate publisher must meet the most conservative common denominator for sexual material in order to avoid constant litigation, or the threat of it, at the whim of local prosecutors. Conversely, the hard-core manufacturer can limit his market to the large, cosmopolitan cities, which have always been the primary outlet for such material anyway.

Even more serious is the chilling effect the Burger decision will have on the arts and the entertainment and information media. Already in several reported instances sheriffs, police chiefs, and local prosecutors have moved against materials that could by no stretch of the imagination be defined as hard core. Soon zealous self-appointed guardians of public morals will demand that some books be removed from public libraries or deleted from school reading lists. In fact, many of the great books, great paintings, and great plays that constitute civilization's heritage, including the Bible, could be called smutty.

Again, as in other types of victimless crimes, the major flaw in any attempt to curb the manufacture and distribution of pornographic material is the public lust for the material. According to some reports, the economics of the pornography business are enough to make other businessmen green with envy. Publication of sex magazines, for both men and women, is flourishing; sex books usually are among the best sellers; at least 50 percent of movie receipts are said to be earned by X or R rated shows. The range of clientele includes illiterates who feed quarters into peepshow machines, college students and military personnel who collect magazines of the trade, businessmen who spend lunch hours watching X rated movies, and professionals who acquire luxurious and expensive materials. People somewhat facetiously suspect that the zeal of law enforcement agents and prosecutors in seizing pornographic material is directly proportional to their eagerness to screen it later.

Certainly the commercial exploitation of sex does have its ugly aspects. Unfortunately, though, because sexuality has been so long subjected to suppression, Americans have never had the opportunity to develop standards of good taste in its depiction and to enforce them voluntarily in a free market.

Sentiment against sex-based diversions may once have been so great and so uniform that government could attempt to enforce certain modes of behavior, but not today. A nationwide survey of American public opinion sponsored by the National Commission on Obscenity and Pornography revealed that most American adults believe that adults should be allowed to read or see any sexual material they wish. Almost half of the respondents said that laws against sexual materials are impossible to enforce (Commission on Obscenity and Pornography, 1970).

In reality, pornography is relatively harmless. In 1970, at the end of the most exhaustive study ever conducted on the effects of sexually explicit material, the National Commission on Obscenity and Pornography (1970) concluded:

In sum, empirical research designed to clarify the question has found no evidence to date that exposure to explicit sexual materials plays a significant role in the causation of delinquent and criminal behavior among youth or adults. The commission cannot conclude that exposure to erotic materials is a factor in the causation of sex crime or sex delinquency. [Pp. 286–87]

According to the Commission, analyses of United States crime rates do not support the idea of a causal connection between the availability of erotica and sex crimes among either juveniles or adults. Similar analyses in Denmark show that as the availability of erotica increased there, sex crimes decreased. Consequently, the Commission recommended that federal, state, and local legislation prohibiting the sale, exhibition, or distribution of sexual materials to *consenting adults* be repealed (Commission on Obscenity and Pornography 1970).

The contradictions inherent in any attempt to control what people can read or watch is best summarized in a story about an antipornography committee in Iowa:

The [Concerned Community Citizens] committee found that their own youth were among their severest critics. An engineering student told them: "Just because you see something like two people make love on the screen doesn't mean you're going to rush home and make love—or, because you see a person raped on the screen, that you're going to rush off and rape a person." "But Mike," his father replied, "you're not the majority. We're trying to protect that majority who can't cope with this filth." "Protect? In what way?" And pretty Stephanie wanted to know why these grown-ups didn't get busy about something *really* important. "Why don't you do something that really helps the community?" Besides, she asked, "Don't you all believe in freedom—you all *do* believe in freedom, don't you?" ... "We," declared Jack, "are going to save you." "You cannot shield your children from life, Jack," said [a] car dealer as he left, "and I don't care how you try." [Neary 1970, p. 25]

Conclusion

A discussion of overcriminalization is touchy; so the ideas in this chapter may offend some readers. People like to believe that the United States is composed of a homogeneous group of people who sooner or later will absorb, in a melting-pot fashion, any newcomer or deviant. Social science research has abundantly demonstrated the incorrectness of such a perspective. Recent American history has shown, often dramatically, that differences and disagreements exist. American society has always been and is becoming increasingly pluralistic. New ethnic, racial, and regional pride emphasizes the richly varied value systems and ways of life that are alive and well here. To maintain that Americans share agreed on values easily enforceable against rebels, misfits, and different people is an illusion. Until we recognize that differences do exist and are healthy, until we integrate differences into the ways we design and implement measures of social control, any effort, short of tyranny, to achieve social order will be self-defeating. The Task Force on Law and Law Enforcement (Campbell et al. 1970) reached the following conclusion:

> The criminal law is society's most drastic tool for regulating conduct. When it is used against conduct that a large segment of society considers normal, and which is not seriously harmful to the interest of others, contempt for the law is encouraged. When it is used against conduct that is involuntary and the result of illness, the law becomes inhumane. When it becomes a means for arbitrary or abusive police conduct, it can cause hostility, tension and violence. Repeal of many such laws is overdue. Where the law merely attempts to enforce a particular set of moral values (as in the case of statutes regulating sexual behavior and preferences), simple repeal is usually justified. Where, on the other hand, a social problem such as drunkenness is involved, other methods, more apt to solve social problems, are needed to substitute for the repealed laws. And where the problem in enforcing the law arises primarily from the attitudes of the police, as with disorderly conduct statutes, it should be dealt with by changing those attitudes through training or different recruitment policies, rather than by repeal or by judicial voiding of the underlying statutes. [P. 617]

CHAPTER 12

Victims, Criminals, and Society

Types of Victims

The Italian school of criminology almost a hundred years ago
initiated a kind of personalization or individualization of criminal
law and criminology. Not the concept of a crime but the person
of the criminal became the center of interest and investigation.
In recent years the crime itself has been viewed as a complex
situation that reflects the interaction between individuals and the
cultural norms and expectations of society, as the product of the
intricate interplay of emotional, rational, chance, and situational
factors.

Consequently, attention and interest have centered on the victim as an integral part of the criminal situation. Scholars have
begun to see the victim not necessarily as a passive object, as the

227

neuter or innocent point of impact of crime into society, but as eventually playing an active role or possibly contributing in some way to his own victimization. The victim, his role and responsibility, the crime motive, and behaviors that could be considered provocative have been subjects for speculation, debate, and research during the last thirty years. The result has been typologies of victims developed in an effort to characterize and analyze the victim and the role he plays in the complex drama of his own victimization. These typologies can be synthesized into four major categories: the innocent and ignorant, the socially disadvantaged, the unwilling precipitator, and the willing precipitator.

The Innocent and Ignorant Victim

Children can be viewed as prototypes of the innocent and weak victim. They are not only physiologically undeveloped but also immature and unable to resist criminals physically or with moral strength. Children become victims in crimes of child molestation, child abuse, and kidnapping. They often do not attempt to escape from their attackers because of fear, curiosity, and physical weakness.

Like children, females often become victims because they lack strength. The greater physical strength of male offenders is important in crimes committed against women. With the exception of homosexual attacks, women occupy a biologically determined victim status in sexual crimes.

Advanced age incurs biological weakness and sometimes diminished mental capability. Thus the elderly are in the precarious position of being easy victims. Older persons hold most positions of accumulated wealth and wealth-giving power; so they often may be victimized in crimes against property.

The mentally defective comprise another class of potential and actual victims. Because they are mentally incapable of avoiding certain encounter situations and often are unable to exercise discretion and make sound judgments, they are ripe for victimization.

The Socially Disadvantaged and Powerless

Socially disadvantaged persons become victims because of their lack of status and the low level of society's response to their legitimate aspirations. They are often referred to as outcasts, downtrodden, disadvantaged. Alcoholics and intoxicated persons display diminished physical and mental capabilities, making them prime candidates for victimization in any type of crime, especially against property. They become targets for pickpockets, thieves, and gamblers. In violent crimes, such as rape and murder, many of the principals, victim and criminal, have been intoxicated.

Prostitutes, especially those who solicit in the streets, are easy targets for victimization. Beatings and abuse from their pimps and customers, as well as robbery by other street people, are common occurrences. Although they may precipitate their own victimization, they are in a sense powerless to do much about their conditions. That they operate outside the law, that their allegiance to a semicriminal code prevents them from notifying police, that reporting may incriminate them—all serve to perpetuate their victimization. Prostitutes and others like them have become so enmeshed in a losing situation that a defensive move is often impossible, or at least more harmful than injury at the hand of a criminal.

The addict's victimization status is based on problems similar to the prostitute's and the alcoholic's. However, the addict's emotional and physical cravings further enhance the victim potential. For example, death by poisoning because of substitutions or overdose makes addicts victims of themselves and others.

Minorities and the poor are victims because they are unable and powerless to protect themselves on an equal footing with the rest of society. Their underrepresentation in the criminal justice system and the system's lack of response to their problems locks them into that position. Economics and prejudice interact to force most of the poor and minority group members to live in urban areas identified as high crime areas. Thus they become live-in victims for criminal and noncriminal elements.

Persons who suffer from emotional disturbances, as opposed to physical defects, also become victims. Depression manifests it-

several ways to analyze this type of victimization takes into account the size of the victimized enterprise. The likelihood of victimization and its extent and dynamics can be markedly different, depending on whether the target is a mom-and-pop corner store, a large warehouse, or a department store (Smigel 1956). Another way is to determine whether an attack is aimed at an individual in an organization, at the organization as representative of something else, or simply at the property involved (Dynes & Quarantelli 1970).

The Public as Victim

Narcotics offenders, weapon offenders, the publicly disorderly or drunk perform acts that the public apparently has deemed to be against its best interest. Then the public becomes the corporate victim. In order to really undrstand this type of victimization and grasp its extent, a question is necessary: Who is the public attempting to protect in each instance?

Narcotics laws ostensibly are meant to protect not only the offender from a dangerous substance but also the public from being victimized in robberies or burglaries that narcotics users commit. Laws on disorderly conduct and drunken behavior aim at protecting citizens from invasions of privacy as well as at keeping undesirables out of respectable neighborhoods. A controversial question that has been addressed quite vigorously is whether people feel really victimized by these actions, and how. Those who propose legalization of some drugs, pornographic material, or homosexuality between consenting adults obviously feel that such acts do not victimize them.

The Victim-Offender Relationship

During the last three decades, interest in the roles victims play in their own victimization has increased among social scientists. Von Hentig's (1941) paper, "Remarks on the Interaction of Perpetrator and Victim," and book, *The Criminal and His Victim* (1948); Mendelsohn's (1940) study, "Rape in Criminology," and paper "New Bio-psycho-social Horizons: Victimology" (1947); Ellenberger's (1955) study of the psychological relationship between the criminal and his victim—all underline the importance of studying the criminal-victim relationship.

In his study, Von Hentig (1948) speaks of the "duet frame of crime":

> ... I maintain that many criminal deeds are more indicative of a subject-object relationship than of the perpetrator alone. There is a definite mutuality of some sort. ... In the long run process leading gradually to the unlawful result, credit and debit are not infrequently undistinguishable. ... In a sense, the victim shapes and moulds the criminal. ... They work upon each other profoundly and continually, even before the moment of disaster. To know one we must be acquainted with the complementary partner. [Pp. 383–85]

M. Wolfgang (1958) analyzed all police-listed criminal homicides in the city of Philadelphia between January 1, 1948, and December 31, 1952. He compared the race, sex, age, methods, temporal and spatial patterns, motives, and the influence of alcohol as they relate to both victim and offender. Wolfgang also discussed his findings on victim-precipitated homicides, which he defines as "those criminal homicides in which the victim is a direct, positive precipitator in the crime" (p. 252). Although Wolfgang's definition is rather restrictive, 150 of 588 homicides —26 percent—were found to fit it.

Wolfgang considers that murder falls into this class only when the victim was the first to use physical force. If he had included within this category murders in which the victim provoked his slayer verbally or psychologically, the incidence of victim-precipitated homicide would have been even higher. In summarizing his evidence on victim-precipitated homicide Wolfgang states:

> In many cases the victim has most of the major characteristics of an offender. ... Connotations of a victim as a weak and passive individual, seeking to withdraw from an assaultive situation, and of an offender as a brutal, strong, and overly aggressive person seeking out his victim, are not always correct. Societal attitudes are generally positive toward the victim and negative toward the offender ... However, data in the present study ... destroy these connotations of victim-offender roles in one out of every four criminal homicides. [P. 265]

M. Amir (1971) also used data collected in Philadelphia. He analyzed a total of 625 police-listed forcible rapes for two years,

1958 and 1960. To better examine the relationship between victim and offender, Amir created a scale that measured the amount of knowledge a victim had of an offender before the assault. The scale was based on offender ratings of:

a. Stranger
b. Stranger but general knowledge
c. Acquaintance
d. Neighbor
e. Close friend
f. Family friend
g. Family relative

Amir found that 48 percent of the victims in the study had had primary contact (c through g) before the rape, and that when the offender was a stranger 54 percent of the victims had consumed alcohol with the offender before the crime. Thus Amir's analysis tends to disprove the assumption that in forcible rape an offender unknown to her attacks a woman without warning, and that the victim's role is a passive one.

Amir defined victim-precipitated rape as that when the victim actually had agreed or had been thought to have agreed to sexual relations and then later refused. Of 646 cases, 122, or 19 percent, conformed to this definition. Accordingly, Amir stated, "These results point to the fact that the offender should not be viewed as the sole cause and reason for the offense, and that the victim is not always the innocent and passive party" (p. 266). We should note here that Amir's conclusions apply mostly to intraracial rapes—that is, to rapes that involve persons of the same race.

Many persons tend to depict criminal behavior in mass disturbances as random and irrational, but R. Dynes and E. Quarantelli (1970) pointed out that a selective pattern can be noted in cases of looting, vandalism, arson, and sniping. Although research and debate on the more influential factors in the selective process is still on-going, Dynes and Quarantelli concluded:

Political powerlessness is reacted to by attacking the symbols of power which indicate repression and control. . . . Retail stores symbolize both lack of economic resources and despised style of life. The police symbolize political and repressive power. . . . Retail stores and the police serve as the victims . . . because they symbolize for the ghetto residents their comparative and enduring deprivations. [P. 190]

The Victim and the Administration of Justice

Some victimologists refer to the era when the victim secured his own compensation as the golden age of the victim (Schafer 1968). Early humans handled law and order on an individual basis; each struggled alone for survival. Since many of the political and legal institutions familiar now did not exist then, the individual made, enforced, and executed rules and judgments. Punishment took the form of personal revenge, blood feud, and vendetta.

As more complex social structures such as the tribe developed, reaction to injury or loss became less severe. Instead of vengeful retaliation, people demanded pecuniary compensation for the victim. If the injured party accepted the offender's offer of something of economic value—compensation—he was revenged. Gradually community, tribe, or state influence and control over compensation grew. Hence the criminal's position was somewhat eased, the victim's personal claim was weakened, and the community claimed a share of the victim's compensation.

Thus slowly ended the period when the victim and his family controlled criminal procedure and so served their private interests. In the Western world during the Middle Ages, as feudalism and ecclesiastical power grew, crime came to be viewed as an offense against the state to be tried in a criminal court. Damage to the victim became a separate issue, called tort, and had to be handled in a civil court, separated from the offense per se.

Thus although law violations often involved harm or injury to individual members of the state, all violations were seen as offenses against the rules of the state. So the state became, for legal purposes, the victim, and nearly all the rights vested in the victim became state rights. The state was compensated and satisfied through criminal proceedings and the collection of fines, while the victim was left uncompensated, unsatisfied, and burdened with civil proceedings.

With a few exceptions the state of the victim's plight now is much the same as then. Consider the victim involved with the law enforcement system. From the time police have been informed of a crime the victim is merely a means of solving the inquiry. Despite his mental state the victim is questioned by the police, and may have to go over and over his story, no matter how painful repetition may be to him. In some crimes, such as rape, victims are subjected to such embarrassment, shame, and degradation that often they are made to feel more like criminals than victims.

The victim often is asked to look for hours at pictures, or to identify suspects in lineups, which often requires absence from work or home and hence causes serious inconvenience and even loss of earnings. The victim often is put off, deceived, and even ignored when he inquires about the progress of a police investigation. If police recover his property, he cannot repossess it until legal proceedings have been completed; so he suffers further hardship.

The victim's lot does not improve when the process moves to the judicial phase. In addition to his expenses and financial losses, the victim must relive the experience of his victimization in prolonged and often terrifying detail on the witness stand. Often he is attacked, ridiculed, and humiliated in the defense counsel's cross-examination. His credibility is a central issue in jury deliberations.

During and after the trial the victim must live in the community with the offender and the offender's family, another possible source of fear and grief. All of these situations continue the victimization and are often more painful than the effects of the crime itself. Moreover, when the criminal trial is over the victim who wants personal compensation must go through the same process in civil court, often a futile exercise since the offender may be indigent or otherwise unable to provide compensation or restitution. Even if the convicted offender can compensate the victim, the trial may be undesirable in that it prolongs the link between criminal and victim, with all the fears and uneasiness that such a relationship creates.

Overall, the victim's forced participation in the criminal justice system is in itself a further imposition. He has no freedom of choice once the system is aware of the crime. He must participate and cooperate throughout all the inconveniences. The revival of interest in the victim, though, has begun an effort to correct the victim's past neglect with regard to compensation and restitution.

Compensation is the counterbalancing of the victim's loss, "an indication of the responsibility of society; it is a claim for compensating action by the society; it is civil in character and thus represents a non-criminal goal in a criminal case" (Schafer 1968, p. 112). *Restitution* is "an indication of the responsibility of the offender; it is penal in character and thus represents a correctional goal in a criminal case" (Shafer 1968, p. 112). The difference is important, both theoretically and practically. Under compensation the victim's task is similar to that of applying for any other type of state compensation or welfare. Under restitution the offender is responsible for making good any harm or loss to the victim.

In 1955 the late English penal reformer Margery Fry began a movement for recognition that the victim deserves remedy more effective than the traditional action in tort. In 1963 the New Zealand Parliament established the first crime compensation tribunal, with discretionary power to award public compensation to the victim or dependents when injury or death occurred in specified offenses. Britain initiated a similar program in 1964.

The first jurisdiction in the United States to adopt the compensation principle was California. Its program was enacted in 1965 to put in operation two years later. Since then similar or related programs have been established in New York (1966), Hawaii (1967), Massachusetts (1967), Maryland (1968), Nevada (1969), and New Jersey (1971). Most of the programs are applicable only to victims whose financial resources are limited or who suffer serious financial hardships. Attempts at introducing federal legislation came from Senator Yarborough in 1965, Senator Mansfield in 1972, and Representative Rodino in 1973. Recent attempts to introduce federal legislation establishing industrial parks near correctional institutions where inmates can work for union wages included provision for criminals' restitution to victims. A different and further step to provide for compensation to the victimized in certain crimes also has been proposed—an insurance system (Starrs 1965).

Treatment of Victims of Sexual Assault

Crime in the United States, as measured by the crime index offenses, declined 3 percent during calendar year 1972 over 1971, but violent crimes as a group increased. Forcible rape was up 11 percent. Of all the violent crimes that scar city life now, rape is the most squalid and least tractable.

Attacked women face an excruciating dilemma: if a woman resists she may provoke her assailant into assaulting other parts of her body and perhaps even murdering her; if she accedes she substantially reduces the chance that her assailant will ever be convicted. The problem arises from current rape laws. Earlier laws were rigged to leave men virtually defenseless against a lying or vengeful woman. Now the victim's testimony alone often is insufficient for conviction, even though the very nature of the offense almost obviates corroborating witnesses.

The pain and humiliation of reciting details prevent many victims from reporting the offense, but those who do often allege improper police and hospital treatment. Many people claim that police who investigate rape cases often intimidate the victim with threats of false arrest charges and questions that apparently satisfy only policemen's curiosity or prurient interests or that border on voyeurism. In hospitals, rape victims are placed in emergency rooms, in the midst of sometimes horrifying emergency cases. Rarely do they receive counseling or psychiatric help.

Reacting to this situation, American women are organizing themselves to combat rape, a crime they believe is being condoned in a male-dominated society. Most groups are concerned with post-rape services, and rape crisis centers have been established in several cities, such as Washington, D.C., Los Angeles, and New York. Some advocated changes in the way rape victims are treated after reports of sexual assault are the following:

Rape victims should be given high priority on admission to hospitals for treatment and examination.

Mental health workers should be on 24-hour duty to counsel and aid women who have been sexually assaulted.

Policewomen rather than male detectives should interview female rape victims.

Victims should never be threatened with false arrest charges.

Rape laws should be rewritten, making conviction somewhat easier and trials less wrenching for the victim.

Conclusion

Scholarly and professional interest in victims and their relationships with criminals has grown significantly. Renewed interest in the victim and the debate over such issues as compensation, restitution, insurance, and treatment are of vital interest to persons who want a more equitable system for administering justice. This chapter is not exhaustive (it does not discuss victims of police force, victims of war, victims of the correctional system, victims of state violence, and victims of any oppression, for example), but it has stressed that just as the criminal has a role, rights, and responsibilities, so also does the victim. It also has shown the utter failure of the criminal justice system to consider the innocent victim. Efforts to reform the current situation should be supported (Drapkin & Viano 1974).

Part IV

Social Control

CHAPTER 13

The Administration of Justice: Ideals and Realities

United States Justice

Human concern with criminal deviance throughout recorded history has led to countless attempts to control both deviants and their impact on society. The thrust of any action, though, has always been toward containment at the least, and eradication at the most.

Even though, as noted, crime and delinquency are to some extent and for various reasons healthy for any society (see, e.g., Durkheim 1950), every civilized society has developed mechanisms for dealing with persons who violate the norms, rules, and laws of the state. From its founding, and most particularly now, concern in the United States for the effects of crime and delinquency, their impact on society, and the processes for control have received considerable attention. Citizens are both alarmed and frightened, and in many political campaigns candidates for public office have suggested that crime is the principal problem in the United States. Law-and-order campaigns are common, especially since the politicians know or suspect that their expressions in favor of law and order gain popular support.

A few years ago, the Joint Commission on Correctional Manpower and Training commissioned Louis Harris and Associates (1968) to survey public attitudes on crime. Their report, *The Public Looks at Crime and Corrections*, reveals the following:

> The public feels that our society has not been able to deal successfully with the problem of crime. There is a sense of disappointment in what has been accomplished through law enforcement, the courts, and corrections. . . . There is little hope for the future unless some change occurs. [P. 1]

Certainly, as Clarence Schrag (1971) has noted, "American justice is in turmoil" (p. 1). A historical pattern of neglect has necessitated major changes. Schrag not only laments the failure of the system to curtail crime, he also indicts the system: "There is evidence that instead of preventing crime, the system of justice —as it is now embodied in our police, courts, and correctional agencies— *is a significant factor in crime causation*" (p. 1; emphasis added).

The average citizen may see as workable the simple progression of crime commission-offender arrest–offender conviction-offender punishment, but for several reasons that process probably is more the exception than the rule. Complainants in white-collar and victimless crimes generally do not want to prosecute. Victims of many predatory crimes, such as rape, burglary, and assault, for one reason or another do not always report the offense. Lack of police personnel often precludes effective investigation when offenses are reported. Frequently when crimes are investigated not enough evidence exists to bring an alleged suspect to trial. Prosecutors and judges, overworked and at times too few in number, screen out many cases and engage in bargaining justice, which adds to the dropout rate in the system. The correctional system is overburdened and consequently unable to effectively reduce recidivism rates.

The inefficiency, ineffectiveness, and burgeoning caseloads for police, courts, and corrections add up to a system basically incapable of dealing with the crime problem. Increased technology, scientific developments, more manpower, diversion from the system of minor offenders and selected juveniles, more training and education, and improved organizational management conceivably have helped. Collectively, however, they and other developments have been insufficient to reduce the effects of the social problem.

Dealing with crime in the United States is a pervasive, complex, and difficult social problem. The extent of crime in the United States now, and the controversy over the figures used to measure its extent, have been discussed (see chap. 8). Crime and juvenile delinquency *probably* are on the rise, but their actual rates of increase are not certain. This, however, does not reduce the debate nor satisfy victims and potential victims concerned for safety of body and property.

Criminology as a Discipline

Concern about the problems of criminal justice administration has centered in part on classes of crimes and the reasons some people are unable or unwilling to live according to societal norms. All sorts of people think about the causes of crime—novelist and statistician, philosopher and physiologist, thief and judge. Each, perhaps, in some way has made some kind of contribution to an understanding of the problem, but none alone nor all collectively have resolved the problem. Concepts of cause related to such issues as economics, physiognomy, heredity, cultural values, criminal associations, family life, education, and recreation have been espoused, but none seems to answer the question, Why?

Although people have written about crime from different perspectives and disciplines, in recent years a new discipline, criminology, has begun to examine all the issues, variables, and concerns related to criminal justice:

... [C]riminology is the field which focuses on the distinctive problems created by society's overt refusal to tolerate certain forms of behavior it has generated in certain of its members. The problems posed by these imponderables range from the moral to the philosophical to the practical and technical, from the ideological and political to the managerial and administrative. What makes their [criminologists'] study particularly intriguing to the adventurous mind is the fact that not one of them has been solved. [Korn 1966, p. 2]

The criminologist's role, then, rests on the classical touchstones of science: explain, predict, and control. His mission is to understand the problems of crime and delinquency, and through theory and practice to help society deal with the problems.

Even though criminology as a discipline has developed rather recently, disagreement about its proper subject matter abounds. Consensus is lacking, for example, on the most appropriate curricula in schools for police, court, and correctional students. Besides disagreement over such fundamentals as etiology, prevention, control, and other conceptual issues, criminologists cannot agree on how criminal justice services are best practiced.

Henslin (1972) suggests:

A major theme running through the writings of those who have expressed themselves on this matter is that criminologists have been overly preoccupied with offenders, to the neglect of more basic, and potentially more fruitful, concerns . . . especially the analysis of how law comes into being, the process by which particular behaviors come to be labelled as criminal . . . [and] on the analysis of the conditions under which criminal law develops such that particular *behaviors* (in contrast to individuals exhibiting particular behaviors) come to be proscribed by law. [P. 1]

The historical analysis of societal reaction to crime and other forms of deviation is fascinating but complex and is subject to considerable speculation and interpretation, especially since only in the last hundred-odd years has accurate documentary evidence accumulated on the feelings, beliefs, laws, and practices of various societies. Thus any present reconstruction of official policies is piecemeal and probably incomplete. Korn and McCorkle

(1965) indicate that not only is the credibility of historical sources questioned, consistency among them is lacking.

Historical Developments

Conceptions of crime and control, of deviance and social order probably are a result of human responsiveness to changes in experience, knowledge, technology, institutions, and physical and intellectual resources. Schrag (1971) says:

> ... in spite of the current clamor about disorder and alienation the capability of implementing man's ideas seems always to be increasing. The goals of crime control, therefore, are not simply to produce uniformity of conduct but to anticipate and, so far as possible, to direct or manage the processes of social change. If the task is more difficult today than before, it is largely because of the increasing disparities in people's beliefs, interests, practices, and resources. [P. 10]

Man has not always been humane or concerned with the welfare of others in society. In fact, information available now indicates that until only a few centuries ago it was commonly believed that deviants, such as criminals, the insane, and heretics, were possessed by the devil or other demons and could be saved only by means of exorcism—that is, by driving the evil forces from the deviant's body. Consequently, severe physical punishments, including flogging, branding, stoning, and execution were regarded as proper and natural forms of revenge. Relatives of the victim originally controlled physical punishment, but later the responsibility fell on government. This change from blood feuds and other forms of personal revenge probably occurred as rulers recognized that only government assumption of responsibility for revenge could control or prevent outbreaks of hostilities among offenders, victims, clans, and/or other interested parties.

During this age of revenge, the preclassical period in criminology, retaliation was the primary method for controlling crime and criminals. Many people believe that retaliation still enters into criminal justice practices and probably reflects the public's endorsement of repressive measures, especially for heinous offenses.

Although we obviously have become more humane in dealing with some deviants—that is, less physically abusive—some people maintain that retaliation is still the cornerstone of our criminal justice system:

> In actuality, no other explanation of criminal codes than the retributive one is possible: they were and still are constructed in accordance with the idea of retributive punishments.
>
> The very possibility of overcoming the retributive structure of punishment is doubtful . . . even the boldest reformers dare not break completely with the tradition based on retaliation. [Timasheff 1937, pp. 400–401]

An age of reason ushered in the classical period of criminology during the late eighteenth and early nineteenth centuries. Several philosophies, especially in the areas of law, governmental responsibilities, and man's conception of man, significantly influenced the development of new ways to control crime and criminals. Physical punishments per se were almost abolished, and prisons became the primary correction device. The emerging philosophies of hedonism and rationalism, the increasing popularity of contract theories of government, which detailed the relationship between government and the governed, and the growing evidence (according to some) of the essential interdependence of men—all helped to support prisons as the ideal punishment.

At this time also the industrial age became a force in society, especially in Europe, where cities began to emerge. Economies were based on industrial production instead of agriculture, and populations shifted, becoming more crowded in certain areas.

Reforms in Methods of Control

> The new ideology maintained that natural law, not the divine right of kings, provides the foundation of social order, that man is endowed with knowledge of right and wrong, that he possesses a free will, and that he operates under the principle of hedonism in the pursuit of pleasure and the avoidance of pain. In this view, crime is a deliberate act, the result of malicious intent and a perverse will. [Schrag 1971, p. 10]

In an effort to establish a fair, equitable, and rational system of justice, punishments were graded by law according to the perceived severity of the offenses committed. Framers of this philosophy hoped that the penalty as the offender and society perceived it would be at least equal to the rewards of the crime. Precise punishments were fixed by law, and judges no longer had complete discretion to do as they wanted. Once an offender was found guilty his fate was sealed. "Let the punishment fit the crime" became the motto of the criminal justice system.

Police and courts were expected to enforce the law without question or option; they were to ensure the certainty of punishment. In short, reformers thought that all persons in society certainly had to know that "crime does not pay!" The process was to have no exceptions. However, in time the very young and the insane were legally exempted from prosecution and unequivocl punishments (a time often referred to as the neoclassical period of criminology).

During this period in classical criminology the crime, or the offense, received primary emphasis; the law was paramount. But during the late nineteenth century several persons began to suggest that man was not completely a free agent, so thoroughly hedonistic that he sought pleasure all the time. Instead, they argued, the only way to control crime was to look at the offender and attempt to find out precisely why he committed deviant acts. Such knowledge, they argued, would allow society to be truly able to control crime, especially since the offender could be treated and potential offenders prevented, or deterred, from engaging in criminal behavior. The new era has been called the age of reform but is more popularly referred to as positive criminology.

Cities predominated then, and industrial production was the basis for the world's expanding economies. Then, too, Freud began to write and his psychoanalytic theories gained acceptance; so reformers argued that if the causes of deviant behavior were not understood it could not be cured. Cure, then, became the primary process for controlling crime and delinquency in society.

Sutherland and Cressey (1970) summarize the reasons for this shift from retribution to precise forms of punishment to rehabilitation. They state:

The official policy of individualized treatment for offenders developed out of the positive school's arguments against the practice of attempting to impose uniform punishments. . . . It was, and is, argued that policies calling for uniform punishments are as obviously ineffective as would be a policy calling for uniform treatment of all medical patients, no matter what their ailments. This led some persons to advocate that the type of punishment be adapted to the individual offender; even today "individualization" is sometimes used to refer to a system for imposing punishments. However, as the treatment reaction has increased in popularity, "individualization" has come to designate a treatment process . . . [involving] expert diagnosis . . . and expert therapy. [Pp. 325–29]

Curing Offenders

As indicated, criminal deviants now are perceived to be sick and in need of expert curative attention. The rehabilitation model presupposes an objective approach to the understanding of deviance; that is, the reasons or causes can be understood best in terms of the offender's actual behavior and the precise social context in which he lives and acts.

Several criminologists approach the problem from a different perspective—namely, the subjectively problematic. They, too, are positivistic in orientation, expressing primary concern for the individual, but they assert that crime and delinquency cannot be accepted on face value alone. They maintain, rather, that deviance is in the eye of the beholder and is no more than a social label applied to persons who are different.

To completely understand the causes of the behavior and the processes for control of the individuals, an understanding of the labeling process and the belief systems of the persons who do the labeling is necessary. This approach requires that the study of delinquents and criminals be structured, not according to the medical model of curing offenders, but according to a model that describes interactions between offenders and agents and agencies of social control who label them as deviants. The model also suggests that the policies, practices, and values of agents and agencies of social control, comprising the criminal justice administration network, sometimes create more deviance among those they attempt to control. In other words, the interaction between offender and controller occasionally results in *more* rather than *less* crime and delinquency.

Transformation to the treatment perspective, from the classical to the positive in criminology, from theory to practice, probably received its greatest impetus in the United States when the first juvenile court opened in Chicago in 1899. Here the notion of rehabilitation was first implemented as a systemic approach, for delinquents were viewed as sick and desperately in need of supervision and treatment. As psychoanalytic theories became popular, juvenile courts and child guidance clinics associated with them increased in numbers. Similar treatment of adult criminals soon followed and continues to be a popular model of crime control.

It may be true, if Platt (1969) is correct, that persons responsible for this child welfare movement, known as "child savers," were genuinely concerned about the need to rehabilitate juvenile delinquents. However, they also seemed just as eager to control the immigrants and poor in large cities, and within the movement they tried to keep these minorities in their assigned geographic and social places.

Platt says:

> The child savers viewed themselves as altruists and humanitarians dedicated to rescuing those who were less fortunately placed in the social order. Their concern for "purity," "salvation," "innocence," "corruption," and "protection" reflected a resolute belief in the righteousness of their mission. [P. 3]

Conservatism and Control

The child savers were, in effect, the moral entrepreneurs of their era—persons who sought increased penalties as the means to control crime and whose legacy still affects the criminal justice system. In fact, these child savers belonged to the same group that at the turn of the century developed and managed settlement houses designed primarily to help newly arrived immigrants to become acculturated. The settlement houses provided many helpful services for the poor and for immigrants, especially in teaching the English language and the cultural norms and values. Some argue, though, that the primary purpose was to teach the Protestant Ethic and to ensure that newly arrived persons maintained their respectful places (see, e.g., Klein 1968; Higham 1967).

Henslin (1972) discusses the nature of such controlling activities and suggests that the approach was very conservative: "Central to conservatism ... is the desire to have people follow normative structures, to obey the rules, and to bring pressure to bear when someone does not act in the expected manner. Conservatism tends to contain within it the desire to control others" (p. 3). Further, Henslin relates the notion of control to conservative biases among many criminologists and criminal justice practitioners:

> Thus we note that at least half the contents of criminology texts deal with the prevention and *control* [emphasis added] of crime [Quinney 1970 *a*], and we even find a book carrying the title *Controlling Delinquents.* [Wheeler 1968] Basic to this book is the idea that "there are systematic types of delinquents requiring different forms of treatment and control." [Wheeler 1968; p. 318] What is "required" is treatment (the assumption, I presume, is that something is "wrong" with these persons, since they are felt to need treatment) and control (based, I presume, on the idea that such persons are either uncontrolled or improperly controlled). To take as one's goal the control of delinquents may very well require replacing their normative system, which may be law-breaking in type, with another normative system, one more accepting of legal codes [cf. Hindelang 1970]. [Pp. 3–4]

Even so, by means of a coalition of altruists and moral entrepreneurs, the juvenile court system became firmly established on the basis of a *parens patriae* philosophy; namely, the state has the responsibility for child care as though it were a parent. Programs of treatment and control developed for delinquents and adults, according to Shireman (1962), were designed to protect society through the rehabilitation process:

> Social protection was to be achieved through the rehabilitation of the juvenile offender. Decisions in each case were to be made upon the basis of mature, clinical judgment. The age-old themes of vengeance,

incapacitation, and deterrent punishment were to be replaced by humane understanding and compassion. [P. vi]

Rehabilitation Versus Reintegration

Correctional practitioners have begun to suggest that rehabilitation of delinquents and criminals has not worked. Hence they have begun to use the term reintegration to reflect the new consensus on how best to deal with and otherwise control deviant behavior. The new model argues in the positivistic tradition that unless offenders are dealt with in the community and unless offender *and* community values are intertwined in the treatment process, it will not be possible to produce change and normative behavior in offenders. Efforts to implement this philosophy include community-based treatment facilities, such as halfway houses, and new programs, such as work-release and furloughs from prisons. Whether or not these devices will be any more helpful in controlling and reducing crime and delinquency remains to be tested.

The historical development of criminal justice programs has been discussed in terms of the movement from classical to positive criminological concepts—from revenge, to reform, to rehabilitation of offenders. Barnes and Teeters (1951) assert that contemporary criminal justice programs are the logical and orderly result of evolutionary practices. That is, criminal justice administration as presently practiced is the result of trial and error—what did not work was discarded, and what remains is a matter of studied choice. They argue further that there has been an incremental effect that has built toward a better system (pp. 342–43).

Korn and McCorkle (1965) argue, conversely, that the Barnes and Teeters analysis is incorrect. They assert that criminal justice as presently practiced is simply a collection of ideas, practices, untested hypotheses, and vague notions, which remain either because of tradition or because persons who hold the most power are unwilling to change (pp. 367–72).

Current Practice

An examination of the realities of current criminal justice practices forces the admission that Korn and McCorkle may be right;

scientifically accurate determination of how best to deal with criminal deviants is impossible. No one is sure about what the primary goals of the system should be or, for that matter, whether a *system* of criminal justice actually exists. For example, is the objective the protection of society, the reduction of crime, or the control and treatment of offenders? Or, perhaps, is the primary mission a combination of these objectives? Obviously proponents and antagonists occupy every position.

The argument over the orderly evolution of a criminal justice system began well over a decade ago, but few persons in criminal justice administration have bothered to explore its meaning or significance. That a criminal justice system has evolved seems to be taken for granted. Scholars discuss problems and issues associated with the system; each implores the others to consider cherished ideas or programs, or argues that others' ideas should be rejected. Each has tried to contribute to the evolution of the system; few have questioned whether a system actually exists.

The President's Commission on Law Enforcement and the Administration of Justice (1967) accepted that criminal justice administration in the United States has been operating as a system, even though they enumerate in elegant and considerable detail difficulties, problems, and issues associated with the concept. The Commission notes, for example, that "any analysis of the criminal justice *system* [emphasis added] is hampered by a lack of appropriate data" (p. 263).

The Commission's (1967*a*) final report, *Challenge of Crime in a Free Society*, also states: "The criminal justice *system* is an enormous complex of operations. Subjecting such a *system* to scientific investigation normally involves making changes in its operations in order to observe the effects directly" (p. 261; emphasis added). The report also refers often to the kinds and qualities of training experiences available to the manpower within the system, generally decrying their lack of effectiveness.

The National Advisory Commission on Criminal Justice Standards and Goals (1973*c*) also accepts the existence of a system. This Commission's summary report, *A National Strategy to Reduce Crime*, discusses numerous issues and problems associated with the system, including the nature and quality of manpower training:

"Fragmented," "divided," "splintered," and "decentralized" are the adjectives most commonly used to describe the American *system* [emphasis added] of justice. . . . Words such as fragmented and divided, however, refer not only to demarcations in authority, but to differences in states of mind, and not only to physical distances, but to distances in philosophy and outlook. [P. 41]

The last statement suggests that the Standards Commission, like the President's Crime Commission, decries the failure of the system to develop a philosophy of operations or a commonly accepted statement of goals and objectives.

The system notion has been challenged from both theoretical and practical points of view. Bilek (1973) comments that a system does not exist and suggests that such a state of affairs has implications for criminal justice administration's apparent "ineffective and inefficient operation [which] exacerbates the problem of high crime urban areas . . ." (Pp. 85–86).

Sigurdson et al. (1971) report that lack of a system impedes effective planning. The American Bar Association (1972), which recently has taken an active role in studying and changing the administration of criminal justice services, particularly in corrections, refers to the "non-system" of criminal justice as it is practiced in the United States (p. 1).

One of the most comprehensive statements to challenge the idea of a criminal justice system appears in *Law and Order Reconsidered,* a staff report for the National Commission on the Causes and Prevention of Violence (The Eisenhower Commission 1967):

It is commonly assumed that . . . three components—law enforcement (police, sheriffs, marshals), the judicial process (judges, prosecutors, defense lawyers) and corrections (prison officials, probation and parole officers)—add up to a "system" of criminal justice. The system, however, is a myth.

A system implies some unity of purpose and organized interrelationships among component parts. In the typical American city and state, and under federal jurisdiction as well, no such relationship exists. There is, instead, a reasonably well-defined criminal process, a continuum through which each offender may pass: from the hands of the police, to the jurisdiction of the courts, behind the walls of a prison, then back onto the street. The inefficiency, fallout, and failure of purpose during this process is notorious. [Freed 1969, p. 266]

These authors may be correct in describing the array (or disarray) of criminal justice services in the United States today as not being a system, or being, actually, a nonsystem. Buckley (1967), an authority on systems theory, does not consider the problems of systems as they may relate to the delivery of criminal justice services, but his definition of a system is most apt:

> ... [a] system ... may be described generally as a complex of elements or components directly or indirectly related in a causal network, such that each component is related to at least some others in a more or less stable way within any particular period of time. ... The particular kinds of more or less stable interrelationships of components that become established at any time constitute the particular structure of the system at that time, thus achieving a kind of "whole" with some degree of continuity and boundary. [P. 41]

Although disagreements on models, theories, and concepts of the notion of systems are numerous (see. e.g. Boulding 1956; von Bertalanffy 1962; and Buckley 1968), all seem to agree that a systemic approach to organizational study must include such issues as interrelationships and goals. Thus, in an examination of the criminal justice system or nonsystem these factors, at least, are essential. No understanding of the administration of criminal justice and all its problems, conflicts, issues, and services is possible without an understanding of the significance of goals, of how individuals relate to organizations, and of how organizations relate to each other.

Discussion of the evolution of criminal justice services and whether the network constitutes a system or nonsystem would be academic were it not for the serious implications the issue has for practical operations and future programming. That is, the so-called criminal justice system has failed to understand and control crime in part simply because it is just not a system.

A value judgment is implied when it is stated that the network of criminal justice services in the United States would be better were it a system, or that crime control could progress if these currently disjointed services were gathered into a genuine system. That such a state of affairs is or would be beneficial must be explored further.

For example, if all services and programs could be brought together to achieve a commonly accepted statement of objectives or goals (e.g., eradication of crime), then the accepted and acceptable techniques for achievement might be primarily those of control. If law enforcement, courts, and corrections accept control as a viable means for achieving, say, crime eradication, then society could become very repressive and suppressive. This philosophy could, in turn, lead to the rejection of all forms of deviance, including political as well as criminal acts.

Durkheim (1950) has commented on the need for a healthy society to have some crime in order to change and prosper. He does not advocate an increase in crime in a conventional sense, but he does indicate that a society free of crime is not only impossible but also undesirable. In a unified, goal-directed system where crime control becomes the primary objective, means could supplant ends, and the democratic form of government consequently would be diminished. In a unified system where all components are so interrelated that conflict is minimal, checks and balances now available in the nonsystem, which partially serve to protect clients, might also diminish, harming democracy in general and individual liberty in particular.

A true system of criminal justice administration in the United States now would require the development and maintenance of a genuine dialogue between and among its potential component parts. Police would speak with judges, probation officials with prosecutors, and defense attorneys with victims. In addition, all units in the system would speak with clients of all the services in ways never before deemed necessary. A genuine dialogue, of course, would alone be beneficial, for the components have never truly been in dialogue before. The danger is that the more powerful in the system probably would have their operational philosophies and goals accepted, leaving the meek and less powerful without adequate voice in their own affairs. Then unification would result not in a genuine system but more likely in a totalitarian organizational state in which clients and victims probably would continue to be the least heard and the least important.

Although such conditions might result from systematizing the criminal justice network of services, no one can predict what actually would happen. But if the situation reasonably could occur, then a reasonable conclusion is that a system of criminal justice administration in the United States should not be a goal. At least, it should not be a goal until and unless the problems are solved.

Practically and realistically, however, benefits undoubtedly would accrue from more systematization—that is, greater efforts to coordinate and integrate services in order to achieve an explicit goal. More positive and constructive interrelationships among and between individuals and component agencies and organizations could be beneficial not only for clients but also for community welfare. Even with the inherent dangers, systematizing the network of criminal justice services probably could lead to greater effectiveness (not just efficiency) of services as well as more balanced concerns for the needs and welfare of all of the component parts.

Legal analyst Herbert Packer (1968) does not discuss the system issue. He does suggest, though, that the problems in criminal justice administration have become more confusing because of the dilemma of deciding between a *crime control* and a *due process* stance in dealing with the problems of persons caught up in the administration of criminal justice services.

The due process model stresses legal safeguards in dealing with offenders. It is based on the notion that nothing should be informal, as in juvenile justice, because of the possibility of error. Everyone is entitled to constitutional safeguards, and persons who hold power, including judges, policemen, and probation officers, must exercise that power judiciously and fairly.

The crime control model stresses speed and finality:

> ... extrajudicial processes should be preferred to judicial processes, informal operations to formal ones. ... Routine, stereotyped procedures are essential if large numbers are being handled. The model that will operate successfully ... must be an administrative, almost a managerial model. [Packer 1968, p. 159]

Some persons argue that neglect of due process and failure to adhere stringently to constitutional safeguards in dealing with offenders are the basic causes of inadequacies in the criminal justice system. Attention to the offender's needs and society's supposed willingness to rehabilitate him have resulted in administrative procedures that "for the good of the offender" are nonetheless illegal and unconstitutional, and provide inadequate amounts of social protection. Kassebaum et al. (1971) assert that from the offender's point of view, treatment procedures designed to help or cure are superficially benign but actually quite malignant, for offenders see cure as nothing more than a fancy name for control.

Network of Services

We have suggested that the so-called criminal justice system is not working. Its failure thus constitutes a serious social problem for us, especially since we apparently are unable to control the crime problem. Police are not sure what communities expect of them aside from the apprehension of known offenders—a task that historically they have been unable to do. The *Uniform Crime Reports* (FBI 1973) states:

> Law enforcement agencies in the Nation cleared 21 percent of the Index Crimes during 1972 compared with 20 percent in 1971.... [T]he clearance rate, which relates the number of known offenses cleared, has declined [over a five-year period, from 1967 through 1972]. [P. 31]

Whether the police are inefficient or unable to keep up with the vast array of cultural, technological, and bureaucratic changes in society cannot be answered now (see Bittner 1970 for a complete discussion of this issue).

Similarly, the exact reasons for the inability of the courts to deal effectively with the crime problem are uncertain. Some have asserted, for example, that courts have backlogs not only because of the superabundance of civil actions (Korn & McCorkle 1959) but also because of overcriminalization in law; that is, far too many laws are on the books. Those who argue for reduced laws and reduced penalties—in, say, "victimless crimes"—assert that society must learn to tolerate deviance that hurts no one (see Schur 1973). Some argue that, like the police, judges are unable to understand their primary mission and do not know what society expects of them.

Corrections, the third basic component of criminal justice administration, receives equally harsh treatment for its concomitant failure to reduce or otherwise control the crime problem. For example, correctional claims to cure, treat, or rehabilitate offenders have been thoroughly analyzed. The results show clearly and conclusively that correction is as ineffective as police and courts. Cohn (1973) and Bailey (1966) indicate that rehabilitation as practiced to date simply does not work, possibly because correctional officials do not have enough tools and techniques, possibly because the push for bureaucracy has led to inadequate management procedures. Research findings, however, point to correctional failure in controlling crime and delinquency.

Certainly police, courts, and corrections are not totally powerless to deal with the crime problem. However, inadequate procedures, improper management, and poor program evaluative processes all add up to criminal justice administration failure. Simply put, crime and delinquency now are beyond effective control. Former Attorney General Elliot L. Richardson (1973) said that federal, state, and local governments have failed to develop ways of judging the effectiveness of crime-fighting efforts.

National Strategy

Some kind of national strategy, then, is needed both to define the actual problems and to find effective and meaningful ways of dealing with them. Such a strategy received impetus from the President's Commission on Law Enforcement and Administration of Justice (1967a), which reported on an eighteen-month study of crime in the United States. The 340-page report, *The Challenge of Crime in A Free Society,* broadly surveys the causes, extent, and nature of crime and delinquency, and examines the operations and effectiveness of police, courts, and correctional services.

The Commission made more than two hundred specific recommendations, ranging from federal action to state and local government programs and suggestions for citizen action. Following the main report are eight Task Force reports: *The Police, The*

Courts, Corrections, Juvenile Delinquency and Youth Crime, Science and Technology, Assessment of Crime, Narcotics and Drugs, and *Drunkenness.* These reports contain supporting documents and materials gathered during preparation of the main report. Research studies and selected consultants' papers also were published.

A primary Commission recommendation was that "in every state and every city, an agency, or one or more officials, should be specifically responsible for planning improvements in crime prevention and control and encouraging their implementation." Consequently, in 1967 Congress passed legislation commonly known as the Safe Streets Bill, which established the Law Enforcement Assistance Administration (LEAA) to assume federal responsibility for assisting states in criminal justice planning. Since 1968, the federal government has poured billions into research and action programs, and $1 billion each has been authorized for fiscal years 1974 and 1975 and $1.25 billion for 1976.

In an effort to understand criminal justice practice, develop meaningful goals, set relevant standards, and formulate needed priorities, the Law Enforcement Assistance Administration in 1971 created the National Advisory Commission on Criminal Justice Standards and Goals. The Commission's final reports, issued in 1973, make specific recommendations for action. In a summary report of its efforts, *A National Strategy to Reduce Crime,* the Commission (1973c) states:

> Americans know that crime reduction is imperative. They know the costs and consequences of crime. They know the fear of crime. They have been the victims of crime. . . . What has been needed, however —and what this Commission now provides—is a plan of action that States, cities, and citizens can implement to reduce crime, protect society, and increase public safety. [P. 2]

Even so, the net effects of both public and private efforts to deal with the criminal justice problem cannot possibly be determined now. What will and what will not work are receiving considerable attention, and someday we may have effective answers. In its concluding remarks and comments on its recommendations, however, the President's Crime Commission (1967) said:

... this report on crime and criminal justice in America must insist that there are no easy answers. The complexity and the magnitude of the task of controlling crime and improving criminal justice is indicated by the more than 200 specific recommendations for action, and the many hundreds of suggestions express the Commission's deep conviction that if America is to meet the challenge of crime it must do more, far more, than it is doing now. It must welcome new ideas and risk new actions. It must spend time and money. It must resist those who point to scapegoats, who use facile slogans about crime by habit or for selfish ends. It must recognize that the government of a free society is obliged to act not only effectively but fairly. It must seek knowledge and admit mistakes.

Controlling crime in America is an endeavor that will be slow and hard and costly. But America can control crime if it will. [P. 291]

In 1973, six years after publication of the President's Crime Commission reports, another set of reports was issued under the direction of the National Advisory Commission on Criminal Justice Standards and Goals (1973*c*). In its summary report, *A National Strategy to Reduce Crime*, the Commission urges that the criminal justice system be turned into a *real* system. In looking at possible standards and goals, the Commission concentrates on four basic priorities: (1) prevention of juvenile delinquency, (2) improvement in the delivery of social services, (3) reduction in delays in the criminal justice process, and (4) an increase in citizen participation to combat crime.

To reach the goal of an effective system the Commission offers hundreds of recommendations and standards. All attempt to establish performance levels of operation for the components of criminal justice administration, especially police, courts, corrections, and for service agencies of government as well.

In six volumes, the Commission (1973*c*) develops a plan that emphasizes

... the need for all elements of the criminal justice system to plan and work together with the social service delivery system. The plan emphasizes the need for greater community support of the police and for the police patrolman to strengthen his ties to the community and to be given greater responsibility and authority for preventing and reducing crime in the community. The plan emphasizes the need for the prosecutor, defender, and judiciary to work toward insuring speedier trials while still protecting fundamental rights. The plan also emphasizes the need for corrections to develop effective programs and procedures for reintegrating offenders into the community as soon as possible consistent with the protection of the community. [P. 3]

If a true system of criminal justice administration is possible, criminologist Wolfgang (1972) believes that it probably can work if a method for accountability is developed within it:

All parts of the criminal justice system should be accountable to the public at large, to the victim, and to the offender. Moreover, each subpart of the system should be accountable to the immediately preceding subpart. The democratic process requires public officials and organizations to be on public display.

What we are getting is excessive accounting within each subsystem to itself to such an extent that the basic and original functions are dissipated. [P. 15]

Conclusion:
A Social Problem
Is Everyone's Business

Social scientists and others frequently sound like prophets of doom. They view with alarm the problems that affect society and thereby often accentuate the problems rather than understand and relieve them. We noted earlier that a social problem is, in effect, in the eyes of the beholder because few see each problematical situation from the same perspective.

To some, for example, the relaxation of restrictions on premarital sexual behavior does not reflect a breakdown of the American family but, instead, is seen as a liberation from Puritanical constraints. Some may see poverty as a debilitating experience, but others believe that the poor in the United States are better off than the poor in any other country, especially since public and private welfare and technology in the United States ensure that the poor are at least to some degree fed, housed, and clothed.

265

We have not attempted to comment here on the rightness or wrongness of approaches to social problems; instead, we have tried to show that numerous issues confront American society and are significant to most people as they affect daily living. Mental illness, crime, alienation, racism, family disorganization, delinquency, and consumer issues are social problems that most Americans would like to see eradicated.

Americans certainly are not demanding a Utopian society in which disease and all other debilitating problems would miraculously disappear. Such a state of affairs is an ideal beyond practicality. However, most Americans want social problems to be understood, at least, and controlled, at best. Crime, poverty, and mental illness frighten people; the expression, "There but for the Grace of God go I," is quite apt. Who understands everything about the human condition or about human societies? Analyses of experiences, research, and common sense tell a great deal, but complete understanding is more often than not quite elusive. What is known now appears to be true; later knowledge can disprove almost anything.

As an example, man was for many centuries convinced that the world was flat; so speculation that another shape was possible must certainly have shocked many. Hence the true shape probably was unacceptable as fact for years. Now the abundance of knowledge makes ridiculous the idea that any rational person could have ever believed the earth was flat.

Americans are strongly tempted to be smug about their knowledge of social problems and may believe they understand the problems well enough to devise reasonable and adequate measures for control. But to fallible humans a present problem may become no more than a historical incident later. Conversely, a current problem may in the past have been an insignificant annoyance.

Mental illness is an example. In earlier times persons who now would be labeled mentally ill were considered to be possessed. They were shunned, killed, banished, or otherwise ostracized from their communities because others feared contamination, and the only possibility for recovery was believed to be through an ecclesiastical miracle. Today, most people recognize mental illness for what it is—a potentially curable illness. Consequently, a once nonsocial problem is now a significant social problem that requires action. A social problem requires not only action but also research into its causes. People now assume that with proper scientific inquiry they can understand the problem and design appropriate measures for action.

We have approached this study of social problems with the view that we must understand before we can act. Wisdom, the Bible notes, is most important; therefore we are encouraged to seek wisdom. However, to know is only a third of the battle, in our opinion. From wisdom should come understanding, for without understanding, knowledge cannot be applied. Comprehension of the meanings of facts leads to the responsible and meaningful action that wins the battle. Wisdom, understanding, and action in proper perspective can change doom preaching to optimism.

More than three decades ago J. Huizinga (1936) wrote the following:

> We are living in a demented world. And we know it. It would not come as a surprise to anyone if tomorrow the madness gave way to a frenzy which would leave our poor Europe in a state of distracted stupor, with engines still turning and flags streaming in the breeze, but with the spirit gone.
>
> Everywhere there are doubts as to the solidity of our social structure, vague fears of the imminent future, a feeling that our civilization is on the way to ruin. They are not merely the shapeless anxieties which beset us in the small hours of the night when the flame of life burns low. They are considered expectations founded on observation and judgment of an overwhelming multitude of facts. How to avoid the recognition that almost all things which once seemed sacred have now become unsettled, truth and humanity, justice and reason? We see forms of government no longer capable of functioning, production systems on the verge of collapse, social forces gone wild with power. The roaring engine of this tremendous time seems to be heading for a breakdown. [Pp. 53–54]

Huizinga may at first reading appear to be a prophet of doom. However, he continues:

> Between the extremes of despairing pessimism and the belief in imminent deliverance stand all those who see the grave evils and

shortcomings of our time, who do not know how they are to be remedied and overcome, but who hope and work, who strive to understand and are ready to bear. [P. 54]

We do not offer panaceas or ready-made solutions for the social problems discussed here, even though descriptions of the problems imply solutions. A sense of urgency about some of the problems may be inherent, but we hesitate to suggest which ones are most critical. Individuals and/or communities must determine which problem they perceive to be most significant.

Social problems that are immediate, painful, and demanding of help differ among people: the offender caught up in what he perceives to be an unjust criminal justice system, the mentally ill patient in the back ward of a mental hospital, the consumer who has been unfairly dealt with, the victim of a malicious crime, the frightened parent whose child has run away, is on drugs, or has been committed to a juvenile training school. To these people we can offer no special relief; society perhaps has not yet understood its problems well enough to design and implement effective processes. Nevertheless, we can offer some hope, for reasonable and concerned individuals do care and do try to understand.

We also agree with Rosenberg et al. (1964), who maintain that social science researchers

> ... sometimes foster in the mind of the public an overconfidence in the efficacy of social science. ... When given the chance they clamor, for economists seldom perform wonders in helping us grapple with our ailing economy, or psychologists with mental disorder, or sociologists and criminologists with juvenile delinquency. [P. v]

We believe that science can help in understanding perceived social problems and can provide guidelines for effective action, but resources and skills are insufficient to complete the task. Society therefore must assist and encourage scientific efforts to understand and deal with social problems. Everyone is responsible for working toward understanding, relief, or control of any problem that affects society. There is an old saying: "If you are not part of the solution, then you are part of the problem." A social problem is everyone's, not just the scientist's, business.

The bewildered layman may ask how an individual can do anything about mental illness, delinquency, or white-collar crime. The answer here is not simple but in fact very complex and personal. What one person can do is not necessarily what others can or should do, but some things *everyone* in society ought to do. Education is important. By education, we mean learning the facts in order to do away with myths and stereotypes. Racial prejudice, which usually results from irrational beliefs based on unique experiences, is a prime example. Discussions about feelings and beliefs with persons who are the objects of those feelings and beliefs can help to set the record straight. Avoidance of contact with the educated perpetuates closed-mindedness and ignorance. Failure to consider new ideas or new approaches perpetuates rather than relieves a problem.

Finally, people in criminal justice administration, and particularly in law enforcement, are most frequently in the front lines, confronted by social problems that beset American society. The policeman on the beat, probation officer, prosecutor, defense attorney, judge, and warden must deal with society's victims and those who victimize. The policeman cannot turn away from social problems. He is forced to face persons whom the problems affect and he must know the issues. Therefore, the policeman must be a student of society; he must learn about and understand social problems; he must work toward their solution.

The policeman is as much a member of society as those he serves, and as such he has equal responsibilities for building a better America. The benefits to the policeman may in fact be quite great. If much of his routine duty time is spent in social welfare types of activities, then relief of community social problems actually will make his job easier. Then he may also be able to spend more time on what many believe to be the first essential duty of law enforcement: crime fighting.

It seems important to respect the views of Weinberg and Rubington (1973), who insist:

> The student of social problems today could become a consumer of solutions tomorrow. If he is to rationally consider alternative proposals, perform the duties and exercise the rights of citizenship, he needs to have a set of values, a body of information, and some notion of contingencies. [Pp. viii–ix]

References

Ahern, J. F. 1972. *Police in Trouble.* New York: Hawthorn Books.

Alex, N. 1969. *Black in Blue: A Study of the Negro Policeman.* New York: Appleton-Century-Crofts.

Allen, F. A. 1964 *a.* *The Borderland of Criminal Law: Essays in Law and Criminology.* Chicago: University of Chicago Press.

———. 1964 *b.* *The Borderland of Criminal Justice.* Chicago: University of Chicago Press.

Allport, G. 1954. *The Nature of Prejudice.* Cambridge, Mass.: Addison-Wesley.

American Bar Association. 1972. *New Perspectives on Urban Crime.* Washington, D.C.: Special Committee on Crime Prevention and Control.

American Friends Service Committee. 1971. *Struggle for Justice.* New York: Hill & Wang.

American Law Institute. 1962. Model Penal Code, Section 4.01 (1 and 2) (Proposed Official Draft).

Amir, M. 1971. *Patterns of Forcible Rape.* Chicago: University of Chicago Press.

Anderson, R. T. 1966. "From Mafia to Cosa Nostra." *American Journal of Sociology* 71:302–10.

Antonovsky, A. 1964. "The Problem: The Social Meaning of Discrimination."

In *Mass Society in Crisis: Social Problems and Social Pathology,* edited by Bernard Rosenberg et al., pp. 108–24. New York: Macmillan.

Ardrey, R. 1966. *The Territorial Imperative.* New York: Dell.

Arnold, T. 1935. *The Symbols of Government.* New York: Harcourt, Brace.

Bailey, W. C. 1966. "Correctional Outcome: An Evaluation of 100 Reports." *Journal of Criminal Law, Criminology and Police Science* 57: 153–60.

Barnes, H. E., and N. K. Teeters. 1951. *New Horizons in Criminology.* 2d ed. New York: Prentice-Hall.

Becker, H. S. 1963. *The Outsiders: Studies in the Sociology of Deviance.* New York: Free Press.

Bedau, H. A. 1973. "Are There Really Crimes Without Victims?" Paper presented at the First International Symposium on Victimology, Jerusalem.

Bell, D. 1953. "Crime As An American Way of Life." *Antioch Review* 13 (June): 131–54.

———. 1962. *The End of Ideology.* 2d rev. ed. New York: Collier Books.

———. 1963. "Crime As An American Way of Life." In *Social Controversy,* edited by W. Petersen and D. Matza, pp. 94–106. Belmont, Calif.: Wadsworth.

Berkowitz, L. 1968. "Impulse, Aggression, and the Gun." *Psychology Today* 2(4): 19–22.

———. 1973. "The Case for Bottling Up Rage." *Psychology Today* 7(2): 24–31.

Biderman, A. 1966. "Social Indicators and Goals." In *Social Indicators.* edited by R. A. Bauer, pp. 68–153. Cambridge, Mass.: M.I.T. Press.

———. 1967. "Surveys of Population Samples for Estimating Crime Incidence." *The Annals* 374 (November): 16–33.

Bilek, A. J. 1973. "America's Criminal Justice System—A Diagnosis and Prognosis." In *The Change Process in Criminal Justice,* pp. 85–110. Washington, D.C.: Law Enforcement Assistance Administration.

Bittner, E. 1970. *Function of Police in Modern Society.* National Institute of Mental Health. Washington, D.C.: U.S. Government Printing Office.

Bloch, H. A., and G. Geis. 1970. *Man, Crime, and Society.* New York: Random House.

Borgstrom, C. 1973. *Focal Points: A Global Food Strategy.* New York: Macmillan.

Boulding, K. 1956. "General Systems Theory—The Skeleton of Science." *Management Science* 2:197–208.

Bremner, R. H. 1956. *From the Depths. The Discovery of Poverty in the United States.* New York: New York University Press.

Brinton, C. 1936. *French Revolutionary Legislation on Illegitimacy, 1789–1804.* Cambridge, Mass.: Harvard University Press.

———. 1959. *A History of Western Morals.* New York: Harcourt, Brace.

———. 1965. *The Anatomy of Revolution.* New York: Vintage Books.

Brown, C. 1965. *Manchild in the Promised Land.* New York: Macmillan.

Brown, J. 1940. *Public Relief, 1929–1939.* New York: Henry Holt.

Brown, L. 1973. "Globe Gobbling: The World Scarcities Ahead." *Washington Post,* Sunday, November 25.

Brown, R. M. 1970. "The American Vigilante Tradition." In *The History of Violence in America,* pp. 45–84. New York: Bantam Books.

Bryant, C. 1971. *Social Problems Today: Dilemmas and Dissensus.* Philadelphia: J. B. Lippincott.

Buckley, W. 1967. *Sociology and Modern Systems Theory.* Englewood Cliffs, New Jersey: Prentice-Hall.

———, ed. 1968. *Modern Systems Research for the Behavioral Scientist: A Sourcebook.* Chicago: Aldine.

Bureau of the Census. 1973. *Current Population Report.* Publication P-60, no. 88 (June). Washington, D.C.: U.S. Department of Labor.

Bureau of Labor Statistics. 1973 *a.* In *Washington Post.* August 17, 1973.

———. 1973 *b.* Personal communication. August 1973.

Burgess, E. W., and H. J. Locke. 1953. *The Family.* 2d ed. New York: American Book Co.

Calverton, V. F., and D. Schmalhausen, eds. 1930. "Parenthood, The Basis of Social Structure." In *The New Generation.* New York: Macaulay.

Campbell, J. S., J. R. Sahid, and D. P. Stang. 1970. *Law and Order Reconsidered.* A Staff Report to the National Commission on the Causes and Prevention of Violence. New York: Bantam Books.

Capen, E. W. 1905. *Historical Development of the Poor Law in Connecticut.* New York: Columbia University.

Caplovitz, D. 1963. *The Poor Pay More.* New York: Free Press.

Cavan, R. 1953. *The American Family.* New York: Thomas Y. Crowell

Chambliss, W. J., and J. T. Liell. 1966. "The Legal Process in the Community Setting." *Crime and Delinquency* 12:310–17.

Chute, C. I. 1949. "The Juvenile Court in Retrospect." *Federal Probation* 13 (September):7.

Clark, R. 1970. *Crime in America.* New York: Simon & Schuster.

Clinard, M. B. 1952. *The Black Market: A Study of White Collar Crime.* New York: Holt, Rinehart.

———. 1971. "A Disorganizing Concept." In *The Study of Social Problems,* edited by E. Rubington and M. S. Weinberg, pp. 77–79. New York: Oxford University Press.

Cloward, R., and J. A. Jones. 1963. "Social Class: Educational Attitudes and Participation." In *Education in Depressed Areas,* edited by A. H: Passow, pp. 190–216. New York: Teachers College Press, Columbia University.

Cohen, A. K., and J. F. Short, Jr. 1966. "Juvenile Delinquency." In *Contemporary Social Problems,* edited by R. K. Merton and R. A. Nisbet, pp. 84–135. 2d ed. New York: Harcourt, Brace.

Cohn, A. W. 1973. "The Failure of Correctional Management." *Crime and Delinquency* 19 (July): 323–31.

Coleman, J. S. 1966. *Equality of Educational Opportunity.* Washington, D.C.: Government Printing Office.

Commission on Obscenity and Pornography. 1970. *Report.* New York: Bantam Books.

Committee on Homosexual Offences and Prostitution. 1957. "Wolfenden Report." London: Home Office, Cmnd. 247, Her Majesty's Stationery Office.

Coser, L. A. 1962. "Some Functions of Deviant Behavior and Normative Flexibility." *American Journal of Sociology* 68 (September): 172–81.

———. 1967. *Continuities in the Study of Social Conflict.* New York: Free Press.

Cressey, D. R. 1950. "The Criminal Violation of Financial Trust." *American Sociological Review* 15:738–43.

———. 1967. "The Function and Structure of Criminal Syndicates." In *Task*

Force Report: Organized Crime. Washington, D.C.: Government Printing Office.

Dancey, C. L. 1968. "Causes of Violence." *Peoria Journal Star,* June 30, p. A-6.

Davies, J. C. 1962. "Toward a Theory of Revolution." *American Sociological Review* 27 (February): 5–19.

Davis, K. 1939. "Illegitimacy and the Social Structure." *American Journal of Sociology* 45 (September): 220–38.

———. 1969. *Discretionary Justice: A Preliminary Inquiry.* Baton Rouge: Louisiana State University Press.

Deevey, E. S., Jr., 1969. "The Human Population." In *The Subversive Science,* edited by P. Shepard and D. McKinley. Boston: Houghton Mifflin.

Dentler, R. A. 1967. *Major American Social Problems.* Chicago: Rand McNally.

Department of Health, Education and Welfare. 1973. In *Washington Post,* Aug. 15.

de Schweinitz, K. 1943. *England's Road to Social Security.* Philadelphia: University of Pennsylvania.

Devlin, P. 1965. *The Enforcement of Morals.* London: Oxford University Press.

Dix, D. 1967. *Remarks on Prisons and Prison Discipline in the United States.* Montclair, N. J.: Patterson Smith, Reprint Series.

Douglas, J. D. 1971. *Crime and Justice in American Society.* Indianapolis: Bobbs-Merrill.

Drapkin, I., and E. Viano. 1974. *Victimology.* Lexington, Mass: D. C. Heath (Lexington Books).

Durkheim, E. 1950. *Rules of Sociological Method.* 8th ed. Trans. by S. H. Solvay and J. H. Mueller. Edited by G. E. G. Catlin. Glencoe, Ill.: Free Press.

———. 1952. *Suicide.* Trans. by J. A. Spaulding and G. Simpson. Edited by G. Simpson. London: Routledge & Kegan Paul.

Dynes, R. R., and E. L. Quarantelli. 1970. "Organization as Victim in Mass Civil Disturbances." *Issues in Criminology* 5 (Summer): 181–93.

Edelhertz, H. 1970. *The Nature, Impact, and Prosecution of White-Collar Crime.* Washington, D.C.: Government Printing Office.

Ehrlich, P. R., and A. H. Ehrlich. 1972. *Population, Resources, Environment.* San Francisco: W. H. Freeman.

Eisenhower, D. D. 1953. Press Conference, March 19.

Ellenberger, H. 1955. "Psychological Relationship Between Criminal and Victim." *Archives of Criminal Psychodynamics* 1:257–90.

Ennis, P. 1967. "Crime, Victims, and the Police." *Trans-Action* 4 (June): 36–44.

Environmental Protection Agency. 1973. *The Quality of Life Concept.* Washington, D.C.: Government Printing Office.

Faltermayer, E. K. 1964. "Who Are the American Poor?" *Fortune,* March. p. 119.

Feagin, J. R. 1972. "Poverty: We Still Believe That God Helps Those Who Help Themselves." *Psychology Today* 6 (November): 101–110, 129.

Federal Bureau of Investigation. 1972. *Crime in the United States—1971: Uniform Crime Reports.* Washington, D.C.: Government Printing Office.

———. 1973. *Crime in the United States: Uniform Crime Reports—1972.* Washington, D.C.: Government Printing Office.

Flacks, R. 1971. *Youth and Social Change.* Chicago: Markham.

Fosdick, H. E. 1947. "Are We Part of the Problem or Part of the Answer?" *National Educational Association Journal* 36: 621–22.

Frederick, C. J., and L. Lague. 1972. *Dealing with the Crisis of Suicide.* Pamphlet No. 406A. New York: The Public Affairs Committee.

Freed, D. J. 1969. "The Nonsystem of Criminal Justice." In *Law and Order Reconsidered: A Staff Report to the National Commission on the Causes and Prevention of Violence,* edited by J. S. Campbell, J. R. Sahid, and D. P. Stang, pp. 265–84. Washington, D.C.: Government Printing Office.

Freeman, H. E., and W. C. Jones. 1970. *Social Problems: Causes and Controls.* Chicago: Rand McNally.

Freud, S. 1953. *Civilization and Its Discontents.* Trans. by J. Riviere. London: Hogarth Press.

Gage, N. 1972. *The Mafia Is Not an Equal Opportunity Employer.* New York: Dell.

Galbraith, J. K. 1958. *The Affluent Society.* Boston: Houghton Mifflin.

———. 1973. *Economics and the Public Interest.* Boston: Houghton Mifflin.

Glaser, D. 1971. *Social Deviance.* Chicago: Markham.

Glenn, N. D. 1963. "Occupational Benefits to Whites from the Subordination of Negroes." *American Sociological Review* 28 (June): 443–48.

Glick, C. 1957. *American Families.* New York: Wiley.

Gliner, R. 1973. *American Society as a Social Problem.* New York: Free Press.

Goldman, N. 1963. *The Differential Selection of Juvenile Offenders for Court Appearance.* New York: National Council on Crime and Delinquency.

Goode, J. 1956. *After Divorce.* Glencoe, Ill.: Free Press.

———. 1971. "Family Disorganization." In *Contemporary Social Problems,* 3d ed., edited by R. K. Merton and R. A. Nisbet, pp. 467–544. New York: Harcourt Brace Jovanovich.

Gordon, D. M. 1973. "Capitalism, Class, and Crime." *Crime and Delinquency* 19 (April): 163–86.

Gould, J., and W. L. Kolb, eds. 1964. *Dictionary of the Social Sciences.* New York: Free Press.

Graham, H. D., and T. R. Gurr. 1970. "Introduction." In *The History of Violence in America,* pp. xv–xxii. New York: Bantam Books.

Gravel, M. 1972. "Corporate Pushers." *Playboy* 19 (9):142, 210–12.

Gross, L., ed. 1959. *Symposium on Sociological Theory.* New York: Harper & Row.

Gurr, T. R. 1969. *Why Men Rebel.* Princeton, N.J.: Princeton University Press.

Halleck, S. L. 1971. *The Politics of Therapy.* New York: Science House.

Hamalian, L., and Fred R. Karl. 1970. *The Radical Vision: Essays for the Seventies.* New York: Thomas Y. Crowell.

Harrington, M. 1962. *The Other America.* Baltimore: Penguin Books.

———. 1969. "Crisis of Affluence." *Center Magazine* 2 (September): 47.

Harris, F. 1973. *The New Populism.* New York: The Saturday Review.

Harris, L., and Associates. 1968. *The Public Looks at Crime and Corrections.* Washington, D.C.: Joint Commission on Correctional Manpower and Training.

Hart, H. L. A. 1963. *Law, Liberty, and Morality.* Stanford, Calif.: Stanford University Press.

Haskell, M. R., and L. Yablonsky. 1970. *Crime and Delinquency.* Chicago: Rand McNally.

Heard, A. 1960. *The Cost of Democracy.* Chapel Hill: University of North Carolina Press.

Henry, J. 1973. *On Sham, Vulnerability and Other Forms of Self-Destruction.* New York: Random House.

Henslin, J. M. 1972. "Toward Refocusing Criminology." Paper prepared for the 1972 Inter-American Congress of Criminology. Caracas, Venezuela.

Herbers, J. 1970. "Special Introduction." In *The History of Violence in America,* pp. viii–xix. New York: Bantam Books.

Higham, J. 1967. *Strangers in the Land: Patterns of American Nativism, 1860–1925.* New York: Atheneum.

Hindelang, M. J. 1970. "The Commitment of Delinquents to Their Misdeeds: Do Delinquents Drift?" *Social Problems* 17 (Spring): 502–509.

Hood, R., and R. Sparks. 1970. *Key Issues in Criminology.* New York: McGraw-Hill.

Horton, P. B., and G. R. Leslie. 1970. *The Sociology of Social Problems.* 4th ed. New York: Appleton-Century-Crofts.

Huizinga, J. 1936. *In the Shadow of Tomorrow.* New York: Norton.

Hunt, M. 1973. "Sexual Behavior in the 1970's." *Playboy* 20 (10): 85–88, 194–207.

Illich, I. 1973. *Tools for Conviviality.* New York: Harper & Row.

Jeffery, C. R. 1960. "The Historical Development of Criminology." In *Pioneers in Criminology,* edited by H. Mannheim, pp. 364–94. London: Stevens.

———. 1971. *Crime Prevention through Environmental Design.* Beverly Hills, Calif.: Sage Publications.

Jensen, A. R. 1969. "How Much Can We Boost IQ and Scholastic Achievement?" *Harvard Educational Review* 39 (Winter): 1–123.

Johnson, L. 1963. Address to a Joint Session of Congress. November 27.

Kadish, S. H. 1967. "The Crisis of Overcriminalization." *The Annals* 374 (November): 157–70.

Kahn, K. 1973. *Hillbilly Women.* Garden City, N.Y.: Doubleday.

Kassebaum, G., D. A. Ward, and D. Wilner. 1971. *Prison Treatment and Parole Survival.* New York: Wiley.

Kelso, R. 1922. *History of Public Poor Relief in Massachusetts.* Boston: Houghton Mifflin.

Kennedy, J. F. 1963. Message to Congress. June 19.

Kennedy, R. F. 1963. "Robert Kennedy Defines the Menace." *New York Times Magazine,* October 13.

Kephart, M. 1955. "Occupational Level and Marital Disruption." *American Sociological Review* 20 (August): 456–65.

Klein, P. 1968. *From Philanthropy to Social Welfare: An American Cultural Perspective.* San Francisco: Jossey-Bass.

Knight, D. 1972. *Delinquency Causes and Remedies: The Working Assumptions of the California Youth Authority Staff.* Sacramento: California Youth Authority.

Kobetz, R. W., and B. B. Bosarge. 1973. *Juvenile Justice Administration.* Gaithersburg, Md.: International Association of Chiefs of Police.

Korn, R. R. 1966. "A Framework for Problem-Solving in Criminology." Mimeographed. Berkeley: School of Criminology, University of California.

Korn, R. R., and L. W. McCorkle. 1959. *Criminology and Penology.* New York: Holt, Rinehart & Winston.

Kwan, Q. Y., P. Rajeswaren, B. P. Parker, and M. Amir. 1972. "The Role of Criminalistics in White Collar Crimes." *The Criminologist* 7 (24): 12–35.

Laing, R. D. 1971. *The Politics of the Family.* New York: Pantheon.

Lapp, R. E. 1973. *The Logarithmic Century.* Englewood Cliffs, N.J.: Prentice-Hall.

Leich, H. H. 1973. "The Terrible Toilet." *Washington Post,* July 15.

Leites, N., and C. Wolf, Jr. 1970. *Rebellion and Authority.* Chicago: Markham.

Lenski, G. 1970. *Human Societies.* New York: McGraw-Hill.

Lerman, P., ed. 1970. *Delinquency and Social Policy.* New York: Praeger.

Lerner, M. 1957. *America As A Civilization: Life and Thought in the United States Today.* New York: Simon Schuster.

Lesy, M. 1973. *Wisconsin Death Trip.* New York: Pantheon.

Leyendecker, M. H. 1955. *Problems and Policy in Public Assistance.* New York: Harper & Bros.

Lipsky, M. 1970. *Police Encounters.* Chicago: Aldine.

Lofland, J. 1966. *Deviance and Identity.* Englewood Cliffs, N.J.: Prentice-Hall.

Lorenz, K. 1966. *On Aggression.* New York: Harcourt, Brace.

Lovering, T. S. 1969. "Mineral Resources from the Land." In *Resources and Man,* pp. 109–55. National Academy of Sciences. San Francisco: W. H. Freeman.

Lubeck, S. G. 1973. Book review in *Federal Probation* 37 (June): 78–79.

Luszki, M. B. 1958. *Interdisciplinary Team Research: Methods and Problems.* New York: New York University Press and the National Training Laboratories.

Lynn, R. 1970. "Violence in American Literature and Folk-lore." In *The History of Violence in America,* pp. 226–42. New York: Bantam Books.

McCarthy, C. 1973. "In Which Our Man Meets the Purring Miss Enzymes and Other Omens of the Future at the Gathering of the Food Technologists' Clans." *Washington Post,* Potomac, September 30.

McDonagh, E. C., and J. E. Simpson. 1969. *Social Problems: Persistent Challenges.* New York: Holt, Rinehart & Winston.

MacIver, R. M. 1937. *Society: A Textbook of Sociology.* New York: Farrar & Rinehart.

Mannheim, H. 1965. *Comparative Criminology.* Boston: Houghton-Mifflin.

———, ed. 1960. *Pioneers in Criminology.* Chicago: Quadrangle Books.

Marcuse, H. 1955. *Eros and Civilization.* Boston: Beacon Press.

Marshall, B. 1973. "Can the F.B.I. Rebuild Itself?" *Washington Post,* Sunday, July 1.

Marx, K. 1959. *Economic and Philosophic Manuscripts of 1844.* London: Lawrence & Wishart.

Matza, D. 1964. *Delinquency and Drift.* New York: Wiley.

———. 1966. "Poverty and Disrepute." In *Contemporary Social Problems,* 2d ed., edited by R. K. Merton and R. A. Nisbet, pp. 619–69. New York: Harcourt, Brace.

Maudsley, H. 1878. *Responsibility in Mental Disease.* New York: D. Appleton.

Merton, R. K. 1951. "A Social Psychological Factor (The Self-Fulfilling Prophecy)." In *Race Prejudice and Discrimination,* edited by A. Rose, chap. 50. New York: Knopf.

——. 1957. *Social Theory and Social Structure*. Rev. ed. Glencoe, Ill.: Free Press.

——. 1966. "Social Problems and Sociological Theory." In *Contemporary Social Problems*, 2d ed., edited by R. K. Merton and R. A. Nisbet, pp. 775–823. New York: Harcourt, Brace.

Mitford, J. 1973. *Kind and Usual Punishment: The Prison Business*. New York: Knopf.

Morgan, N. 1973. "Running Out of Space." *Harper's* 247 (1480): 59–60, 65–67.

Moyer, K. E. 1973. "The Physiology of Violence." *Psychology Today* 7 (2): 35–38.

Murdock, P. 1949. *Social Structure*. New York: Macmillan.

Murton, T. 1972. *Accomplices to the Crime*. New York: Grove Press.

Myrdal, G. 1944. *An American Dilemma*. New York: Harper & Row.

——. 1963. *Challenge to Affluence*. New York: Pantheon.

National Advisory Commission on Civil Disorders. 1968. *Report*. New York: Bantam Books.

National Advisory Commission on Criminal Justice Standards and Goals, 1973 *a*. *Community Crime Prevention*. Washington, D.C.: Government Printing Office.

——. 1973 *b*. *Corrections*. Washington, D.C.: Government Printing Office.

——. 1973 *c*. *A National Strategy to Reduce Crime*. Washington, D.C.: Government Printing Office.

National Center for Health Statistics. 1973 *a*. Personal communication from Division of Vital Statistics, August 29. Washington, D.C.

——. 1973 *b*. *Monthly Vital Statistics Report*. Provisional Statistics, Annual Summary for the United States. Washington, D.C.

National Commission on the Causes and Prevention of Violence. 1970. *Violence in America: Historical and Comparative Perspectives*. New York: Bantam Books.

National Commission on Marijuana and Drug Abuse. 1972. *Marihuana: A Signal of Misunderstanding*. Washington, D.C.: Government Printing Office.

National Institute of Law Enforcement and Criminal Justice. 1970. *Police Training and Performance Study*. Washington, D.C.: Law Enforcement Assistance Administration.

National Institute of Mental Health. 1970. *Mental Illness and Its Treatment*. DHEW Publication no. (HSM) 73-9056. Washington, D.C.: Department of Health, Education and Welfare, National Institute of Mental Health.

——. 1972. *Pollution: Its Impact on Mental Health*. Washington, D.C.: Government Printing Office.

Neary, J. 1970. "Pornography Goes Public." *Life* 69 (9): 19–35.

Newman, O. 1973. "A Theory of Defensible Space." *Intellectual Digest* 3 (7):57–64.

Nisbet, R. A. 1966. "The Study of Social Problems." In *Contemporary Social Problems*, 2d ed., edited by R. K. Merton and R. A. Nisbet, pp. 1–24. New York: Harcourt, Brace.

Norman, S. 1972. *The Youth Service Bureau: A Key to Delinquency Prevention*. Paramus, N.J.: National Council on Crime and Delinquency.

Orshansky, M. 1965. "Counting the Poor." *Social Security Bulletin* 28 (January): 3–26.

Packer, H. 1964. "The Crime Tariff." *American Scholar* 33:551–57.

————. 1968. *The Limits of the Criminal Sanction.* Stanford, Calif.: Stanford University Press.

Pettigrew, T. F. 1971. "Race Relations." In *Contemporary Social Problems,* 3d ed., edited by R. K. Merton and R. A. Nisbet, pp. 407–65. New York: Harcourt Brace Jovanovich.

Piliavin, I., and S. Briar. 1964. "Police Encounters with Juveniles." *American Journal of Sociology* 69:206–14.

Platt, A. M. 1969 a. *The Child Savers: The Invention of Delinquency.* Chicago: University of Chicago Press.

————. 1969 b. "The Rise of the Child-Saving Movement: A Study in Social Policy and Correctional Reform." *The Annals* 381 (January):21–38.

President's Commission on Law Enforcement and the Administration of Justice. 1967 a. *The Challenge of Crime in a Free Society.* Washington, D.C.: Government Printing Office.

————. 1967 b. *Task Force Report. Crime and Its Impact: An Assessment.* Washington, D.C.: Government Printing Office.

————. 1967 c. *Task Force Report: Juvenile Delinquency and Youth Crime.* Washington, D.C.: Government Printing Office.

President's Task Force on the Mentally Handicapped. 1970. *Action Against Mental Disability.* Washington, D.C.: Government Printing Office.

Quinney, R. 1970 a. *The Problem of Crime.* New York: Dodd, Mead.

————. 1970 b. *The Social Reality of Crime.* Boston: Little, Brown.

Raab, E., and G. J. Selznick. 1964. *Major Social Problems.* New York: Harper & Row.

Ramo, S. 1969. *Cure for Chaos.* New York: David McKay.

Report of the President's Commission on Crime in the District of Columbia. 1966. Washington, D.C.: Government Printing Office.

Richardson, E. 1973. In *Washington Post,* August 6.

Richmond, M. E. 1917. *Social Diagnosis.* New York: Russell Sage Foundation.

Rienow, R., and L. T. Rienow. 1969. *Moment in the Sun.* New York: Ballantine.

Robison, S. M. 1966. "A Critical View of the Uniform Crime Reports." *Michigan Law Review* 64 (6):1031–54.

Rodgers, W. H., Jr. 1973. *Corporate Country: A State Shaped to Suit Technology.* Emmaus, Pa.: Rodale.

Rongy, A. 1933. *Abortion: Legal or Illegal?* New York: Vanguard.

Rose, P. I. 1970. *The Study of Society.* New York: Random House.

Rosenberg, B., I. Gerver, and F. W. Howton, eds. 1964. *Mass Society in Crisis: Social Problems and Social Pathology.* New York: Macmillan.

Rosenhan, D. L. 1973. "On Being Sane in Insane Places." *Science* 179:250–58.

Roszak, T. 1969. *The Making of a Counter Culture: Reflections on the Technocratic Society and Its Youthful Opposition.* New York: Doubleday.

Saar, J. 1973. "Experts Assess Effects of Long D. C. Smog Siege." *Washington Post,* Sunday, September 16.

San Francisco Project. 1965. Berkeley, Calif.: School of Criminology, University of California.

Schafer, S. 1968. *The Victim and His Criminal.* New York: Random House.

Schrag, C. 1971. *Crime and Justice: American Style.* Rockville, Md.: National Institute of Mental Health, Center for Studies of Crime and Delinquency.

Schramm, G. L. 1949. "The Juvenile Court Idea." *Federal Probation* 13 (September):21.

Schumach, M. 1965. "F.B.I. Crime Data Called Misleading by Sociologist." *New York Times,* March 22.

Schur, E. 1969. *Our Criminal Society: The Social and Legal Sources of Crime in America.* Englewood Cliffs, N.J.: Prentice-Hall.

———. 1973. *Radical Non-Intervention: Rethinking the Delinquency Problem.* Englewood Cliffs, N.J.: Prentice-Hall.

Schur, M., ed. 1964. *The Family and the Sexual Revolution.* Bloomington: Indiana University Press.

Sellin, T., and M. Wolfgang. 1964. *The Measurement of Delinquency.* New York: Wiley.

———, eds. 1969. *Delinquency: Selected Studies.* New York: Wiley.

Shepard, P., and D. McKinley. 1969. *The Subversive Science.* Boston: Houghton Mifflin.

Sheridan, W. H. 1967. "Juveniles Who Commit Non-Criminal Acts—Why Treat in a Correctional System?" *Federal Probation* 31 (March): 26–30.

Shireman, C. R. 1962. "Foreword." In *Justice for the Child,* edited by M. K. Rosenheim. New York: Free Press.

Shuey, A. M. 1958. *The Testing of Negro Intelligence.* Lynchburg, Va.: J. P. Bell.

Sigurdson, E., R. Carter, and A. McEachern. 1971. "Methodological Impediments to Comprehensive Criminal Justice Planning." *Criminology* 9:246–67.

Smigel, E. O. 1956. "Public Attitudes Toward Stealing as Related to the Size of the Victim Organization." *American Sociological Review* 21:320–27.

Sparks, W. 1965. "Terror in the Streets?" *Commonweal* 82 (11):345–48.

Srole, L., T. S. Langner, S. T. Michael, M. K. Opler, and A. C. Rennie. 1962. *Mental Health in the Metropolis.* New York: McGraw-Hill.

Starrs, J. E. 1965. "A Modest Proposal to Insure Justice for Victims of Crime." *Minnesota Law Review* 50 (December):285–310.

Storey, J. R. 1972. "Public Income Transfer Programs: The Incidence of Multiple Benefits and the Issues Raised by Their Receipt." *Studies in Public Welfare.* Paper no. 1. Washington, D.C.: Joint Economic Committee, U.S. Congress.

Storr, A. 1968. *Human Aggression.* New York: Atheneum.

Sutherland, E. H. 1940. "White-Collar Criminality." *American Sociological Review* 5 (February): 1–12.

———. 1949. *White Collar Crime.* New York: Dryden Press.

Sutherland, E. H., and D. R. Cressey. 1970. *Criminology.* 8th ed. Philadelphia: J. B. Lippincott.

Szasz, T. 1961. *The Myth of Mental Illness.* New York: Harper & Row.

Taft, P. 1964. *Organized Labor in American History.* New York: Harper & Row.

Tappan, P. W. 1949. *Juvenile Delinquency.* New York: McGraw-Hill.

Task Force Report. 1967. *Juvenile Delinquency.* Washington, D.C.: Government Printing Office.

———. 1967. *Organized Crime.* Washington, D.C.: Government Printing Office.

Taylor, K. K., and F. W. Soady. 1972. *Violence: An Element of American Life.* Boston: Holbrook Press.

Timasheff, N. S. 1937. "The Retributive Structure of Punishment." *Journal of Criminal Law and Criminology* 28 (September-October): 400–401.

Turk, A., J. Turk, and J. T. Wittes. 1972. *Ecology, Pollution, Environment.* Philadelphia: W. B. Saunders.

United States Bureau of the Census. 1973. In *Washington Post,* August 27.

United States Civil Rights Commission. 1964. "Some Questions and Answers on the Civil Rights Bill." Washington, D.C.: Leadership Conference on Civil Rights.

U.S. Department of Health, Education and Welfare. 1964. *Converging Social Trends, Emerging Social Problems.* Washington, D.C.: Government Printing Office.

U.S. Department of Justice, Law Enforcement Assistance Administration. 1973. *Police Guide on Organized Crime.* Washington, D.C.: Government Printing Office.

U.S. Department of Labor. 1965. *The Negro Family ("The Moynihan Report").* Washington, D.C.: Office of Policy Planning.

U.S. National Commission on the Causes and Prevention of Violence. 1969. *Violence in America: Historical and Comparative Perspectives.* Edited by H. D. Graham and T. R. Gurr. Washington, D.C.: Government Printing Office.

U.S. Public Health Service. 1968. *Trends in Illegitimacy: United States—1940-1965.* Washington, D.C.: Government Printing Office.

Urban America, Inc., and the Urban Coalition. 1969. *One Year After,* as reported in *The New York Times,* "One Year Later: Still Two Societies." March 2: IV–5.

van den Haag, E. 1964. "Intelligence or Prejudice?" *National Review* 16 (December 1): 1059–1063.

Vanderbilt, A. P. 1967. In *Task Force Report: Juvenile Delinquency and Youth Crime,* President's Commission on Law Enforcement and the Administration of Justice, Washington, D.C.

Virginia Education. 1973. In *Washington Post,* Aug. 21, pp. 1, 3.

von Bertalanffy, Ludwig. 1962. "General System Theory—A Critical Review." *General Systems* 7:1–20.

Von Hentig, H. 1941. "Remarks on the Interaction of Perpetrator and Victim." *Journal of the American Institute of Criminal Law and Criminology* 31 (March-April):303–9.

———. 1948. *The Criminal and His Victim.* New Haven, Conn: Yale University Press.

Walker, W. 1972. "Games Families of Delinquents Play." *Federal Probation* 36 (December):20–24.

Waller, W. 1967. *The Old Love and the New.* Carbondale: Southern Illinois University Press.

Washington Lawyers' Committee for Civil Rights. 1972. "Victimless Crimes and the Inner City." Monograph.

Waxman, Chaim I., ed. 1968. *Poverty: Power and Politics.* New York: Grosset & Dunlap.

Weber, M. 1947. *Wirtschaft und Gesellschaft (Society and Economics)*. Trans. by T. Parsons and A. M. Henderson. New York: Oxford University Press.

Webster, J. A. 1970. "Police Task and Time Study." *Journal of Criminal Law, Criminology and Police Science* 61:94–100.

Weinberg, M. S., and E. Rubington. 1973. *The Solution of Social Problems*. New York: Oxford University Press.

Weisberg, B. 1970. "Raping Alaska: The Ecology of Oil." In *Divided We Stand*, pp. 63–71. San Franoisco: Canfield Press.

West's California Codes. 1957. St. Paul, Minn.: West Publishing Co. Modified by supplements through 1968.

Wheeler, S., ed. 1968. *Controlling Delinquents*. New York: Wiley.

White, L. 1969. "The Historical Roots of our Ecologic Crisis." in *The Subversive Science*, edited by P. Shepard and D. McKinley, pp. 341–51. Boston: Houghton Mifflin.

Wilkins, R. 1973. In *Washington Post*, Aug. 28, p. 28.

Wolfgang, M. 1958. *Patterns in Criminal Homicide*. Philadelphia: University of Pennsylvania Press.

———. 1970. *Youth and Violence*. Washington, D.C.: Government Printing Office.

———. 1972. "Making the Criminal Justice System Accountable." *Crime and Delinquency* 18 (January):15–22.

Worcester, D. L. W. 1929. "The Standard of Living." In *Proceedings of the National Conference of Social Work*. New York.

World Health Organization. 1973. In *Washington Post*, July 15.

Name Index

283

Subject Index

About the Authors

Emilio C. Viano, Ph.D., is associate professor at the Center for the Administration of Justice, The American University, Washington, D.C. He also has served on the research staff of the National Council on Crime and Delinquency.

He has published two books, *Victimology* and *Victimology: A New Focus;* his articles have appeared in the *International Journal of Criminology and Penology, Canadian Journal of Criminology and Corrections, Quality and Quantity: The European Journal of Methodology, Sociology and Social Research, Sociology, Journal of Criminal Law and Criminology,* and *Federal Probation.*

Alvin W. Cohn, Ph.D., is president of Administration of Justice Services, Inc., and a principal in Planning Research Corporation/Public Management Services.

Dr. Cohn has held several academic positions, most recently with the Center for the Administration of Justice at The American University. He has prepared numerous training programs for police and correctional agencies, and has served as consultant to the National Criminal Justice Reference Services, the Federal Bureau of Prisons, and the Federal Judicial Center.

His articles have appeared in a number of professional journals, including *Federal Probation, Crime and Delinquency, Popular Government, Canadian Journal of Criminology and Corrections,* and *Criminology.*